DEVON
THATCH

DEVON THATCH

AN ILLUSTRATED HISTORY OF THATCHING

AND THATCHED BUILDINGS IN DEVON

JO COX
&
JOHN R L THORP

DEVON BOOKS

First published in Great Britain in 2001

British Library Cataloguing-in-Publication Data
A CIP record for this title is available from the British Library

ISBN 1 85522 797 5

DEVON BOOKS
OFFICIAL PUBLISHER TO DEVON COUNTY COUNCIL

Halsgrove House
Lower Moor Way
Tiverton, Devon EX16 6SS
Tel: 01884 243242
Fax: 01884 243325
email sales@halsgrove.com
website www.halsgrove.com

Devon Books gratefully acknowledges the support of
English Heritage towards the publication of this book.

ENGLISH HERITAGE

Printed and bound in Great Britain by Bookcraft Ltd, Midsomer Norton

CONTENTS

Dedicated to Helen Cox and Mary Thorp

PREFACE

Athatched roof was once unremarkable but today is an object of special pride. Thatch is in some ways the most unlikely material to use for roofing, especially in a county with a wet climate, needing regular attention and periodic renewal. Nevertheless it is held in the highest regard, actually increasing the value of a country house or cottage. Indisputably a thatched roof has a wonderful appearance and this accounts in part for this regard, but there is more to it than this. Thatch is a reminder of values and ways now mostly lost, but still remembered with affection. The sight of a thatcher at work on a roof, or corn stooked for thatching, is a link to a world which is nearly gone. Thatch provides a continuity with a picturesque rural past, something particularly appropriate in Devon with its still unspoilt countryside.

Famous as Devon is for its thatched roofs, nobody has attempted properly to research its origins and significance before this book. With the one exception of Pam Egeland's *Cob and Thatch*, of 1988, there has been no specific work on the subject. Interest in thatch, and in particular its local variations, has been stimulated by English Heritage's three recent volumes on the subject, of which Jo Cox was one author. Her research, commissioned by English Heritage, combined with John Thorp's enormous knowledge of local building traditions, has made possible the writing of this book which for the first time defines the origins and character of Devon thatching. They demonstrate that not only does Devon possess a unique tradition in the use of combed wheat straw for thatching – a tradition that it must be crucial to maintain – but that many of its surviving thatched roofs are of extreme antiquity, outstanding reserves of botanical and agricultural history. It has always been a thrill in the course of my work to be able to put my head through a ceiling trap door and see not only the roof timbers blackened by medieval smoke from the hearth below but also – and just as blackened – the very thatch that a farmer first put on the roof in the fifteenth or sixteenth century. *Devon Thatch* traces the direct line from these medieval roofs through to the present day when we have significant new issues of materials and techniques to address; this book will be a major contribution to the debate.

Devon County Council's awareness of the importance of thatch to the county and its buildings led it to commission this book from the authors. The County Council is committed to the support of thatch both as a vital local tradition and because it is quintessentially a sustainable technique. Unlike many building materials, thatch is a material which extracts virtually no price on the environment. Growing wheat for local thatching moreover has a potentially important role to play in today's changing agricultural scene.

The book would not have been possible without generous support from English Heritage, who, like the County Council, recognise that full and accessible information is key to maintaining local traditions. This support is very gratefully acknowledged.

In recent years the authors have become well known nationally as leading historic buildings consultants and Devon is very fortunate to be able to count them among its residents. Their enthusiasm for the County's history gives an extra dimension to the work. It has been a great pleasure for me to have been closely involved in the evolution of this volume – I am sure that the owners and aficionados of thatched buildings in Devon will gain equal pleasure from the story it tells.

Peter Child
Historic Buildings Adviser Devon County Council, August 2001

ACKNOWLEDGEMENTS

The support of Devon County Council has been the foundation for the production of this book. We are especially grateful to Simon Timms and to the unflagging interest, comments and good cheer of Peter Child of Devon County Council during all stages of writing. There is a long list of other people to thank for their help. We would like to give an especial thanks to Dr Anita Travers, who helped with the research both locally and in the Public Record Office and Guildhall Library. Other members of the Keystone team, past and present, contributed in different but crucial ways: Sandi Ellison, Rupert Ford and Sophie Sharif.

We are very grateful to numerous Devon house-owners who have given us access to their buildings over a long period of time, to many Devon thatchers for information and advice and to local conservation officers for information.

Good advice, comment, information and access to illustrations came from:

Ann Adams; John Allan; Dr Paul Brassley; Peter Brockett; Professor Chris Brooks; Neil and Bernadette Carr; Roy Brigden; Jack Dodson; Gordon Elston; Harold Fox; Sue Frewin; Alan Fuchs; Gordon Glover; Dr Todd Gray; Dr Tom Greeves; Ray Harrison; Val Harrison; Professor Avril Henry; Mr Geoffrey Hoare; Bill Vellacott; Terry Hughes; Tristan Johnson; John Letts; Jack Lewis; Fred Lister; Ian Maxted; Dr James Moir; David Morgan; Mike Nevitt; Paul Norman; Richard Parker; Sarah Pearson; John Pullen; Geoff Pyne; Alan Prince; James and Robin Ravilious; Marjory Rowe; Jenny Sanders; Colin Shears, Peter Smith; Robin Stanes; Dave Stenning; David Trezise; John Winstone.

Staff at:
Beaford Archive
Cookworthy Museum, Kingsbridge
Cornwall Record Office
Countryside Agency (formerly the Rural Development Commission)
Devon and Exeter Institution Library
Devon Record Office
English Heritage
Guildhall Library
National Monuments Record
Public Record Office
Rural History Centre, Reading
University of Exeter Library
West Country Studies Library

Notes for Readers

Virtually all the buildings illustrated or described in this book are privately owned. They are therefore not open to the public and we ask that readers respect the privacy of the owners.

Most of the buildings in the book are listed as being of special architectural or historic interest by the Department of Media, Culture and Sport. Copies of the lists for Devon are available for consultation by appointment at County Hall, Exeter, District Council offices and at some libraries. They may also be accessed on the Images of England web site: www.imagesofengland.org.uk

Where historic prices are quoted in the text these are in pre-1971, pre-decimal currency and have not been converted into today's decimal currency. The pound remained the same unit after decimalisation, but before 1971 was divided into 20 shillings, each equivalent to 5 of today's pence. Each shilling was divided into 12 old pence (240 to the pound), each equivalent to 0.4 of one penny today.

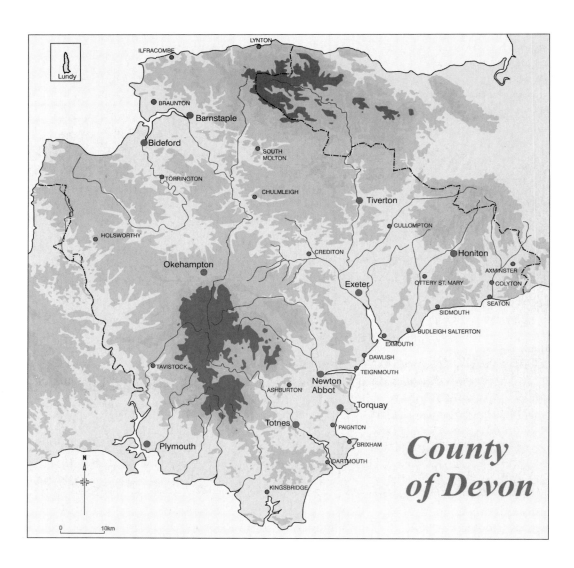

THE SURVIVAL OF A TRADITION

The Importance of Devon Thatch

Locally-produced building materials are as much a part of a sense of place as are local landscapes. They represent the transformation of what landscapes have to offer – usually in the way of underlying geology – into buildings and they are a live connection between buildings and their local setting. Devon thatching would rank high on most contemporary lists of what makes the county visually distinctive. As a grown material, traditional Devon thatch is not localised around quarries or areas of woodland, but is tied more broadly to the county's landscape through farming. While most is found on buildings before 1900, the county's thatching tradition has continued to the present day as the maintenance of thatch on old buildings.

Thatch in the Devon landscape at Barton Lands, Culmstock.

© John R L Thorp 1997

The use of plant stems or whole plants as a roof covering is an ancient building technique, widely distributed in both tropical and temperate climates. Although direct archaeological evidence for prehistoric thatching is 'almost nonexistent', the lightness of construction of many of the earliest domestic buildings known from excavation suggests that they were roofed with some form of thatch.[1]

Thatching today is one of the characteristic roof coverings of rural houses in the south of England, thinning out north of a diagonal line drawn between the Severn and The Wash. South of this line it is found, often or occasionally, from Norfolk, Suffolk, Essex and Kent all the way down to the narrowing wind-swept Cornish peninsula, where it is a minor theme among roofs of Cornish slate. The greatest concentration, however, is in Devon. Devon is now the foremost county in England for numbers of thatched buildings, and the premier region for numbers of thatched buildings in Europe. This is not because thatch was, historically, an especially favoured roofing material in the county, but is a matter of the survival of a local tradition. Survival today is limited almost exclusively to houses. Thatch on a broad range of other buildings has disappeared and short-lived thatch is no longer found on workaday structures.

Thatch as the ancestor of the tarpaulin, providing a temporary cover at St Giles in the Wood in 1900. Six sound-looking men in front of a very basic short-lived thatch on a store, perhaps bracken for bedding animals. This is a type of thatching that has disappeared.

Although the precise number of English thatched roofs today is not known for sure, some idea of the figures can be judged from the numbers of listed buildings with thatched roofs. Devon has 3 983, or 17 per cent of the national total of thatched buildings of special historic or architectural interest, with Dorset second with 2 052. The true figure in the county, including unlisted buildings is certainly more than 4 000. There are also 816 listed buildings in Devon identified as having been thatched in the past but now with some secondary roof-covering, usually corrugated iron or asbestos. The total then, of all the surviving buildings in the county with some evidence of a period of thatched roofing is probably about 5 000. This is only a tiny percentage of what once existed, considering that most farm buildings were originally thatched and every farmhouse had its yard with at least a shippon (cowhouse) and a barn.

Devon does not have ideal conditions for thatch. The relatively high rainfall and humidity encourages the speed with which thatch decays. Norfolk and Suffolk both have a much kinder climate for thatch, with less rainfall and dry winds to keep moisture out of the roof. Nevertheless, both counties have fewer thatched roofs than Devon. The disadvantages to thatch of the local climate are exacerbated by what is described as the 'slack' or shallow pitches of the roofs of local traditional buildings. Slack pitches slow down the drainage of water off the roof, keeping the plant stems damp for longer than on steeply-pitched roofs and this, too, speeds up the natural decay of thatch. The minimum recommended pitch for a new thatched roof is 45º. Pitches as steep as 60º can cause difficulties for the thatcher. A small sample of twenty-one thatched or formerly thatched buildings in Devon shows that the earliest roofs, which date from before c.1340, are the steepest, with a pitch of 48º. The later

Thatch in the wet Devon climate. Mr Webber at White Cleave, Burrington, photographed by James Ravilious in 1974.

roofs, dating from c.1400–1650, have pitches that vary from 43° to 45°, with single examples of 46° and 47°.[2] South East thatched roofs are generally steeper than this.[3] So neither climate, nor the pitch of roofs can explain the amount of thatch in the county.

Below left: *The characteristic slack pitch of a Devon thatched roof in High Bickington, photographed in the early 20th century.*

Above: *A Suffolk cottage with a steeply-pitched roof covered in crushed straw thatch.*

If we had been able to take a birds-eye view of England in the 1760s, Devon would not have stood out from the crowd for numbers of thatched roofs. Thatch was then far more widely spread, along with regional variations, obvious and subtle, including different materials and types of thatch used from region to region. Some of the thatching types that could have been seen are extinct now. Thatch would have been seen everywhere, unevenly distributed, of course, according to what else was available, cost-effective and customarily used for roofing. Heather thatching, dark in appearance compared with straw or water reed, was used in the north of England, parts of Kent and in the New Forest. Water reed thatch would have been found close to the big wetland and estuarine reed beds, for instance on the Ouse below Bedford, but with the greatest concentration in Norfolk. The rural areas of the Midlands and inland East Anglia would have revealed crushed straw ('long straw') roofs, a shaggier, more bristly type of straw thatch than in the South West. Turf thatch was used in

Cumbria. On the Cornish coasts, as in Ireland and Scotland, some thatch would have been tied down with nets or ropes from which stones were hung, to prevent it blowing off the roofs in high winds.

In each area, examples of other roofing materials would have been found too, sometimes side by side with thatch, but in concentrations close to their sources, whether slate quarries, tile manufactories or woodland for producing shingles. The spread of these materials was determined by customary use, and by the routes down which they could conveniently be transported: canals, toll roads, and coastal shipping runs.

The principal competing roofing material in Devon in the 1760s was slate, less common than thatch but found, we can guess, concentrated as pockets of roofs of small pegged slates or large rag slates, close to the Devon slate quarries. At a greater distance from them, it would be found on a few better-quality farmhouses, gentry houses and the big roofs of most parish churches. Slate would also have been seen in many small coastal towns, threaded together by shipping routes between the harbours from which it was exported, to harbours where the heavy, fragile material was unloaded. There would have been some surprises on individual buildings: wooden shingles on some Devon church roofs, even buildings roofed with an early form of roofing felt, constructed of thick tarred paper. Most of the urban areas like Plymouth, Exeter and Barnstaple, as well as smaller market towns, especially in the west of the county, would have been slated.

The traditional Devon roofing options of thatch or West Country slate, each with local variations, as they survived in Torcross, on the south coast of Devon, c.1890. Both thatched roofs have plain flush ridges. The thatched house in the foreground has slate verges, a technique known to have been used occasionally in Devon from at least the early 19th century. There are two types of slate roof shown. The house facing the sea has small pegged slates with larger slates at the eaves and verges and the front is partly slate-hung. The smaller house with a collapsing roof has a rag slate roof using large slates nailed to the rafters.

By the 1860s the same birds-eye view would have shown variations in the relationship of thatch to other roofing materials all over England. James Moir has estimated from insurance records that the numbers of thatched buildings in England then was about 842 000, compared with a survival of about 35 000 in

1960. By the early 1860s new buildings erected to house the increasing population were less likely to have thatched roofs in some areas, particularly the North of England. Here slate and tile roofs had begun to appear in greater numbers in the expanding towns and cities. Many older houses, which had previously been thatched, had been re-roofed likewise. The numbers of thatched buildings in the Midlands would have been only slightly less than in 1800, new ones having been roofed with other materials, with the thatch on older buildings mostly maintained. In the south the numbers of thatched buildings actually increased between 1800 and the early 1860s, while in the South West there was a sharp decline.[4] The differences reflected different kinds of economic development from region to region, combined with variations in access to alternative roofing materials.

In Devon there was an increasing dependence on agriculture as the economic backbone of the South West in the second half of the 18th century, compared with the rise of manufacturing industries in other regions. Even in rural Devon, though, by 1860, most villages would have had a mixture, in different proportions of thatch or south-west slates. Some buildings, especially those erected since the 1850s, as well as some churches, would have had uniform roofs of Welsh slate purchased in standard sizes.

Taking a birds-eye view of England in 2001, the regional differences in roofing materials have to be looked for more carefully amongst the many new roofing materials that were produced in the 19th century and later. These include factory-made concrete tile and artificial slate, as well as natural slate from Wales or imported from other countries. There is still a discernible regional pattern at the core of most old cities and towns, where either tile or slate will dominate, but we have to look to the rural areas for the survival of thatch, whether in villages, or in farmsteads. Even in Devon where, comparatively-speaking, so much thatch remains, the surviving thatched roof of the farmhouse is now unlikely to be off-set by ranges of thatched farm buildings: these will have been re-covered in slate, corrugated iron or tile. Many smaller village houses and their minor outbuildings are now covered in slate sourced from all over the world and, as in the towns, late 19th century and later village houses are not usually thatched.

Below: *A complete yard of thatched farm buildings at Sampford Courtenay in the first half of the 20th century. Thatched farmbuildings are now extremely rare.*

Left: *Thatch in the mid 20th century surviving on a Devon farmhouse but, typically, lost on the farmbuildings by this date at Afton, near Berry Pomeroy.*

Inner Hope Village c.1930, showing the earlier thatched houses in the village centre and later villas and bungalows on the outskirts with slate roofs.

Devon is the pre-eminent county in England for numbers of thatched buildings today, not because it always has been, but because some (but by no means all) thatch has survived the forces for change which have replaced it elsewhere (*see colour page 1*). The survival of straw thatch identifies Devon as a county of exceptional agricultural continuity, particularly from 1750 and, perhaps most importantly, from the last quarter of the 19th century to the present day. This is the period in which thatch disappeared most comprehensively in other regions. The survival of thatched roofs is intertwined with the character and, especially, the survival of Devon farming. This continuity is not just the outcome of what has happened in the county historically, but also of what has not happened.

Devon is now primarily a rural county. The hinterlands of its only city of any size, Plymouth, and its much smaller capital, Exeter, may have been filled up with new satellite settlements and massively expanded villages but, with the exception of the unsettled areas of Dartmoor and Exmoor, the county is principally made up of farmland. Most of the farmsteads are very ancient sites, their field boundaries created and their farmhouses built at a time when many other counties still had large areas of unenclosed land, out of which farms were carved in the 18th and 19th centuries. Relatively few new farms were established in Devon after the period when canal and rail transport meant that new building materials for a mass market were at hand.

It is easy to think of the county as a place where small farms have forever been the order of things, farming has always dominated, and the pace of change has been slow. This is because Devon's great periods of wealth and industrialisation came early by comparison with other regions and then failed as other regions began to prosper. Devon's economy grew faster than any other English shire between 1334 and 1535.[5] One direct reflection of this is the enlargement of nearly every Devon parish church in the period. Another is the thorough rebuilding of many Devon farmhouses to a size and standard that could comfortably accommodate centuries of future change. The wool industry and the development of trade in the late 16th and 17th centuries produced surplus wealth that was used to build prosperous merchants' town houses, smart enough to compare with any in England. Profits from mining made landlords rich in the 17th century, a century in which the county's population grew massively. National commentators admired the remarkable level of agricultural improvement and progress in Devon, spurred by the need to feed an increasing population.

The scale of change that medieval and early modern wealth, based not just on agriculture, but also on industry and trade, brought to the appearance of buildings was significant. The balance between the use of locally-available building materials altered. Materials were used in novel ways that sharply distinguished urban houses in the late 16th and 17th centuries from their country cousins. In the larger towns builders not only adapted house plans to cram new houses on to valuable urban sites, but introduced showy timber-framing for constructing external walling (a technique that never appeared in rural areas), and exploited local slate, not only for roofing, but for cladding walls with plain and fancy slate-hanging. Nevertheless thatch remained the commonplace roofing for rural housing and farm buildings in the boom period of the late 16th and 17th centuries, acceptable across a range of building types, from the houses of the gentry to farm buildings and cottages. It was excluded only from the most superior buildings and in the centres of the larger towns.

© Jo Cox

Woodlands Farm, Bridford, in the 1980s. The farmhouse is probably 16th century and was thatched from the outset. Thatch continued to be used as the farmstead was developed with buildings in the 17th century.

The late 16th and 17th centuries added massively to the stock of thatch in the county, including many well-constructed buildings that have survived to the present day. Devon is a geologically complicated county, with a good range of building stones as well as a subsoil that provides earth for cob building. Combed straw thatch can be found roofing just about every type of walling material available in the county before 1700 (*see colour page 2*). However, thatch was slowly and gradually abandoned as a roofing material in the larger towns, pushed into second place and most likely to survive on the margins, where urban expansion had incorporated older farmhouses. Gradually it was also squeezed out of the smaller towns. The changes to the distribution and status of thatch in the 16th and 17th centuries were important, but they were changes within the recognisable vernacular tradition of locally-sourced building materials. They were neg-

Above: *Houses of different dates in the Devon village of Broadhembury are given visual consistency through the use of thatch. Some of the houses are still part of an estate.*

Right: *Thatch and granite on Higher Shilstone, Throwleigh, a Dartmoor longhouse built on the edge of the open moor near the 305m (1000ft) contour.*

ligible compared with those that 18th and 19th century industrialisation eventually brought to both the rural and urban buildings of other regions.

After 1750 the golden age of economic prosperity and building in the county was over. When the Cheshire farms serving Manchester were turning to intensive dairy and beef production to supply city dwellers, or West Kent farmers adapted their production to feed London, Devon farms experienced change on a much lesser scale. Devon landlords, with a handful of exceptions, such as the Dukes of Bedford, did not profit massively from late 18th and 19th century industrialisation. This meant less investment in agriculture and a slower pace of change, both to agriculture and to country buildings. The mechanisation of the corn harvest in the shape of threshing machines and, latterly, the combine harvester, was slow to develop in a county where the acreage of grain was comparatively small, and this contributed to the survival of traditional straw thatching. The isolation and backwardness of the county in the second half of the 18th century and the 19th century may have been over-emphasised in the past, but it became an agriculturally conservative place without the focus of the big cities that grew in the North and the Midlands.[6] Devon was not a county of particularly small farms in the 19th century, but it never had many large farms or fell under the influence of great improving landlords. In the 19th century it became, relatively speaking, plain and undramatically poor, probably suffering somewhat less from the late 19th century agricultural depression than counties where there were less flexible farming systems, or where there had been greater previous investment in farming progress, making the fall from prosperity more apparent.

After the agricultural depression the pattern nationally was of farms swallowing up their impoverished neighbours and becoming larger. In 1881, Devon had exactly the national average number of farms under 100 acres. In the 20th century, however, it remained a region of small farms, and indeed, a place where small farms were the centrepiece of its economy.

The historic pattern of change in the county established exactly the right environment for the survival of thatch. Building development was intense in the late medieval and early modern period when vernacular building materials were the norm, the thatching tradition was strong all over England, and thatch was used on the houses of the wealthy as well as cottages and farm buildings. Change was sluggish in the period when new harvesting technology could have brought the thatched tradition to an end and when local materials in other places were increasingly pushed aside by mass-produced building materials transported a long way. The demand for thatch, although much reduced, was strong on enough small farms and in villages during the late 19th and early 20th century to keep thatchers busy maintaining what was already there, even though few new thatched houses were built after the arrival of the railways and new farm buildings were roofed with slate.

Thatch in Thurlestone in 1900 on homes of different dates and sizes. The village shop to right, advertising the Western Morning News *is clearly a 17th century or earlier building.*

The developing tourist industry of the late 19th and 20th centuries also played its part in the survival of thatch. Visitors brought a new perspective to thatch, which was seen through the tourist's camera and as views on postcards. Tourism strengthened a self-conscious attachment to the thatched cottage as a distinctive element in the Devon landscape. This gave weight to campaigns to preserve thatch as its cost crept up in the 20th century, until demographic change and decline in Devon farming combined to transfer many old thatched farmhouses to non-farming owners who were keen to own thatched houses and could afford the costs of maintaining them.

If Devon is fortunate in the sheer quantity of thatching that survived, it is the traditional use of straw, rather than any other thatching material, that has given the

Changes to the Devon thatching tradition as it was consciously preserved and went on show for the tourist industry. Cockington in Torbay c.1860 with a thin rick-thatch on the house to the left. Over a century later in the 1960s, Cockington had become a major tourist attraction. The acceptable standards for the appearance of thatch had changed and the same house has a more substantial thatch with a block-cut ridge and more usable space in the attic.

Changes to the Devon building tradition driven by improvement. Government sponsored rebuilding of cottages for rural workers in Ilsington in the 1920s involving complete re-roofing and rethatching of the same building. More space, better ventilation and the arrival of a patterned ridge on the thatch are among the improvements.

county a bonus in the sheer bulk of historic thatch that survives on its roofs. When rethatching takes place, the old thatch on most Devon roofs is not stripped off right back to the roof timbers, but the thatcher removes only what is necessary of the existing, rotted thatch to reach a sound base into which a new overcoat of thatch can be fixed. Water reed thatch, by contrast to thatch using straw, is often stripped back to the roof timbers when roofs are rethatched, the old material being removed and disposed of. If we do not know why or when the technique of 'overcoating' straw thatch was begun in Devon, it was used on some houses as early as the 14th century and has been continued since. Today it has the practical advantage of sparing the thatcher or the owner the inconvenience of disposing of tons of old material. From an historical viewpoint, it has supplied us with a unique legacy, not just of old straw, but of information.

The technique of rethatching by overcoating leaves layers of old thatch underneath the new coat. If the new thatch overcoat was grown and harvested the season before it was fitted, the layers below were grown, harvested and fitted decades, even centuries before. In some surviving houses, pre-1550 thatch can

Above: *The technique of overcoating combed straw thatch in progress on the Cott Inn, Dartington c.1959. The landlord and landlady seem to be giving the thatcher a hand, perhaps for the benefit of the composition of the photograph.*

Left: *The tradition of overcoating has practical advantages. Stripping back to the rafters, which may be necessary if the roof has been very neglected, involves disposing of an enormous amount of old thatch, as shown at this house in Landkey in the 1920s. Regulations about the disposal of rubbish, as well as transport and labour costs, make it expensive for thatchers today.*

still be identified as the coat that is the one attached to the roof timbers. Here we have an extraordinary stock of actual crops – albeit rather dried out and dusty – that were growing in the fields from the medieval period. This is the largest resource of the study of historic plant remains – archaeo-botany – left in Europe. Examination of this material can show precisely what types of grain were being grown in different centuries. The heads, where they survive, can indicate the crop yields of the past and the thatch may include examples of the weeds and flowers that grew alongside the grain. Since little enough was written down about how England was farmed in the medieval period, this evidence is rich, direct and probably the most convincing source of documentation we shall ever obtain about early cereal farming in the county. Later layers of thatch, including those on houses that were built after c.1550, continue the story, right through to the present day overcoats. The thatched roofs of Devon farmhouses are libraries of unwritten information about the farming past. If we can learn how to translate that information accurately it can add enormously to our understanding, not just of techniques for fitting thatch in the past, but of grain-growing, harvesting and the ecology in former times.

Remarkable for the survival of numbers of thatched buildings, its old straw thatch a storehouse of information on historic farming, the county is the best place to investigate the history of the combed straw tradition, one of the three types of mainstream thatching that have continued in use in England to the present day. Nowadays combed straw is usually called 'combed wheat reed' or 'wheat reed' or sometimes 'Devon reed'. In this book it is called 'combed straw' because historically wheat was not the only plant used for thatching; rye was also commonplace.

It is not possible to understand just how remarkable the combed straw tradition is without reference to the other major surviving thatch types, water reed, and crushed straw, today called 'long straw'.

Water only penetrates a short way into the surface of the thatch, the rest remains dry. This can be seen on the underside of the eaves in the contrast between the darker, weathered thatch and the lighter colour of the thatch which remains dry.

All three types of thatch use long-stemmed plants, which are traditionally fitted to timber roof constructions. The objective of the thatcher is to produce an even roof, without any dips or hollows, to allow rainwater to run off swiftly and evenly. Rethatching a new house in any of these materials usually starts at the bottom of the roof. The thatch may be fixed to the roof structure in a number of different ways which have changed over time and, like slate or tile, is laid in courses, although these courses are not usually visible once the roof is completed. The early method of attaching the bottom layer of thatch to the roof timbers was stitching, using pliant organic materials and, later, tarred cord. Later, metal nails with a hooked end, called 'crooks' were used for some types of thatch, driven into the rafters, holding the thatching material down with lengths of split hazel or willow called 'sways'. This method was first used for water reed and was later extended to combed straw. In modern times wire sometimes replaces the lengths of willow or hazel. Today, some water reed and combed straw thatchers use screws, which are inserted into the rafters using a cordless electric screwdriver, with lengths of wire in place of the willow or hazel. This avoids knocking crooks into the rafters which can shake and damage old ceiling plaster. The last part of the roof to be thatched is the ridge, the finish of which may be managed in a number of different ways but which is built up over a long roll of thatching material sometimes called a 'dolly'.

As an organic material, thatch begins to age and decay from the day it is fitted. Over a period of time, the ends of the material exposed to the elements rot, until finally the fixings of the courses of thatch below begin to show. The ridge is the most vulnerable, and needs rethatching soonest, before the main pitches of the roof. Sometimes the rate of decay of a roof is uneven and a patch of new thatch may be needed to keep the roof covering sound. There comes a point where rainwater may start to penetrate and the roof needs rethatching.

Although all three of the major surviving English thatches have similarities in the general way the roof is approached, there are important and striking differences between them. There is also a great deal of variation, even today, in the way they are detailed. Thatch is the only roofing material today for which there is not a British Standard, although many thatchers work, formally or informally to minimum standards that were developed in the 1940s. This means there is still a wide variety of techniques employed by individual or regional thatchers, who may disagree on what makes the best roof. Methods may be used in one part of the country that would be frowned upon by thatchers in another. Sometimes it is possible to suggest practical reasons why this should be, but frequently it seems that it is a case of 'the way it has always been done'. All this can make thatching rather mysterious to a non-thatcher, along with the terminology of thatching which includes traditional names for fixings used, for the units in which thatch is moved about and the way it is measured.

Water Reed

Water reed thatch uses the long, stiff stems of a plant called *Phragmites australis*, grown in managed reed beds in wetland areas. Water reed is a familiar sight in most counties, growing wild in wet roadside ditches and big ponds, but a roof thatched with water reed absorbs a large acreage and reed beds need to be carefully maintained and regularly harvested to produce suitable thatching material. Norfolk is by far the largest and best-known English source of water reed for thatching but water reed is now also imported into England from as far afield as Turkey, Hungary and Austria. The reed arrives on site in bundles, with the flag of the reed all at one end. It is fitted to the roof with the ends of the reeds given a 'kick' at the eaves, giving each stem a slight bend. This means the underside

A water reed roof in Norfolk in the 1950s.

of each stem is in tension and the upper side in compression. The butt ends of the reed (the thickest part of the stem, at the bottom) show on the surface. Water reed used to be stitched on to the roof timbers, but today it is usually fixed into the rafters with metal crooks, the courses of material held down by wire. A bat-like tool is used to 'dress' the material into position, knocking it upwards, tightly into its fixings. This produces the cropped or quill-like appearance of water reed. Water reed is too stiff to bend over the ridge of a roof so a different, more pliant material, either straw or, where it is available, sedge, is used for the ridge. As previously stated, as a very general rule (to which exceptions are known from the early 1900s and many after 1945), when water reed is rethatched today, it is usual to strip all the old thatch back to the timbers, dispose of it and start again from the skeleton of the roof construction.

The Straw Thatches

1 – Crushed Straw ('Long Straw')

The other two thatches, crushed straw and combed straw, both use straw for the whole roof. Crushed straw, as far as we know, was not a thatching technique used in Devon, at least from the medieval period, and appears never to have been used in the county, although until World War Two it was the common straw thatch throughout southern England. Any plant, wheat or rye, with a reasonably long stem 0.9m (36ins) minimum is considered suitable for either type of thatch today. In spite of the modern common name for crushed straw, 'long straw' does not need a straw of any greater length than combed straw. Unlike water reed, it is rare today to strip a crushed straw roof right back to the timbers on rethatching. There are distinct differences in appearance between the two surviving straw thatches because of the way the straw is processed between the field and the roof and the way in which it is fitted to the roof. Experts, including thatchers, do not always agree on the definition of what is a crushed straw (long straw) roof. There is no simple blueprint and techniques vary from region to region and between thatcher and thatcher. Most people, however, would be able to recognise one, especially if was set side-by-side with a combed straw roof. Crushed straw has long lengths of straw visible on the roof, some of the straw lying with the ear end (empty of grain, which has been threshed out) outwards, some with the butt end outwards. When is has been laid, it has a rougher surface texture than combed straw, partly because the thinner, ear ends of the straws are mixed up with the butt ends, and partly because it is not dressed into position with a tool. Because it is not pushed into its fixings, as water reed is, crushed straw has external hazel

A crushed straw roof in Hampshire in the 1950s showing the typical external rodding at the eaves.

or willow rodding called 'liggers' to secure the thatch at the eaves. There are characteristic crushed straw techniques for finishing the verges of a gabled roof, and shaping and finishing the thatch around half-dormers.

The crushed straw thatcher carries out a lot of preparation on the ground before the material is taken up the ladder and fitted. The straw arrives on site loose and crushed from the threshing process. The thatcher makes a heap of straw on the ground, composed of layers wetted with buckets of water. The heap is then manhandled and teased out into 'yealms' on the ground. A yealm is a kind of raft or tile of straw, the stems mixed so that they do not all lie in the same direction, but the thicker butt ends and the thinner tops (formerly supporting the ears of grain) lie side-by-side at the edges of the yealm. After the eaves and verges have been thatched with special bundles or 'bottles' of straw, either tied or crooked to the rafters, the yealms are laid on the roof and fixed down with hazel or willow rods held in place by 'spars' a U-shaped staple made by twisting a length of hazel or willow in the middle and sharpening both ends. Because the ears and butts are mixed up and the straw is softened from threshing, the material 'hangs' and is not dressed into position with a tool.

2 – Combed Straw ('Combed Wheat Reed')

A combed straw roof on a house in Dartington, Devon, in the 1950s.

The straw thatch for which Devon has been famous, originated in the West Country and is now called combed wheat reed. The name combed wheat reed is a confusing one, because the 'reed' makes it sound as though water reed is used, but this thatch uses straw. Although the straw today is almost always from wheat plants, in the past rye straw was also commonly used. There are still many thatched roofs in Devon which have a recent overcoat of combed wheat straw and layers of earlier combed wheat or rye straw below. The material for the fixings may have changed, the varieties of wheat and the length of the straw may be different from layer to layer, but the basic technique has simply been continued. Crushed straw, as far as we know, was not a thatching technique ever used in Devon, at least from the medieval period, and appears never to have been used in the county, although, until World War Two, it was the common straw thatch throughout southern England. The South West: Cornwall, Devon, Somerset and parts of Dorset, did not use crushed straw but used combed straw which was not found outside the South West much before 1945.

Combed straw is a straw thatch but the result of a process that is markedly different from crushed straw. The straw may be from exactly the same plants but, unlike crushed straw, particular attention is paid to keeping the plant stems unbruised by the threshing process and maintaining it in neat bundles, in which the stems are all laid the same way, the butts at one end, the ears at the other. Both the threshing process, and the combing process (to get rid of short and broken straws, any rubbish and leaves) have been carried out in many different ways over the centuries, but both are now mechanised. The 'combing' of the straw to remove short or broken straws and weeds is not in itself unique to combed straw thatching. Crushed straw thatchers carry out much the same process on site, when they are making 'yealms' out of straw, using their hands as a rake but, in contrast to combed straw, mixing butt ends and ear ends. Combed straw demands special attention paid to the straw when it is processed, but there is less work on the ground for the thatcher, compared with crushed straw, before the material is put on to the roof.

Combed straw arrives on site where the house is to be thatched in 'nitches'. Historically a 'nitch' was a tied bundle of straw weighing about 12.7 kilos (28lbs). Today a nitch weighs about 6 kilos (14lbs). These are usually wetted before thatching and not untied until after they have been carried up onto the roof where the thatcher keeps them in a special cradle. There are various methods of obtaining a kick at the eaves and verges. The distance between the ends of the rafters and the outer edge of a thick masonry or cob wall may provide suffi-

A thatcher at Addisford, Dolton, in 1983 carrying a nitch of combed straw up to the roof. Photographed by James Ravilious.

cient kick, or a piece of timber may be attached to the ends of the rafters or the top of the wall.

Handfuls of straw are tied together and then tied on to the roof at the eaves and verges, being pushed together to keep an even surface. Above the eaves a layer of loose straw or backfilling is laid over the laths. In modern combed straw thatching, the courses above the eaves, laid in large handfuls, are temporarily secured with horizontal straw bonds pinned to the rafters. This allows the thatcher to knock the straw into position with a leggatt, a bat-like tool, giving an

even surface. As the thatcher proceeds, the courses are more permanently fixed to the rafters, either with a horizontal sway of hazel or with wire, held down by crooks, knocked into the rafters. This allows the ends of the straw to be dressed more securely with the leggatt. In the past, the courses above the layer of loose straw were usually stitched on, using a needle and some pliant organic material from the hedgerow or a twisted straw rope or cord, the needle being passed through the thatch, round the rafters and back to the thatcher on the outside. It is difficult to see how this would have been practical without an assistant inside the roof. Today, as with water reed, crooks are usually used. The ridge is created with a series of rolls of straw of diminishing size, the length required achieved by tying bundles of straw together with cord or straw bonds. The first roll is tied to the ridge, the upper rolls are fixed to it with spars. Spars must be fixed ensuring that their angle does not direct water down into the thatch. For a flush 'wrapover' ridge straw is bent over the upper roll, and sparred into it, the ends sheared to continue the pitch of the courses below. For a block-cut ridge, a modern ridge type in Devon, the plane of the ridge projects out from the rest of the roof.

Nigel Gard at Beaford pinning down a straw bond with a spar in a 1977. Photographed by James Ravilious.

Nigel Gard at Beaford in 1977, photographed by James Ravilious. The leggatt is a tool used by all combed straw thatchers to dress the straw into position. Water reed thatchers use a tool similar in shape but the diagonal ribs on the working surface are peculiar to combed straw.

A thatcher at Addisford, Dolton, making a ridge. The long horizontal roll is the foundation of the ridge. Photographed by James Ravilious in 1983.

Verges and eaves of a combed straw roof are cut into their final shape with an eaves hook and the surface of the roof is lightly raked and sheared to give an even finish and to clear away any bent straws. The objective for the thatcher is an even roof, with no dips to interrupt the flow of water, with rainwater carried efficiently away from any awkward junctions.

A combed straw thatcher at work. William Martin of the Rural Industries Bureau shearing the eaves of a combed straw roof with an eaves hook c.1950s.

Unlike crushed straw the butt ends of the stems only are visible on the surface of the combed straw roof, like the quill ends of a feather. This makes combed straw much closer in appearance to water reed than to crushed straw, as does the system of fixing the straw with a kick, which allows it to be dressed into position with a leggatt.

When a combed straw roof needs rethatching the usual practice is to strip the eaves and verges down to the roof construction and replace the old thatch there completely. The rest of the roof, however, is not stripped back to the rafters but only as far as a sound base of old thatch. This must be even and free from rot. The new overcoat is fixed into this base using horizontal sways which are secured into the old thatch using spars.

Since the 1950s, in addition to traditional straw roofs in Devon there is also an increasing number of roofs where combed straw has been overcoated, or sometimes replaced altogether, with water reed. Although there are strong visual similarities between water reed and combed wheat reed – both thatches being dressed into position and showing the butt ends of the straw as a series of little circles – there are points of difference.

As the stiffest of the thatching materials, water reed tends to give a roof a more angular appearance than either of the other two thatches. The comparative smoothness and weight of a stem of water reed, makes it more difficult to 'overcoat' one layer on to another. It tends to slip out of its fixings, especially on a steep roof. By comparison, both the straws can be overcoated relatively easily, the protruding nodes along the length of the straw helping to wedge the new coat into the old layer below. Single coat water reed tends to reflect the shape of the roof structure more precisely than an overcoated straw roof. Combed straw can be more easily shaped and turned around protrusions in the roof than water reed and subtle changes of angle are more easily managed. This, along with the shallow pitches of Devon roofs, has given a characteristically dumpy appearance to the outline of Devon houses and farm buildings.

Cliff Cottage, Paignton, probably 18th century, photographed in 1890. The curved roof on the outbuilding shows just how accommodating thatch is as a roofing material.

As a new overcoat of combed straw is fixed into old thatch, which has first been stripped down to a secure base, the new straw layer is added, not to the hard and distinct shape of a timber skeleton, but to a surface that is already soft and shaped by the surviving straw. With every new thatch, the shape of the roof takes on a new life of its own. As the layers of thatch build up over time, considerable depths of thatch may be found on a roof, rising slowly up the chimney shafts over the centuries. A point comes when the depth of thatch may need to be reduced, perhaps to relieve the roof timbers of the weight, or because a new overcoat (which can flatten the roof by several degrees, depending on the length of the material and thickness of the thatch laid), would flatten out the pitch to a point where the run-off of water would be unacceptably slow. Working chimney shafts also need to be a safe distance from the surface of thatched roof. The method of overcoating makes a major contribution to the beauty of Devon's traditional buildings as well as to the preservation of old thatch.

There are good reasons why Devon should have had a strong tradition of straw thatch, rather than water reed. There are estuaries and wetlands in the county where water reed grows, but nothing to compare with the Norfolk Broads and other favourable historic sources for water reed. It would have been impossible to supply all the county's needs from local water reed, even if transport had always been as effective as it is today. It is not hard to understand why Devon had a healthy tradition of slate roofing. Slate occurs naturally in the county, which it does not in the South East of England, and many of the slate quarries were conveniently sited close to the coast, making coastwise transport economical. The most promising locations for water reed are the coastal marshes of the South Hams, which also happen to be the very places where, historically, Cornish and Devon slate was traded coastwise. But straw was found everywhere on farms in the days when every farm was 'mixed' up to a point. Why was it used as combed straw in the South West and crushed straw in other regions? What is most obscure and in some ways most fascinating about the tradition is its origins. Having been established, the tradition took on a life of its own and stubbornly survived, even though the circumstances in which it was created were radically transformed.

The earliest complete surviving Devon houses (rather than fragments) were built c.1300. There is nothing primitive about their construction. By the date they were erected, there were already well-developed building traditions in the county, with cob and masonry walling and cruck roof carpentry. Combed straw thatching, too, was clearly a fully-developed tradition by this date and must have had a considerable past for which we simply do not have the evidence.

The earliest description of West Country combed straw found to date is in Fitzherbert's 1534 *Book of Husbandry*. This popular publication (it appeared in numerous editions in the 16th century) gave detailed advice on farming practice. In the section 'Howe to shere wheate' Fitzherbert comments:

> *And in Sommersetshire, about Zelcester [Illchester] and Martok, they doo shere theyr wheate very lowe, and all the wheate-strawe that they pourpose to make thacke of, they do not thresshe it, but cutte of the eares, and bynde it in sheues, and call it rede: and therwith they thacke theyr houses. And if it be a newe house, they thacke it under theyr fote: the whiche is the beste and the surest thacking that can be of strawe, for crowes and douues shall neuer hurte it.*[7]

Although Fitzherbert's description of cutting the ears off the wheat before threshing does not seem to have been common in Devon, where other techniques were used (judging from what survives), the principle he describes of keeping the stem of the plant unbruised is the same. The explanation Fitzherbert gives for treating the straw this way is given as keeping 'crows and doves' away. With crushed straw thatch birds can be attracted by the visible heads of the grain, where the odd ear may survive, and can pull at the thatch and cause damage, this is one of the reasons why crushed straw roofs are usually netted today. What Fitzherbert means by 'they thatch it under their foot' is a mystery. Later writers provided other reasons for the combed straw tradition they observed. In 1796 William Marshall noted that:

> *It is not for the purpose of thatch, only, that the straw of wheat is carefully preserved from the action of the flail; but for the purpose of litter also; it being found to last or wear much longer, in this capacity, than softly bruised straw ; which may be said to be already on the road of decay, and to have past the first stage toward the dunghill.*[8]

There was then, at least one good agricultural reason, generated by animal husbandry for the peculiar methods of threshing and combing devised in the county. Combing produced durable bedding for livestock as well as combed straw for thatching. This made good sense in a county which grew less grain than many others, making straw a relatively scarce commodity. Perhaps conserving straw for bedding purposes encouraged the management of the crop from the field in ways that influenced the county's thatching tradition. There is a chicken-and-egg element to this argument, as it may have been the demand for relatively scarce supplies of straw for a roofing material as much as for bedding that prompted the peculiar threshing and combing techniques in Devon, and these were found advantageous for livestock. Another possibility is that the method of combing straw was designed to overcome the natural disadvantages of the slack-pitched roof. If the run-off of water from a roof is comparatively slow, perhaps the technique of combing straw was thought to be a remedy. However, in Devon, given that many of the county's old rural houses were built from the outset to be roofed with thatch, we might ask why carpenters did not build steeper roofs to ensure that water ran off the thatch faster?

The origins of the combed straw tradition must remain a matter of conjecture. What is beyond question is that it was strong enough and long-lasting enough to have given the county a very special inheritance, one that is a direct link between the land and standing buildings and makes a major contribution to the history and the present character of the county.

Footnotes

[1] Letts, 1999, 3.

[2] Brockett and Wright, 1986.

[3] For example in Kent, Dormer Cottage Petham with evidence of early thatch, has two pitches, the lowest of which is 52°. Other recorded Kent houses where thatch was a possible original roof covering all had pitches of over 50° (*pers.comm.*, Sarah Pearson).

[4] Moir and Letts, 1999, 15, 18.

[5] Kowaleski, 1995, 16.

[6] As Sarah Wilmot argues in her thesis, 'Land ownership, farm structure and agrarian change in South West England 1800-1900: regional experience and national ideals', PhD Thesis, University of Exeter, 1988.

[7] *The Book of Husbandry by Master Fitzherbert*, reprinted from the edition of 1534 and edited by the Rev Walter W Skeat, 1882, 35-36.

[8] Marshall, 1796, Vol.1., 183.

2

MEDIEVAL THATCHING IN DEVON

Surviving Medieval Thatch

As the previous chapter showed, Devon is remarkable in having surviving early thatch due to the common practice of overcoating rather than stripping the thatch back to the roof timbers at rethatching. The earliest layer of thatch is visible from inside the roofspace, so long as later plaster has not concealed it. Traditionally in Devon, this layer and the one immediately above is left undisturbed at rethatching, unless the thatch has been very neglected. The thatch attached to the roof construction of Devon houses can be medieval in date which, in terms of house design, is usually pre-c.1550.

Rethatching only takes place when the overcoat has rotted back to its fixings, either in patches or altogether. This means that a complete historic topcoat in good condition would normally never be encountered. Thus we have no evidence for the external appearance of a medieval thatched house in Devon. Layers of moss or lichen (e.g. found at Broomham, King's Nympton) sandwiched between layers of straw, are an obvious sign of former overcoats. They indicate rethatchings where there was no stripping off at all, as well as providing physical evidence of a long history of moss growth on Devon thatch when the conditions were right. However, they also represent the state of the thatch at a time when it was due to be recoated and the thatch below the moss is usually very decayed.

The only chance of finding a medieval overcoat or ridge, visible and in good order, would be on a part of a thatched roof that had been protected from the weather for centuries. This is not an impossibility. Extending one end of a house, or adding a wing, might enclose part of the roof of the existing house and leave parts of the original covering roofed over and sheltered from the elements. There is at least one known Devon example of this, at Greenway, Luppit, though it dates from after c.1550. However, any thatch overcoat that has been roofed over by an early addition to the building would be a really precious survival.

In theory, disregarding the overcoat (which is not likely to be more than about 35 years old in Devon), it would be possible to peel off successive coats of thatch, travelling back in time with each layer, to eventually encounter the first thatch that was fitted. If the roof has never been stripped, this layer will be the same date as the roof timbers. In practice, however, the archaeological examination of old thatch is more complicated than this.

Firstly, opportunities for this kind of investigation are limited. Historic thatch is an important part of the structure and interest of an old building and is best left where it is. Even if some, or all of the roof timbers are failing, it is usually possible to design a repair that will save them, along with the thatch which is attached to them. There are exceptional circumstances where an archaeological excavation of old thatch can be justified. Extreme neglect (for example on

© Jo Cox

The addition of the wing on the front right of Greenway, Luppit, has left a portion of the main roof thatch inside the roofspace. This was not stripped off when the wing was added and has been protected from the elements. Additions of this kind are the only way that an ancient top coat of thatch could survive.

an abandoned house) might mean that no old thatch can be saved *in situ* but a close examination of the layers, as they are removed, could add to our understanding of past techniques and materials.

Secondly, examples of thatch excavation show that the pattern of 'layers' is usually a complicated one. The layers of thatch of particular dates are rarely evenly distributed over the whole roof. Before World War Two patching was much more frequent than the comprehensive rethatching that is common today, where at least one of the pitches (and often both) is rethatched at the same time. Patching would be applied to an area or areas of the roof that were showing signs of serious wear. Understanding the pattern of layers uncovered in an archaeological investigation of a roof is complicated by patching, which makes some layers a complex mix of differing dates. The practice of stripping back the eaves and verges to the timbers when rethatching means that ancient layers are rarely found at the outside edges of an old combed straw roof.

Thirdly, if a roof suffers a period of neglect, with water penetrating deep into the thatching material, the thatcher may need to strip off several historic layers left by his predecessors in order to find the sound base he needs into which to fix a new overcoat. This means that several layers may be sacrificed at one time at any rethatch, leaving gaps in the record.

The identifiable medieval thatch found in a number of Devon houses is the bottom layer, the one laid over the roof construction. Layers immediately above, may have survived too. C-14 radiocarbon dating of samples of straw is being explored but, at present, it is a method that is still being developed.[1] Until straw samples can be dated with accuracy, the most promising technique for dating thatch is to date the roof timbers by tree-ring dating. This means that, as long as the thatch can first be identified as contemporary with the roof timbers, it can then be dated, by inference, from them. As an indirect method this can never produce a certain date. There is always a possibility that the thatch, even though from a medieval phase, might be a replacement of a previous medieval layer, especially if there are several early phases to the roof timbers. However, if the roof timbers appear to be of one medieval period there is a very good chance that thatch attached to them is of the same date as the timbers.

The earliest known dated roof which still retains a medieval layer of thatch in Devon, The Old Rectory, Cheriton Bishop, has a felling date for the timbers of 1299-1300. If the thatch is the same date as the timbers, which in this case is probable, it is over 700 years old. This is an unusual combination of an exceptionally early Devon roof with thatch that has never been stripped off completely. There are approximately 180 houses known in Devon that retain thatch which is very likely to be pre c.1550 and undoubtedly more which have not yet been identified.

Thatch as Part of the Open Hall House

Before c.1550, most new Devon rural houses were built with open halls. The principal room of the house, the hall, was open from the floor to the roof timbers, with either one end of the house, or both, usually two storeys. Sometimes the house was open to the roof timbers throughout, with low partitions creating the rooms inside.

The open hall was a multi-purpose room and the focus of a largely communal way of life. It was often used for dining and hospitality as well as serving as a kitchen, and possibly used for sleeping too. It was usually heated by an open hearth fire, not contained in a chimney stack but burning on a hearthstone on the floor. The smoke from the open hearth fire rose into the roofspace and dispersed, occasionally with some help from a roof louver, but usually just

Above: *The Old Rectory, Cheriton Bishop. Medieval thatch attached to the earliest dated medieval house roof in Devon, c.1300. When the straw was growing, the present cathedral in Exeter was only partly rebuilt.*

Left: *Smoke-blackened thatch at Lower Woodbeer, Kennerleigh.*

clearing away by seeping through the thatch. The smoke discoloured both roof timbers and thatch, first tanning them brown but, after a longer period, leaving them thoroughly smoke-blackened with an incrustation of black soot which can be seen adhering both to the timbers and to the thatching straw. It is usually not difficult to distinguish this from localised smoke-staining from a leaky chimney. When the underside of a thatched roof is dark brown or black all over, it must be the roofing material that was on the house when an open hearth was in use.

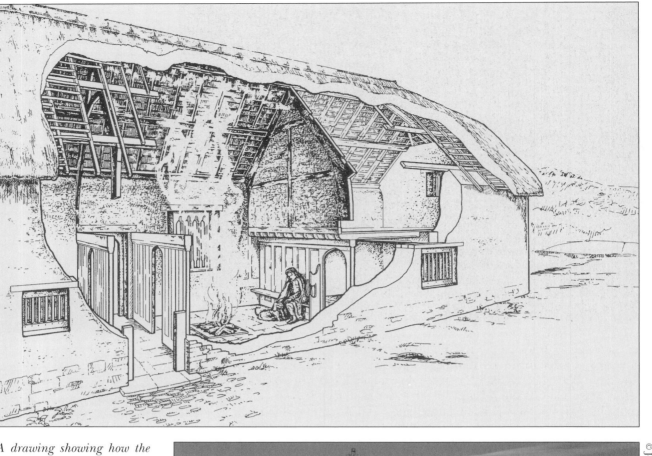

Above: *A drawing showing how the underside of the thatch in a Devon open hall house is blackened from the smoke of the open hearth fire. From a thatcher's point of view this is a relatively uncomplicated roof shape, all one height, with no chimneys projecting through the thatch and no awkward junctions with wings.*

Right: *Middle Clyst William, Plymtree. When the open hall design was modernised, the chimney stack to heat the hall was added on to the front of the house. This is quite a common arrangement in Devon and slightly less complicated for the carpenter and thatcher than introducing a stack projecting through the roof.*

As social life lost some of the communal character associated with the open hall, this type of house design gradually fell out of fashion and a larger number of more private rooms was considered desirable. This was a general change that was lamented as early as the late 14th century by the poet, William Langland, who recognised that the new remoteness of the master of the house was not only an architectural change but had social consequences for all the members of the household:

> *The hall is wretched, each day in the week*
> *Neither lord not lady like to sit there.*
> *The rich now have a rule to eat by themselves*
> *In a private parlour, to avoid the poor*
> *Or in a chamber with a chimney, and leave the main hall*
> *That was built for meals, for men to eat in,*
> *And where any spilled food was spare for another.*[2]

Langland was describing the houses of the rich on whom a substantial community might depend. At lower gentry and yeoman level in Devon, where a house-

In the roofspace of Middle Clyst William, Plymtree, the high quality of the roof carpentry and the smart coat of smoke-blackened thatch reveal the quality of the open hall phase. The horizontal trimmer timber between two of the rafters is part of a medieval smoke louver for directing smoke outside from the open fire in the hall. The straw bond that is not blackened probably relates to thatching over the louver after the chimney stack had been added.

hold consisted of the extended family and farm servants, abandoning the open hall came later. It was not until after about 1550 that new farmhouses were built with two storeys throughout their length and the fire was contained in a chimney. This gives a date for smoke-blackened thatch as usually pre-c.1550, before the introduction of fireplaces in stacks into open halls. Over a period of time, the older open hall houses were modified to provide the same arrangement of two storeys throughout, although there must have been an extended period in which some houses kept their open halls and open hearths, even when most farmhouses had been updated. This means that there may be some examples of smoke-blackened thatch that are late 16th century or even later, but most are likely to pre-date 1550.

After 1550 chimney stacks and first floors were introduced into the open hall section of the house, so long as the original design allowed enough height for this change. This provided extra first floor space by making the houses two storeys throughout. In many Devon houses there was enough room within the height of the original open hall to insert a good-sized first floor and a tier of first floor windows. In others the original height of the open hall may have been too low for this kind of conversion so it was necessary to raise the height of the walls and rebuild the roof altogether in order to fit in a ground floor and first floor room, each of a decent height, in what had been a single-storey space.

The alterations to open hall buildings in the late 16th century must have extended the skills of Devon thatchers. The gabled or half-hipped roof of an open hall house, with no projections or awkward junctions, required, as it still does, real skill to weather-proof with thatch. The thatcher has to ensure that the thatch is laid evenly to avoid surface dips where water may collect. The angle at which the thatch is laid, particularly at the corners of the building and the verges, must be carefully managed to ensure that the thatching material will shed water as quickly as possible. The thatcher must adjust this angle to produce a diagonal run-off at the corner but a straight run-off along the length of the eaves. The introduction of stacks to open hall houses involved projections out of the planes of the thatch which demanded additional skill from the thatcher, presenting awkward junctions and little valleys, and potential weak points where leaks might occur. In the 16th century these junctions were probably made with lime mortar, a technique that some thatchers continue to use. Lead for flashing, which is often used in modern thatching, would have been too costly and difficult to obtain then.

Right: *A thatched open hall house, probably 15th century, in Bickington, near Barnstaple. This one acquired a chimney stack, but was too low in height to introduce a floor and second storey in the hall and was still single-storey in 1949. The projecting oven and porch hood are both slated.*

Below right: *The interior was still 'open' in 1949 when the photograph was taken. The only modernisation of the space of the open hall was a plaster ceiling introduced below the thatch. Above the ceiling, the underside of the thatch was almost certainly smoke-blackened. The settle was a good draft-excluder and creates a 'room within a room' in front of the fire.*

Distribution and Survival of Smoke-Blackened Thatch

Smoke-blackened thatch is mostly a rural survival. There are relatively few urban houses of open hall origins surviving in the county. Houses in the large and middle-sized towns in the county were energetically rebuilt from 1550.

Exeter preserves an outstanding group of early clergy houses in Cathedral Close, but the Dean and Chapter owned a slate quarry in Staverton and these buildings were slate-covered from the outset. Bye-laws following severe fires in some of the middle-sized Devon towns gradually excluded thatch from urban areas. The evidence of pre-1550 thatched houses in groups or rows is confined to market towns that grew so little they are now regarded as villages. Silverton, in Mid Devon district, can claim two adjacent medieval open hall houses built together where smoke-blackened thatch survives.[3] Nos 26 and 28 Fore Street, Ide, in Teignbridge, may also be adjacent open hall houses, each with smoke-blackened thatch below later roofing materials.

© John R L Thorp

In the 1980s a resurvey of buildings in rural Devon was undertaken for the former Department of the Environment, to identify buildings in need of statutory protection ('listing') for their historic and architectural interest. Using the descriptions of those buildings, along with some additional information that has come to light since, it is possible to map the distribution of surviving smoke-blackened thatch in the county. Smoke-blackened thatch survives in far greater numbers in the county east of a diagonal line from Bideford on the north coast, to Dartmouth, on the south coast. West of this line there are far fewer surviving houses with known, or possible medieval roofs; the unoccupied uplands of Dartmoor take up some of the area. The western part of the county is also the area of the Devon slate quarries. East of this line there is a rich legacy of houses where pre-1550 timbers are either known to survive, or were suspected to survive on the resurvey, but this could not be confirmed because there was no access to the roofspace when the houses were visited. On the map shown on p.40 the dots that are half black and white represent houses that were definitely identified as having timbers blackened by an open hearth fire.

The map clearly shows that by no means every house with smoke-blackened timbers has preserved smoke-blackened thatch. Only a small percentage of houses, identified as black dots, also have smoke-blackened thatch. Some have a 'clean' coat of thatch, clearly applied at some date after the open hall phase of the house, others have modern slate roofs. Smoke-blackened thatch is a real rarity, even in Devon, which has far more of it than any other county. There is a handful of crushed straw roofs with smoke-blackened thatch in counties outside the South West. Why more have not survived is not clear.

A long thatched row of late 15th of early 16th origins in Fore Street, Silverton. Two of the houses still have smoke-blackened thatch. Silverton, now a village, was then a small town with a market charter and the row was built for merchants. The houses look very much like thatched farmhouses put end-to-end. They contrast with the more showy early 16th century timber-fronted, slate-roofed houses in large towns like Exeter, Totnes, Plymouth and Barnstaple.

SMOKE – BLACKENED THATCH IN DEVON

- ● sooted thatch roof
- ◐ smoke-blackened roof timbers
- ○ uncertain – medieval roof suspected
- ☐ major Devon towns

EXMOOR

305 metres

N

DARTMOOR

305 metres

SOUTH HAMS

0   10   20
kilometres

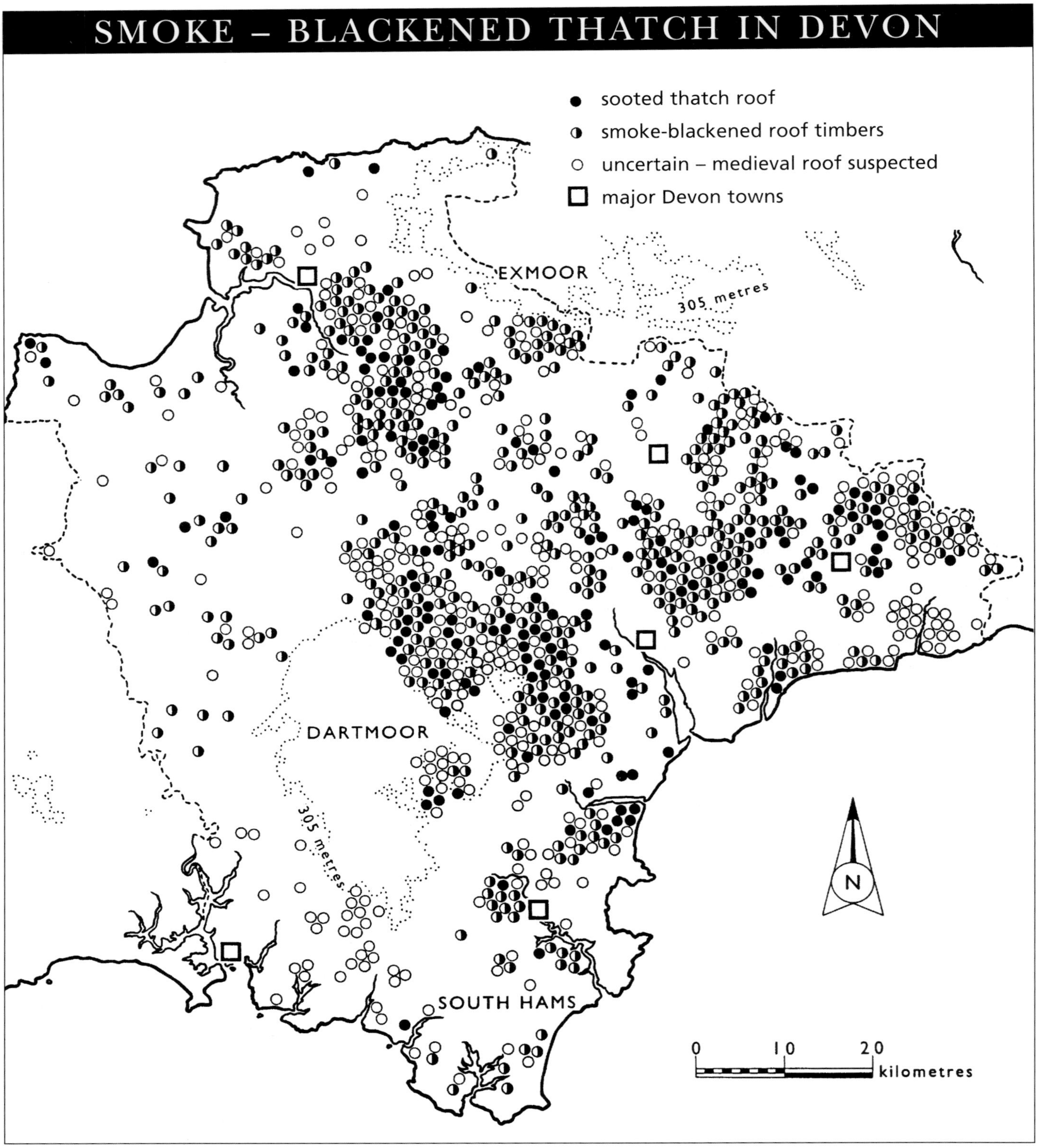

Map showing the distribution of smoke-blackened thatch and its survival compared with that of smoke-blackened roof timbers. Based on the listed buildings register.

The striking disparity on the map between the good survival of open hall roof timbers and the much rarer survival of the thatch that was laid on them needs explanation. A small number of open hall houses, usually superior in status, originally had Devon or Cornish slate roofs. These would have had smoke-blackened slate, rather than thatch, in the open hall phase of the house. In time, if the slate failed and was replaced with thatch, the open hall timbers would survive, but there would be no evidence of smoke-blackened thatch. There is a handful of open hall roofs in Devon where the archaeological evidence for this is plain because some smoke-blackened slates survive, either *in situ* or on the walltops. This suggests that although the original owner could afford slate, one of his successors did not have the means to repair or replace it, and decided to have the house thatched instead when the slates needed attention. Evidence of slate preceding thatch has been found in houses in Chittlehampton in North Devon and two houses in Mid Devon: Traymill in Thorverton and Moorstone Barton, Halberton. At Yeo Barton in Mariansleigh, a fairly complete smoke-blackened slate roof is visible in the attic, surviving underneath a later thatched roof which has been fixed over the top. Owners of other houses may have made the same change, but had the earlier slate covering removed to make fixing easier for the thatcher.

The surviving medieval window at Traymill, Thorverton, announces the early date of this house. The design of the roof construction is very high status. There is archaeological evidence that this house was originally slated. The replacement with thatch suggests a downgrading from the original covering by a later owner or occupier without the means to replace slate with slate.

Yeo Barton, Mariansleigh, where the originally open hall has a relatively complete medieval slate roof surviving under later thatch.

Yeo Barton, Mariansleigh. It is only inside the roofspace that the smoke-blackened pegged slates can be seen. Some of the damage to the slates and the laths over which they are hung on timber pegs is probably due to the ends of the thatching spars.

Bury Barton, in Lapford parish, is a superior open hall house now with a modern slate roof. It has evidence of smoke-blackened thatch below the modern slate. However, recent observation has also identified medieval smoke-blackened pegged slates, replaced before c.1550 with thatch, strangely enough following a fire. This roof tells a complicated story of switching from slate to thatch in the open hall phase as well as a change from thatch to slate afterwards.

To date, the evidence suggests that only a small number of open hall houses were originally slated, rather than thatched, but there is a possibility that there were rather more slate roofs than we know of in the county, subsequently replaced with thatch, at least by the early 17th century. A map of Halberton produced between 1603 and 1608 was used as evidence in a case about disputed water courses, but also shows a number of houses in the parish with chimneys, indicating that the open hearths had gone by this date.[4] *(See colour page 3, plate 9)*. The map-maker clearly shows roof coverings in two different colours, the larger buildings with blueish-green roofs, the smaller brown. This suggests that a good number of the larger houses were slated, while the smaller houses, mostly comprising only one range, without any wings, were thatched.

Where an unsooted base coat of thatch is fitted to sooted timbers, we have to assume that, if it was not slated originally, the thatch was stripped back to the rafters, including the sooted thatch, at some point after the open hall period. The thatch may have been neglected for so long that a sound base for fixing the new thatch just did not exist. The thatcher was thus obliged to start again from the roof timbering. If the thatching laths in an open hall roof are not smoke-blackened it may be that they had failed too, probably as a result of the furniture beetle, or stress as a result of the slippage of the thatch. The rarity of smoke-blackened thatch in the county, given the good survival of smoke-blackened roofs, suggests that a large number of thatched roofs suffered a period of serious neglect, almost certainly associated with times of economic hardship, and had to be stripped back to the roof timbers after the open hall period. Others may have been stripped back in the second half of the 20th century as a result of changing thatching practice, explained in chapter six.

When the hall was still open to the roof, the underside of the thatch in the hall was visible and was presented neatly to complement the roof carpentry. If the house had storeyed ends, the thatch would also have been visible from the first floor rooms and is likely to be as early and as well-presented as the smoke-blackened thatch over the hall. The underside of the roof covering in first floor rooms was not concealed by plaster between the rafters, or by flat plaster ceilings much before 1600, sometimes much later. If the ends of the house were divided from the hall by internal walls, this thatch, although likely to be just as old, will not be smoke-blackened like the thatch above the old open hall.

Materials and techniques used in pre-1550 Devon house thatching

The Roof Structure

The roof structure to which pre-1550 thatch is attached is usually oak. The thatching laths fixed to support the thatch on the backs of the common rafters are generally riven oak. When laths are used they may be quite wide and are usually pegged, rather than nailed, to the rafters. The system of using oak pegs for joining not only the main timbers of the roof, but also for fixing the laths to the rafters, may be one of the reasons why (comparatively speaking) so many examples of smoke-blackened thatch have survived in Devon. Pegs are a particularly long-lasting method of joining timbers; iron nails eventually rust through. The use of pegs has contributed to the survival of laths, the failure of which is likely to mean the stripping back of a roof to replace them.

Laths were only one method of fitting out a roof structure for thatch. Wattling is sometimes found as a substitute for riven laths in Devon. Wattling must have been less labour-intensive and presumably cheaper than laths, the wood simply trimmed clean of twigs rather than cut and split, and requiring fewer fixings to attach it to the roof construction. In regions where water reed is abundant, a layer of woven water reed is sometimes found as an alternative to laths or wattling and is called a 'fleeking'. This woven base of water reed is sometimes found below crushed straw roofs. No fleekings of this kind have been found in Devon, either in open hall or later houses. However, John Letts has identified one smoke-black-

Hendicott, South Tawton, is one of many houses of open hall origins in Devon where some of the original smoke-blackened roof timbers survive, including the carpentry of the half-hipped end and the medieval laths to support the thatch. The base coat of the original thatch was lost on both pitches at this end of the house in the late 19th century, along with most of the timbers on one pitch. Smoke-blackened thatch survives over the hall.

ened use of water reed in Devon, in a house in Otterton in East Devon. This is not woven and is used, not as an alternative to laths but in conjunction with them. It is composed 'c.60cm segments of water reed, laid in a thin layer from eaves to ridge, each course overlapping the top of the course below it'.[5] It is used to support lightly blackened cereal straw laid on top. It is the only water reed that has been identified to date in a pre-1550 thatched roof in the county.

Cereal Straw

Botanical sampling of smoke-blackened thatch in Devon by John Letts has established that it is usually composed of a mixture of rye or bread wheat.[6] The wheat and rye were not varieties with standard names, of the kind grown today, but tall, genetically diverse 'land races'. These ripened over a longer period of time – some individual plants ripening before others – than modern varieties which have been bred to ripen conveniently together, ensuring an efficient harvest over a short period of time. Just how tall the medieval cereals were is difficult to judge from what may be pulled out of a thatched roof, because each straw will have suffered a certain amount of weathering, reducing its length. The height of bread wheat in the field in the medieval period may have been up to 1.5m (5ft) tall. This would accord with many early illustrations, from all over Europe, of chest-high crops in the fields at harvest. The rye and bread wheat found in pre-1550 thatch is a direct reflection of the cereals that were grown in the local fields at the time and is part of the story of Devon farming.

Documents relating to the demesne lands of Devon (the lands of the lord of the manor, cultivated by the tenants of the manor) has shown that oats were the most common cereal crop grown in the county in the medieval period. They were well-suited to a damp climate and poor soil. To date, however, only one sample of oat straw has been found in the roofs of medieval Devon thatch, although it has been identified in other counties. Oat straw was the standard thatching material: 'used in many parts of Scotland, Wales and Northern England well into this century'.[7] Most thatchers today would regard it as a soft straw, compared with wheat or rye, and inferior for roofing. Oat straw may yet be discovered in more Devon roofs, and even if it is not, may have been used in the countless medieval houses that have lost their medieval thatch or have disappeared altogether. Its apparent rarity in Devon smoke-blackened thatch sampled to date may be a sign that oat straw was usually reserved for feeding livestock and when it came to thatching there was a preference for wheat or rye, even though they were less commonly-grown cereals.

After oats, rye was the favoured cereal on the demesnes of North and Mid Devon, with wheat preferred in South and East Devon.[8] Although the number of sampled roofs with medieval thatch is small at present (23 published) and most are from North Devon, the types of cereal found certainly support the view that rye was grown extensively in the county. The samples have raised some extremely interesting issues, though. More than half are from North Devon, where rye is known to have predominated on demesne lands but the samples include combinations of straw from rye and bread wheat. One Devon sample, taken from Pump Cottage, Harpford, in the east of the county, seems to show clear evidence of a mixture of rye and bread wheat, which may have been grown together as a mixed crop in the field.[9] Whether this means that our understanding of which cereals were favoured in different regions needs to be reconsidered, or whether thatchers regularly made use of bread wheat, even though it was a relatively scarce resource compared to rye or oats in some parts of Devon is, at present, uncertain. Medieval thatch is another kind of evidence that can help to amplify what is understood from paper records about the pattern of farming, as well as thatching, in the county in the medieval period.

In the 17th century, as agricultural ground was improved by liming and marling, rye began to be replaced by wheat, but continued in use on poorer ground. It was still being grown in Devon in the late 18th century, but seems to have largely disappeared by 1808:

> *There is no rye, cultivated for a crop any where in this county ; in some instances a small portion is sometimes sown with tares for spring food. An opinion prevails, that this grain was formerly cultivated to a considerable extent through the county at large, excepting only upon those extensive commons lying in Venville, and abutting on Dartmoor and Exmoor Forests. This conjecture seems confirmed in a striking degree, from the vast quantity of rye-straw which is found to form the lower layer in all the ancient thatched buildings, and the vestiges of an ancient cultivation, which are clearly to be traced on all the extensive moors and commons which occupy so large a proportion of the county. Here large fields of rye are said to have been cultivated, although the soil and substrata are by no means suited to the nature of that grain.[10].*

It would be helpful if we could assume from this comment, that when rye is found in any Devon thatched roof, it is always a pre-1800 layer.[11] However, thatching is full of exceptions to rules. As late as 1903, Crossing noted that 'a little rye' was still grown on Dartmoor and that this was done especially for thatchers.[12] It seems from this that the strength of the tradition of rye straw for thatching on Dartmoor survived in the form of a cereal crop dedicated to the thatcher.

If most of the samples show that both rye and bread wheat were used for thatching, other materials have also been identified, including rivet wheat, found on the eastern border of the county, in Chardstock.[13] This was a type of wheat with strong, thick-walled stems, which grew taller than the medieval bread wheats, 'averaging 140cms or more with varietal heights ranging from 120 to 180 cms'.[14]

Other Materials

Pre-1550 thatching was not confined to cereal crops, at least for the base coat. Broom (*Cytisus scoparius*) has been identified (on a rough base of brushwood, rather than riven laths) on the Dartmoor fringes at East Down Farm, Dunsford, overlaid by rye.[15] A sample of smoke-blackened broom from the base coat of the roof of the house has been kept by the owners of Higher Tor, Widecombe-in-the-Moor, also on the edge of Dartmoor.[16]

The Term 'Reed' and Water Reed

The term 'reed', found in the names 'combed reed' or 'combed wheat reed' or 'Devon reed' is something of a poser. It derives from the Old English '*ihreod*'. The Oxford English Dictionary identifies it as usually referring to water reed, the tall-stemmed plant that grows in wetlands and ditches. Does this mean that Devon straw 'reed' was copying an earlier or contemporary thatching tradition, which used water reed? The use of the word in Middle English, however, was quite a broad one, including a 'reed rope', a rope made of reeds and used for securing thatch to a roof and an 'oten reed' – a pipe made of an oat stalk, which was obviously straw. There are also 14th and 15th century examples of the term used to mean a stalk, or a branch or twig. It is clear from the context of the term 'reed' in old Devon documents that it usually means cereal straw and that the confusing use of 'reed' in modern English for thatching straw in the region is an ancient one.

Water reed thatch might be expected close to extensive reed beds, say at Dartmouth (where water reed was certainly cut for thatching in the late 19th century), or Slapton Ley. The absence of evidence for water reed, apart from the single example at Otterton, used to support straw thatch, might be a matter of lack of survival. It could be explained by a method of rethatching with water reed that involved stripping back to the rafters. This method is the one employed for water reed in Norfolk today, and is regarded as traditional there. It might seem obvious that since water reed must have grown on river banks, in ditches, ponds and estuaries in Devon, it would have been a choice of roofing material. However, John Letts has calculated just how time-consuming it would be to harvest enough thatch from these sources to satisfy the demand for even a single house.[17] At present no evidence has been found to indicate that water reed was used to cover Devon thatched roofs before 1550, and no certain evidence that it was used in the county before the late 19th century, with the exception noted on p.42/43.

From Field to Roof

The details of how straw was grown and processed from the field to the roof in pre-1550 Devon mostly derive from what can be seen in thatched roofs or have to be inferred from a variety of sources, not all specific to Devon, or from assumptions that there was relatively little change until the 18th and 19th centuries and later, after which written descriptions do survive.

What is known is that Devon farmers followed a peculiar system of planting as many as three cereal crops in succession, followed by putting the land down to

SOWING

REAPING

grass for several years. Fields were not left fallow, as was the practice in other regions. Wheat and rye were grown in the autumn. By 1667 it was reckoned that Devon wheat was ready to harvest at the end of July.[18] The cereals grown were taller, but of less even height than modern varieties and ripening was comparatively uneven between individual plants.

Unlike today, hand-harvesting was a slow process and harvest may have taken several days if not weeks. Hennell, collecting oral history of old practices

Medieval sowing, reaping, stacking and threshing corn by Sophie Sharif after various medieval manuscript illuminations. The threshing method shown is one that keeps the stems of straw in the same direction, as must have been the case in Devon, but here the corn has been cut off high on the stem. In Devon it would have been cut nearer the ground, giving stems of greater length.

THRESHING

MAKING A RICK

(although not specifically in Devon), in the 1930s, records cases where reaping took a month although, as today, the pressures of the weather might keep reapers out all night, working in the moonlight.[19] The usual method of harvesting wheat and rye was to reap it with a sickle, rather than mowing it with a smooth-edged scythe. The sickle, saw-edged until about 1800, is the harvesting tool recorded in most English manuscript illuminations showing harvest scenes.

Reaping well and all day, was hard work, as an 1871 description of using a sickle illustrates. The harvester (who might be of either sex and worked in teams) had to bring his or her body as close as possible to the ground to allow the sickle to sweep parallel to it. The reaper stood with feet apart and knees bent:

> *The body, on being bowed down, its weight is mostly borne upon the right leg, and while the sickle in the right hand is reaping the standing corn, the left hand gathers the cut corn.*[20]

A team of reapers at work, from Henry Stephens' The Book of the Farm, *published in 1871 Vol II, p.298. The technique in 1871 was probably little changed from the medieval period.*

There was another method of cutting cereals with a sickle. Documentary evidence indicates that, in some regions from the medieval period to the early 19th century, the ears of the corn were first cut off quite high on the stem, leaving a tall stubble or 'haulm', that was then separately harvested, keeping the sickle close to the ground. This practice is documented in other regions from the late 16th century.[21] To date we have no evidence, either documentary or archaeological, that this method of a double harvest, first of ears of grain and then of straw, was practised in Devon, either in the 16th century or before. In the early 19th century the absence of a double cut was noted, wheat in Devon being described as: 'cut so low as to leave nothing to answer what is called haulming in other parts of England'.[22]

Judging from medieval illustrations, the cut corn was gathered into sheaves by binders during the reaping process, all the stems lying in the same direction. Each sheaf was secured by a rope of twisted straw with a knot in it. Knot-tying had regional and personal variations which were noticed and illustrated as late as 1934 in Hennell's *Change in the Farm*. The sheaves were leant together in the field to form well-ventilated stooks to encourage the sap in the corn to evaporate. In 1667 Colepresse notes that in Devon this took from ten to twelve days.[23]

The crop, whether wheat, rye or oats, did not have to be threshed at a given time, but was one of the farm jobs that could be spread across the winter. The sheaves may have been temporarily stored in the field or in a rickyard, built into a rick and thatched over to keep the rain out. Alternatively, they may have been taken direct into the barn and stored in the dry until ready for threshing. The practice of storing sheaves in a building rather than in ricks may have been the more common method in Devon, where the quantities of cereal were comparatively small. By the late 17th century it was recorded that storage in barns was the common method in Devon, although cereal was stored in ricks in Cornwall. But rick-making was certainly part of the rural scene in 18th and 19th century Devon.

Whether stored in ricks or in a barn, threshing could be done either outside or on the threshing floor inside the barn doors which gave a well-lit, well-ventilated space for using the flail. The method before 1550 (and for long afterwards) was hand-flailing. This was applied to the whole of the crop and not only to wheat or rye set aside for thatching. The hand-flail, known locally as a 'drashel', was a vicious instrument consisting of two stout timber sticks, jointed together with leather, or a knot of twisted wood.

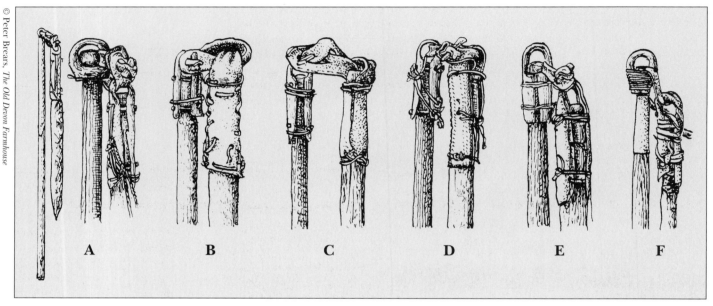

A   B   C   D   E   F

Various hand-flails (drashels) in the Torquay Natural History Museum. A: Pine, holly and rawhide, probably from Hartland. B: Pine, holly, horn and rawhide, from Thorverton. C: Ash, holly, horn and rawhide. D: Pine, unidentified hardwood, horn, leather and rawhide, the shaft stamped 'James Finla…' E: Pine, holly, bent wooden kibble and rawhide, used at Lower Tor Farm, Poundsgate, in 1934. F: Ash shaft with iron swivel and bound wooden kibble, blackthorn flail, rawhide middle band, probably from Oxfordshire. The illustration appears in The Old Devon Farmhouse *by Peter Brears and includes material from the Laycock Collection held in Torquay Natural History Museum.*

One of the riddles in the 8th century *Exeter Book* of poetry, held in the Exeter Cathedral Library, refers to a flail with a chain joint and its use by women. The lighter stick was the handle and usually of a different wood from the actual flail, which was stouter and cudgel-shaped. The flail was swung over the head and brought down rhythmically on the corn. The head of the handle was brought right down to make contact with the threshing floor and the bounce of the flail on the heap of grain and straw loosened and shook the grain out of the ears by vibration.

We do not know the details of how rye and wheat were threshed when thatching straw was required in the pre-1550 period. If they were the same methods that are recorded as continuing into the late 18th century there were several variations. One method was to whack a bundle of wheat or rye, the straw held by the butt end, over a stone or some kind of timber trestle or other device which would free the grain and keep most of the length of the straw undamaged. In the late 18th century, casks – which would have been common on Devon cider-producing farms – were sometimes used. When the flail was used, it must have been applied expertly to the ears of the corn only, shaking out the grain and leaving the straw destined for thatching undamaged. Samples of smoke-blackened thatch show evidence of what has been called 'apex flailing', the plant struck only on the ear of grain or just below.

There are modern descriptions of old-fashioned hand-flailing where sheaves were untied and arranged in two rows, with the ears together and butts outwards, the threshers standing at either end applying the flail to the ears only.[24] The ears of each sheaf might have been cut off and threshed separately with the flail, although this seems to have been more common in Somerset and Dorset than Devon. This would have spared the straw from coming into direct contact with the flail, and kept the stems unbruised and stiff.

The details of the combing process, undertaken to clean and straighten out the stems of the corn before 1550, are not known either from archaeology or documentation, but systems known to have been in use in the 1790s were simple enough to have had a long history. A small rake might be used on bundles of straw suspended from a kind of noose. A fixed rake system may have been employed, moving the straw, rather than the tool, and drawing the bundles through a large comb attached to a timber structure. A North Devon comb described in the early 20th century was about a foot wide with long teeth set about an inch or more apart and, after flailing the ears only the straw was pulled through the comb, first from heads to butts and then from butts to heads.[25] How ancient this practice was is unknown. Evidence of some crushed straw in medieval Devon roofs does indicate that parts of the corn crop were more comprehensively flailed and not all straw was treated with care. At the end of the process bundles of the combed straw known as 'nitches' were stumped on the ground to level the butts and tied up, ready to be used by the thatcher. These bundles are still known as 'nitches' and the term appears in historic records of Devon thatching.

Achieving a kick for combed straw thatching at the eaves and verges today is often managed by a piece of timber, as explained in Chapter One. However, rolls of straw, constructed like a ridge roll, could be tied horizontally to the roof at the eaves and verges, slightly projecting out beyond the walltops. Pre-1550 thatch might be fixed to the roof structure with a number of different materials.

Part of a smoke-blackened ridge roll from Pixie Cottage, Alphington, removed during rethatching in 1999 and held by the Royal Albert Museum, Exeter. The roll was constructed by tying bundles of straw together with knotted straw bonds. Although this was never intended to be seen, it is a fine example of pre-1550 thatch craftsmanship.

Above the loose layer of straw spread over the laths, any flexible plant might be used for tying the thatch on to the rafters. Straw could be twisted into a strong fixing. Old Man's Beard (*clematis vulgaris*) was noticed at a house in Rose Ash parish, North Devon.[26] Blackberry, the thorns stripped off, and wild rose also provided good pliant ties and have been noted in other counties. The technique of stitching the thatch to the roof would have been difficult for the thatcher without an assistant inside to pass the tie back out once it had been turned around the rafter. Most thatchers' 'needles' known from museum collections are metal and straight. Curved needles are also known but these are probably 20th century. In the Bicton Botanical Gardens, East Budleigh, there is one example from Devon of a curved needle patented for rick-thatching during World War Two.

The most simple 'needle' in the Bicton collection is a flat wooden one, tapered at both ends with a single hole in it, probably intended for use with twine. Like straight metal needles which were also used, this would have needed someone inside to guide it out around the other side of the rafter. We can assume that most medieval farmers had ladders long enough to reach the eaves of a house, and the 'thatcher's ladder', that can be hooked into the roof as the thatcher outside proceeds upwards, may be an ancient device. If an assistant was used inside the roof, how he got up to the apex of the roof of an open hall is unclear. A thatcher's 'palm' in the Bicton collection was a very simple fingerless glove of thick leather to protect the palm of the hand, presumably both when using pressure to push a needle or spars into the thatch and for using the hand as a tool for shaping and knocking the thatch up into its fixings. Kneepads were, and are, commonly used by thatchers whose work puts a lot of strain on the knees as well as the back.

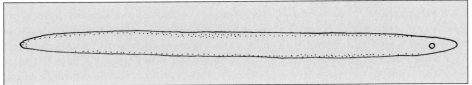

A wooden thatching needle from Otterton, presented to the Rural Life Collection at the Bicton Botanical Gardens, East Budleigh by Mrs Bastin of Pitson Farm. It is 545mm (1ft 9 ½ ins). The thatcher on the outside of the roof would probably have needed an assistant inside the roof to use a straight needle.

The Appearance of the Roof

The size, height and quality of the roof carpentry of a medieval house was the principal indication of the status of the owner. The appearance of the underside of the thatch in the open hall was also a mark of the owner's standing. Looking at blackened thatch that survives over what were the old open halls in Devon farmhouses today, it is quite clear that some thatchers went to considerable trouble to make something attractive out of the practicalities of fitting the layer of thatch over the timber structure of the roof. The first layer of straw over the laths contributed to the support of the rest of the thatch (most of the weight being carried by the rafters) and formed an even barrier preventing any odd ends of straw poking out. This layer in Devon is often rye straw laid, with what seems incredible neatness and care. The thin vertical lines of the straw contrast with the thicker horizontal stripes of the thatching laths. The regular positioning of the ties that attach the thatch to the rafters gives another layer of interest to the pattern. This would have been very difficult for one man to achieve working alone from the outside of the roof. Lower Chilverton, Coldridge, is a good example of patterned fixing. *(See colour page 4)*. The patterning is sometimes disrupted by age in the shape of slipped laths or broken ties but it is impossible to dismiss the impression that there was a strong element of display in the underside of the thatch in open halls and that it was intended to be admired.

A conscious attempt to make something decorative out of thatch that was visible inside would be perfectly consistent with the pre-1550 decoration that we know to have ornamented the better-quality Devon farmhouses. These houses are externally plain compared with those in timber-framed regions where the oak skeleton of the building could be exploited to external decorative effect. In Devon, dressed stone was sometimes used but mass wall construction of stone rubble or cob did not provide the same opportunity for external display. The interiors, however, used texture and pattern to good effect. Houses of much the same size might reveal, in their internal use of pattern, as well as long-disappeared furnishings, significant differences in the status, social pretensions, and disposable income of their owners.

If thatchers could produce thatch that was a practical waterproof covering and also decoration for the interiors of new houses before 1550, it is impossible to know whether this was at the request of the owner or just something that was done without discussion because both craftsman and client expected it. The development and spread of this aspect of the thatcher's craft deserve to be better understood. Did the client ask for his thatch to look like, or look better than, the one in a neighbour's admired house? We know that this was the way that some features of medieval church design were copied and improved on, and it may have been the same in domestic buildings.

The underside of smoke-blackened thatch is not always smart. When wattling is used to support the thatch as an alternative to laths the appearance is striking, but not so neat, as at Townsend Farm, Stockland.[27] The brushwood base at Down Farm, Dunsford, Mid Devon is a rustic affair. At Tytherleigh Cott, Chardstock, East Devon, however, wattling is associated with a superior medieval house with cusped decoration to the roof carpentry. *(See colour page 5, plate 14).*

We do not know whether some thatchers always provided a neat layer of straw over the laths and took a pride in them, or whether the same thatcher, working for a less important or less fussy client in the same parish, might have chosen wattling or brushwood instead. It is more likely perhaps that, as today, some thatchers were simply more skilled than others. The more skilled may have been distinguished from those who had thatched inferior buildings and structures and may have been sought out for better-quality, more showy work.

© John R L Thorp 1987

Stoney Court, Talaton. This medieval roof has a rough brushwood base supporting the base coat of thatch.

West Hele, King's Nympton. The ties woven round the thatching battens contribute to the decorative craftsmanship of the underside of the thatch.

© John R L Thorp 1994

Selective archaeological sampling has shown that the precise neatness of the layer against the laths was abandoned for the layer of thatch above it. This can consist of a fairly rubbishy collection of what has been called 'thatching waste', including short and broken straws, to bulk up and create an even surface for the layer of thatch above. At Broomham in King's Nympton, North Devon *(see colour page 6)*, the thatcher used handfuls of straw bent into a U shape. In Devon these are known as 'plugs' and may still occasionally be used to repair dips in the surface of the thatch by pushing them in under the surface with a tool shaped like a cricket bat *(pers. comm.* Tristan Johnson). At Broomham they seem to have been used, not as a repair, but to construct a sound, flat surface for the layers above. Some of the plugs are smoke-blackened and some are not, which suggests that at least one rethatch on the house involved stripping back to the 'plug' layer after the open hall phase of the building and adding more plugs to make up an even surface for the new overcoat.

Surviving smoke-blackened thatch that includes evidence both of ties and of smoke-blackened spars indicates that the original thatch was created as a series of layers: a loose and often neatly-arranged layer of straw on the laths; a layer stitched to the rafters; a packing layer to provide an even surface if the roof construction itself was not very even, and a final coat sparred on over the top. As Moir and Letts point out, the stitched coat could use ties round the laths, although these were a less secure fixing than rafters and there was some risk of them being pulled away from the rafters.[28]

We can only judge the appearance of pre-1550 thatch from the underside of a small number of surviving pre-1550 houses, most of which are high-quality structures. We know nothing of medieval thatch either higher up, or lower down, the social scale. A late medieval chapel at Bury Barton that is thatched today has been stripped back to the timbers at some point in its history. How many medieval parish churches were thatched is unknown. In East Anglia, there are still some medieval churches thatched with water reed. It seems certain that some Devon churches were thatched. The remains of thatch were found on the chancel of North Bovey parish church during an early 20th century restoration, but it is not known when it had been replaced with slate. Most Devon parish churches, however, have major phases of enlargement in the 15th and early 16th centuries and it seems most likely that when they were enlarged, thatch was replaced with wooden shingles, local slate or, where it could be afforded, lead. Some churches are recorded in the 17th and 18th centuries as having wooden shingle roofs, although it can be difficult, from the terminology used in documentation, to distinguish these from slates. Wooden shingles, pegged into oak boards, survive in at least one Devon domestic building, Cottles Barton in North Tawton, an Elizabethan manor. The roof has been thatched over the shingles. The photographic record shows that in the late 19th century churches were in the forefront of a general change from local slates pegged over laths to Welsh slates nailed into battens. From this one might expect that they also led the way in the change from thatch to slate in the late medieval period. The sheer size and height of parish church roofs would have made the regular maintenance of thatch more onerous than on domestic buildings.

A late medieval chapel at Bury Barton, Lapford.

We do not know whether the techniques that can be examined where smoke-blackened thatch survives today also applied to the modest cottages and hovels of the same period. No pre-1550 thatch survives on farm buildings, except over the shippon end of some longhouses. We must assume that just about every pre-1550 farm building was thatched. Relatively few complete agricultural buildings survive from this period in the county, but even if the requirements for buildings for livestock were limited then, compared with today, there must have been, in addition to the ubiquitous barn, medieval cowhouses, stabling for draught animals and storage buildings for implements.

Agricultural thatching may always have been lower quality and we do not know whether early farm buildings were given coats of thatch thick enough to use the technique of overcoating. Surviving examples of thatch that may be 19th century (under later corrugated iron or asbestos roofs) are usually notably thin. Whether or not this was the case from the medieval period is unknown. Farm buildings are certainly more likely than houses to have suffered periods of neglect and to have needed stripping back to the timbers.

Thatch was also a useful precursor of the tarpaulin, and short-lived thatch, which must have been commonplace pre-1550, was still being used in the 1950s. A thin thatch could keep the weather off not only ricks and hay stacks, but stacks of wood for fuel were certainly thatched. Cob boundary walls in towns may have been thatched, as some still are today.

The Combed Straw Tradition and Devon Farming

To understand, or speculate about the origins of the combed straw tradition, we have to look at Devon farming which produced the raw material and the special systems of processing the straw for thatch. The combed straw tradition depends on cereal growing. Up to a point, all farms mixed some kind of animal husbandry with cereal farming before the 20th century, since the two systems were interdependent. Livestock was needed to manure the fields for cereals, and every farm probably grew some kind of grain for home consumption, if not enough to take to market and sell. The percentage of land under cereal production in the county has varied a good deal from century to century and district to district. The South Hams, for instance, in contrast to most of the rest of Devon, produced cereals in cash-crop quantities from the medieval period. Nevertheless, the wet climate, mild winters and heavy soils made the county ideal, not for grain-growing, but for grass.

Good husbandry could produce acceptable grain yields in Devon, as Finberg's analysis of the records of Tavistock Abbey show.[29] The general picture, however, is one where cereal-growing, relative to some other regions, did not predominate in the 14th century. This was a pattern that became more marked in the late medieval period, when Devon farming became more skewed towards animal husbandry. When twenty out of thirty acres was given over to arable farming in East Somerset, the proportion in Devon was ten out of twenty.[30] North Devon specialised in livestock rearing, East Devon in dairying. The development of the cider industry in the 17th century also saw a reduction in the acreage of arable land, as the favoured site for orchards.[31] The simplest evidence of the balance in favour of pastoral farming systems in Devon can be seen in the relatively small size of farm barns in Devon compared with, say, Kent. In Kent it is not uncommon to find two large 16th or 17th century barns on farms of modest acreage, sometimes supplemented by a third added in the 18th or 19th century. Far fewer early barns have survived in Devon and those that have survived are small.

An agriculture that was not weighted in favour of cereal might seem an odd background for a specialised straw thatching tradition, particularly one that required especial care taken on the farm in the method of threshing and combing. However, as James Moir has argued, given the demand for bedding for livestock (as well as straw for other purposes), straw was a scarce resource and therefore a more precious commodity in the Devon agricultural system, than in regions where more grain was grown. The system for producing crushed straw thatch in the Midlands and East Anglia, where straw was not combed as part of the harvesting process, may have been the result of simple abundance. All this does suggest that combed straw thatching was considered a 'better' method than crushed straw in Devon, and in the other south-western counties, or at least the best that could be managed given Devon's unfavourable climate for thatch.

Footnotes

1. Letts, 1999, 11.
2. This is a free translation of lines 96-102 of Passus X, The B text of *The Vision of Piers Plowman* edited by A V C Schmidt, 1978, 103.
3. Thorp, J, 1982, 173.
4. Ravenhill and Rowe, 2000, 28, 30, 31.
5. Letts, 1999, 58 and plate 67d.
6. Letts, 1999, 52-59.
7. Letts, 1999, 23.
8. Kowaleski, 1995, 14.
9. Letts, 1999, 58.
10. Vancouver, 1808, 170-171.
11. Vancouver's information that rye had been grown extensively on the fringes of Dartmoor is supported by an 1854 prize essay. The author repeats the information that 'for many years past its culture has not been carried out on Dartmoor, yet from the general use of rye-straw as thatch on the old cottages and farm-buildings, we may infer that is has been extensively cultivated.', *'The Cultivation of Dartmoor'*, April 7th 1854.
12. *Crossing*, 1992 edn., 32.
13. Letts, 1999, 54-55.
14. Letts, 1999, 20.
15. Letts, 1999, 55.
16. Jenny Sanders, *pers. comm.*
17. Cox & Letts, 2000, 12.
18. Colepresse, transcribed and edited by Stanes, *TDA*, Volume 96, 1964, 296.
19. Hennell, 116, 120.
20. Stephens, 1876, Vol 2, 298-299.
21. One of the later editions of Thomas Tusser's *A Hundred Good Points of Husbandry*, first published in 1557 refers to this practice, the 'haum' used specifically for thatching. Neve also refers to thatching with 'Helm', 1726, 256.
22. Vancouver, 1808, 142.
23. Colepresse, transcribed and edited by Stanes, *TDA*, Vol.96, 1964, 296.
24. Hennell, 1934, 170.
25. Hennell, writing in 1934, 156, notes that this 'old' North Devon method was described by Mr Passmore of Reading University.
26. By Ray Harrison.
27. Beacham, 1990, 51.
28. Moir and Letts, 1999, 195.
29. H P R Finberg, *Tavistock Abbey*, 1969.
30. Harold Fox, *pers. comm.*
31. Thirsk, J., *The Agrarian History of England and Wales, Vol 5*, 1640-1750, 1984, 384, citing primary sources in the PRO.

3

THE GOLDEN AGE
1550–1750

Devon was a prosperous place in the late 16th and 17th centuries, much of its wealth coming from the cloth industry. This was an economic activity that spread across the rural and urban population, from farming to weaving on farms and in village houses, to the finishing processes and trading in the towns. After 1640 'The South West was one of the country's foremost industrial areas and, after Middlesex and Yorkshire, Devonshire probably contained more people than any other county in England'.[1] Late 16th and 17th century wealth is witnessed by an explosion of building activity in Devon. This was of a quality and soundness for much to have survived today. While the grander buildings kept up with the latest styles and fashions, the great majority of more ordinary buildings were created or improved in the strong regional building traditions and finished with combed straw roofs.

Hole Farm, Black Torrington. A late seventeenth-century house and probably not much changed externally, apart from some enlargement of the windows, between then and this photograph of c.1900. The patched condition of the thatch at this date is typical of standards judged on the basis of keeping out the weather rather than the pristine appearance that is often expected since the mid 20th century. This house is little changed externally today.

Above: *Gosses at Wembworthy, new-built in the 17th century.*

Right: *Thatch covers a 17th century or earlier cob and stone farmhouse, South Hall Farm, Meshaw, shown in a photograph of c.1910, and extends across the adjoining agricultural building.*

At the same time agricultural improvement in both Devon and Cornwall impressed contemporaries and this, too, increased the demand for thatch. Hooker, writing in 1600, recorded the abundance of sheep to serve the cloth trade, efforts to cultivate new land, and the improvement of arable land using ashes, sea sand, seaweed, straw, ferns, stable manure, lime and marl.[2] In some places between 1500 and 1640 rents rose ten times over and farms for which it had previously been difficult to find a tenant 'were in great demand'.[3] Feeding the population was a profitable and expanding business. An increase in arable land meant a demand for short-term thatches over ricks and the need to increase barn sizes for storing grain. It also supplied the raw materials for the thatch that was needed for building. Progress in farming and an increase in farm capacity and output were also reflected in new buildings for animal husbandry. If there was competition with slate as a roofing material for buildings at the top end of the scale, thatch continued to be the roofing material for most Devon farm buildings until the 20th century. It is on farm buildings that the loss of the thatched tradition is most striking and some imagination is needed to reconstruct the sheer quantity of thatched roofs in farmyards that must have been such a familiar part of the rural scene.

The majority of formerly thatched farm-buildings have been re-roofed with slate or corrugated iron like this linhay at West Ford, Cheriton Bishop (right), and this modest c.1700 cob threshing barn at Lower Lovaton, South Tawton (below).

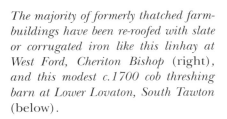

Materials and Techniques

To date published scientific analysis of historic thatch in the South West has concentrated on medieval open hall roofs, but there are some published examples where layers above the sooted medieval thatch, or the coat attached to the rafters, are probably 17th century. Broadway House, The Square, Whimple, for example, has a thin layer of combed straw tied to battens with both straw rope and twine.[4] This is probably contemporary with the early 17th century roof timbers. The references to the use of needles in the 17th century thatching accounts (see below) suggests that twine (probably hemp) was commonly used to stitch the thatch to the roof construction. As a maritime county, rope-making and cordage were well-developed industries in Devon, and hemp was grown extensively in the hinterlands of fishing villages. However, it is striking that no references to 'cord' in thatchers' accounts have been found before the 18th century. Thatchers' accounts are few and far between and it is difficult to generalise from them, but it may be that plant stems and straw rope continued to be the common material for stitching thatch to the roof construction in the 17th century. 'Crooks', hooked iron nails, would have been expensive. The date at which crooks began to be used in Devon may emerge from more archaeological excavation.

In 1572 prices for grain given in the *Calendar of State Papers* show increasing costs from Dorset west to Cornwall, reflecting abundance fading out to scarcity from east to west as the conditions for grain-growing deteriorated. Best quality wheat fetched 16s a quarter in Dorset, 20s in Somerset, 26s 8d in Devon and 48s in Cornwall. Rye rose in price across the four counties from 10s in Dorset to 16s in Somerset, 21s 4d in Devon and 32s in Cornwall.[5]

Arable farming underwent changes in the late 16th and 17th centuries which affected thatching. Rye was a useful corn crop on poor soil. The improvement of land, noted by Hooker, meant that it could better support wheat. Wheat, rather than rye, must have been increasingly available to thatchers, although availability would have varied according to the type of land, the investment in improvement and to the conservatism of tradition. There is good evidence that the fringes of Dartmoor continued to have a strong rye-growing tradition when other areas had switched to wheat. Sampling more old thatch should help to develop the picture of where and when this happened. Devon thatchers must have gradually become accustomed to thatching with straw that was changing as regards variety and availability. It would be interesting to know whether the older thatchers grumbled about the disappearance of rye straw, which is somewhat thinner and more wiry than wheat straw, and what they thought of the relative merits of the two.

Contemporary sources on arable farming with direct relevance to thatch are hard to come by. In 1667, Samuel Colepresse described many of the types of wheat used in Devon, along with brief descriptions of their preferred soil type and the ailments they were prone to. Some types he mentioned were:

> Red, (subject to rust in low, and fatt ground) white, (most subject to Blacke-wheate,) Bald (or bearded), like barly, ear'd, 4 square, of more graines than other sorts, higher and greater straw'd, or reed: yet not profitable for the Bakers in respect of colour tho'e good yielding bread-corne.[6]

The reference to bald or bearded wheat 'higher and greater straw'd, or reed' does suggest that at least this type of wheat was recognised as particularly suitable for thatching, because of its length of straw, and was perhaps specifically grown for thatch by the late 17th century, despite shortcomings in colour for the baker. To date, there is no convincing evidence of the use of water reed for thatch in the period, although there is one thatcher's account (see below) that might be interpreted as referring to water reed being used close by the most promising source of water reed in the county.

Until more information comes to light we have to assume that the simple methods of production and the same kind of tools were employed for thrashing and combing as were recorded at the end of the 18th century and which are assumed to have been similar to those employed before 1550.

Rural Thatch

The conversion of the pre-1550 medieval open hall houses into comfortable two-storey farmhouses did not in itself provide more roofed space, just more rooms under the medieval roof. In line with rising expectations of comfort, plaster ceilings were introduced to the upstairs rooms, usually following the lower slope of the roof up to a flat ceiling at collar level. Such ceilings were increasingly installed from the 1560s onwards. Whilst this produced warm,

A plaster ceiling of c.1600 on the first floor of Clysthayes, Silverton. This is an example of very high quality plaster-work below thatch. Plain ceilings were more commonplace.

clean and comfortable bedchambers, it also marked the beginning of the end of the tradition of showpiece oak roofs with the underside of the thatch designed to be seen in the principal room. It was not only in upper rooms that thatch was concealed. At Flood Farmhouse in Drewsteignton, the only known cob longhouse in Devon, the exposed thatch above the 17th century staircase was obliterated by plastering between the rafters, directly on to the thatch. The spaces between the rafters were completely filled with plaster which was carried over the rafter faces to give a smooth surface in a single plane. The arrival of plaster ceilings in upper rooms depended on the pocket and taste of the owner, as well as the status and use of the rooms, and this applied to new 16th century and 17th century houses as well as to improved medieval ones. Nevertheless the master bedchamber was usually ceiled and, if money allowed, it sometimes featured ornamental moulded plaster decoration. Essentially, from the late 16th century onwards, thatch was meant to be seen from the outside. The introduction of plaster ceilings on the first floor obstructed the thatcher's access to the inside of the roof. If the thatch on a roof fell into disrepair and had to be stripped, it would have made it difficult to stitch a new coat on to the rafters without sacrificing the plaster, and this must have been a motive for keeping thatch in good repair.

Domestic Buildings

Conversion to two storeys throughout was often accompanied by some enlargement of the building. Many houses added lean-to outshuts along the rear to provide a more convenient space for storage, dairying or service rooms to the kitchen. The inner room was sometimes extended by a bay to create a parlour with a generous master chamber above, or the service end extended for a kitchen. It is interesting that the roof carpentry in such extensions was sometimes built higher than the old medieval trusses so that the outside roof ran continuously across both. In this way the builders adjusted design to accommodate the thickness of thatch over the pre-1550 roof which had already built up several coats. This can be seen at Hill Farm, Christow, where the rafters of the open hall are lower than the 17th century parlour extension.

Prowse at Sandford. This is a medieval farmhouse enlarged and remodelled in the 16th and 17th centuries. The farmer today grows wheat for combed straw thatching.

Archaeological analysis of Devon farmhouses has shown that, in general, the pace of change quickened from the 16th century into the 17th century. For instance, Great Moor at Sowton underwent a series of alterations in the 17th century. It was first built as a two-room open hall plan house but was progressively enlarged and modernised through no less than eleven building phases up until c.1720. By this date it had become a spacious house with a large kitchen, a three-storey parlour block and service range. It seems that each generation had sufficient disposable income to make their mark on the building. Most of the improvements dated from the 17th century with, for example, three rearrangements of the kitchen between c.1650-1700. By the 1690s the house had risen in status to become the home of an Exeter physician and included some elegant polite joinery and plaster features. However, it kept a thatched roof throughout all these improvements and this stayed little changed up until the 1970s, when the house was demolished.

The quality of craftsmanship in many of the new or modernised thatched farmhouses of this period is very high. They bear comparison with those of the same date from anywhere in the country. This is evidence that combed straw thatch was not just a serviceable form of roofing but also very acceptable in appearance on well-built houses throughout the greater part of Devon. Even quite high-status gentry houses were thatched, as for instance, Hayes Barton in East Budleigh, the home of Sir Walter Raleigh, which was rebuilt in 1627.

Above: *Westacott, Coldridge. A 17th century remodelling of an earlier house.*

Right: *Buddle Cottage and Bowdel, a 17th century house at Cheriton Fitzpaine, later divided into two.*

Right below: *Hayes Barton, East Budleigh, the home of Sir Walter Raleigh. It is mansion-sized, dating from a 1627 rebuilding, but has always had a thatched roof.*

Chaffcombe Manor in Down St Mary and Langford Court, Cullompton, are typical examples of superior properties where the houses were massively enlarged in the mid 17th century, finished to a high quality but retained thatched roofs. Presumably their owners benefited from proximity to the then prosperous market towns of Crediton and Cullompton. Both featured two-storey porches with richly moulded outer arches, and Chaffcombe has 17th century gabled dormer windows with carved bargeboards. The gabled dormer was a design that required a good deal of skill from a thatcher, to accommodate the junctions with the main roof. When required, thatchers could, and did, adapt to the demands of more complex roof forms in the 17th century and the skills in fitting combed straw thatch kept pace with changes in roof design. There are countless examples of smaller new or modernised medieval houses, such as Basclose, Otterton, which maintained their thatched roofs, but particularly in Mid, North and East Devon.

Above: *Chaffcombe Manor, Down St Mary, mid 17th century. The gabled two-storey porch and gabled dormers, which have original shaped oak barge-boards, make for complicated thatching by comparison with the simple roof form of an open hall house.*

Left: *Smaller than Hayes Barton, Basclose in Otterton is still a very substantial house. It is dated 1627 on the chimney stack. Like Hayes Barton, it is probably a modernisation and rebuilding of an earlier house, reflecting a flourishing economy in the early 17th century.*

As in the pre-1550 period, thatch was not found everywhere, given that West Country slate was a roofing option for some owners. For new 17th century houses, some owners chose thatch, as at Spence Combe, north of Crediton *(see colour page 7, plate 20)*, Gosses, Wembworthy, and Great Gutton, Shobrooke, while some chose slate, as for instance Whitehall in Hemyock, erected in c.1651. Whitehall was not far from the Somerset slate quarry at Treborough. As the

Great Gutton at Shobrooke. A 17th century thatched house unusual for Devon in preserving nearly all its original mullioned windows

more expensive option, slate covered the houses of the very rich or very superior, as for instance Cadhay, Ottery St Mary, enlarged by Richard Hayden in 1617, Poltimore House near Exeter, the late 16th century mansion of the Bampfyldes and Richard Reynell's Forde House at Newton Abbot, built in 1610. By the end of the 17th century, following the Restoration, the larger mansions favoured a metropolitan classical style, all covered with slate. There are examples from Youlston in the north of the county near Barnstaple, to Puslinch in the south, near Plymouth, or Stedcombe House near Axmouth.[7]

It is telling that all the houses illustrated in the late 17th century manuscript, the *Spoure Book*, these being the Devon and Cornish homes of a well-connected family with gentry pretensions, are shown with slate roofs. Minor and agricultural buildings are shown thatched, even when close to the house. The Prideaux drawings (made on tours of 1716 and 1723) of Devon mansions, mostly 16th and

Hoe Barton near Plymouth, in 1694, from an illustration in the Spoure Book. *The formal garden shown to left of the house and the domestic chapel indicate a house of high status. The artist has shown peaked clay ridge tiles on the domestic buildings to indicate slate roofs. The barns in the outer courtyard are shown without ridge tiles and were almost certainly thatched.*

17th century, show all of them slated. These examples indicate that there was a threshold of status in rural Devon above which thatch was unlikely to be found between 1550 and 1750.

Where there is evidence of a change from slate to thatch it can usually be attributed to a downgrading and loss of status to the building. For example, the gatehouse of the Cistercian Abbey at Dunkeswell, certainly slated before the abbey was surrendered, was recast as a thatched farmhouse afterwards. Downgrading the roof covering did not always mean that the interior of the house suffered a loss of status. For example, Yeo Barton, Mariansleigh, had a pegged slate roof when it was built as an open hall house in the 15th century (see page 41). No other farmhouse of open hall origins in the area has evidence of an early slate roof and this must have identified the owners as a cut above their neighbours. In the 17th century the house was thoroughly enlarged in a high quality programme of work. In spite of this upgrading and modernisation, the owner chose to cover over the old slate roof with thatch, perhaps making a choice between exterior ostentation and interior comfort and space.

Three-storey 17th century rural houses are rare in Devon. Their height must always have made roofing more laborious for a slater or thatcher having to carry old material down and new material up extra-long ladders. Nevertheless, Brooklands Farmhouse in Chulmleigh, a fashionable mid to late 17th century three-storey house with a three-storey porch retains its 17th century roof structure and seems to have been thatched from the outset.

© Devon County Council 1986

Brooklands Farmhouse, Chulmleigh. A fashionable house, new-built in the mid to late 17th century and thatched from the outset. This house, unusually, is three storeys, requiring the original and subsequent thatchers to work at an exceptional height for Devon.

Below gentry level there seems to have been a choice of either slate or thatch. This choice must have been affected by the relatively high cost of slate and its carriage, balanced by perceptions of status and fashion on the part of the owner. Where the cost of slate was comparatively reasonable, it might appear on lower status houses. On the eastern fringes of Dartmoor many of the farmhouses are built of larger blocks of neatly-shaped granite ashlar, and some, like the longhouse at Hole, Chagford, are built on a generous scale, but many had thatched roofs. On the other side of the moor, John Woolcombe, an owner with interests in the tin industry, built a relatively small house, Yeo Farm, in Meavy parish, in 1610. This was smaller than Hole at Chagford, but was more smart and fashionable with a symmetrical, multi-gabled front and a slate roof. Upcott Barton in Cheriton Fitzpaine and Dira, Sandford, lie in the heartlands of the thatched tradition yet both acquired slate roofs in the 17th century. But again both are houses with some architectural pretension.

Yeo Farm, Meavy, built for an entrepreneur in tin. This is not a large 17th century house, but it has an up-to date plan, dispensing with the traditional cross-passage entrance. It was slated from the outset.

A thatched roof found in conjunction with the latest fashion for brick in the late 17th century at Hawthorn Cottage, Talaton.

An early 18th century thatched brick gazebo at Elliott's Farm, Venn Ottery, associated with a posh front garden with gatepost finials in the shape of pineapples. The house was thatched too. The gazebo has been re-roofed with concrete tile since the photograph was taken in the c.1940s.

The new style of polite architecture that affected the appearance of the post-Restoration mansions brought with it a fashion for building in brick. Until the second half of the 17th century, brick had not been a traditional building material in the county. Its introduction and growing popularity were part of a national trend as well as the style of the fashionable London buildings. A particularly fine example of the new style, and one of the earliest brick buildings in Devon is the Exeter Customs House, built in 1681 with a slate roof. Most Devon towns acquired stylish new brick houses in the following decades.[8] The outskirts of Exeter included a number of fashionable brick villas from the late 17th century and early 18th century, all slated. The fashion soon spread to the countryside, particularly (but not exclusively) to East Devon where there was an absence of good building stone and the subsoil provided suitable clay for brick-making. Here the use of slate or thatch in association with brick seems to mark out the social distinction between the gentry and the richer farmers. Plymtree Manor and Great Aunke Manor in Clyst Hydon were large late 17th century brick mansions with slate roofs. Smaller and less urbane brick houses, however, continued to use thatch. The earliest examples come from Talaton parish: Harris's Farm near the church, dated 1687, *(see colour page 2 , plate 6),* and the picturesque Hawthorn Cottage on the Escot Estate. Both had thatched roofs. In Payhembury, Glebe Farm has a brick house of c.1700 with polite interior detail but the owner was evidently content with a thatched roof. Some older houses in East Devon were given smart brick fronts around this time whilst retaining their thatch, e.g. Lower Southwood, Rockbeare. Brick and thatch were also found together in an early 18th century gazebo at Elliott's Farm, Venn Ottery.

A number of 17th cottages were built sufficiently well to have survived, reflecting high standards in building associated with general prosperity, even down to unpretentious houses for labourers and artisans. These cottages were usually cob or stone rubble and had thatched roofs. One of the earliest known surviving examples is a pair of mid 17th century one-room plan cob cottages, reputedly built for coal miners, which are now joined together as Widden Cottage, Newton St Cyres, Mid Devon. It seems that most of the surviving 17th century examples of cottages were built in pairs, such as Nos 1 and 2 Church Road, Clawton, West Devon (originally thatched but the roof covered with corrugated iron by 1986), and Mellow Thatch, Morchard Bishop, Mid Devon.

Larger cottages with two- or even three-room plans survive in increasing numbers from the mid 17th century onwards. Many can be seen in the hamlets, villages and smaller market towns of Devon, or alongside the lanes. They are plain vernacular buildings with plastered mass walls, and most originally had thatched roofs.

There were also humble thatched cottages in farmyards. This type of accommodation ensured that the labourer was on hand, but not housed with the family. They are rare survivals in Devon, but must have once been commonplace and a reminder of how much thatch there once was on modest buildings whose survival into the 21st century has been very patchy. Two good examples are the very unaltered early 18th century thatched cottage in the yard of Lower Netherton, Haccombe-with-Combe, next to a thatched 17th century cider house, *(see colour page 8, plate 23),* and Upcott, in Uppacott, Tedburn St Mary, part of a thatched row including a good 16th century house, a barn and a cottage.

Farm buildings

The rebuilding and extension of farm buildings with thatched roofs have to be inferred from the improvements in farming and the survival of 17th century agricultural buildings. Unlike domestic houses it seems that just about all farm buildings, even those close to gentry mansions, were thatched in the 16th century and 17th century, by-passed by the dictates of fashion that applied to superior houses. Very few retain thatched roofs today.

The barn is the most common agricultural building found on historic Devon farms. They occur even on Dartmoor farms where arable farming plays such a small role today. Some of the barns on Devon farmsteads can be shown to have pre-1550 origins but most have been enlarged or altered in the 16th and 17th centuries, no doubt to match the increase in cereal farming. There may have been some slated barns associated with the finest gentry mansions, or mansions near quarries, but thatched examples are known both from early prints and drawings associated with many gentry houses and from surviving examples. For instance there is still a large thatched barn close by Colleton Barton, the manor house of the Bury family up until the 19th century.

An unusually large 17th century barn close to Colleton Barton, Chulmleigh, where a thatched roof survives.

At a lower status level at Dira, Sandford (a house that was slated in the 17th century), there is a fine thatched double barn, dating from the late 17th century or early 18th century, one of the largest in Devon to survive from before c.1800 *(see colour page 9, plate 24)*. Other notably large barns, such as the probably early 17th century six-bay barn at Whelmstone Barton, reflect the prosperity of the rural economy of the time. Similarly on the Blackdown Hills there is a five-bay cob barn with a thatched roof at Pound Farm, Luppitt, which was founded on marginal ground in the late 17th century. These 16th century and 17th century barns were where the grain was stored and the wheat or rye was threshed (although threshing might be done outside too), including material destined for thatching. Inside the barn the crop was threshed between the opposing double doors that would be opened to let in enough light for the laborious process of hand-flailing. In parts of Devon the term 'winding' barn is still remembered, referring to the draught of wind that the open door provided to blow away the chaff during winnowing. These cob and thatch threshing barns, were not only places where straw was processed and stored for thatching on the farm, or selling on for use in the nearby village or town. They were effectively built of straw; they were roofed with it and their cob walls incorporated chopped straw, probably the thatching waste of a previous harvest, put to good use to bind the material together.

A large 17th century barn at Creely Barton, Farringdon, which still had its thatch when this photograph was taken in 1948.

Other types of more specialist farm buildings begin to appear in the period. Apart from the shippons associated with Dartmoor longhouses, no cattle sheds are known from the medieval period. The distinctive linhay, a building type, found in Cornwall, Devon and East Somerset, makes its appearance in the 17th century. These are open-fronted sheds with haylofts (known locally as tallets) above. In rural areas they were used as cattle sheds and their survival from c.1600 onwards reflects the confidence of the farmers to invest in substantial farm buildings. At Shute Barton, Shute, the linhays (originally thatched) were generous enough in scale and sound enough in construction to be functioning in the 1980s.

A probably late 17th or early 18th century linhay in the yard at Westcott Farm, Thelbridge c.1900, along with the Blackford family and their pigs, hens and Devon cattle.

At Widhayes, Uplowman, a large double thatched barn was built in the mid or late 17th century along with a well-built eleven-bay thatched linhay, its beams chamfered with scroll stops as might be found in a domestic house. This is unusually fine but there are a large number of linhays from the 17th century and early 18th century in Devon. Other buildings which might be found on farms from this time include stables, cider houses, granaries, etc., all which would have been thatched. There is, too, the pretty little thatched building from Middle Henstill, Sandford, *(see colour page 9, plate 25),* used for the collection of ashes that were used in land improvement.

Urban Thatch

In the larger towns, Barnstaple, Exeter and Plymouth, there was probably relatively little thatch left in the town centres by 1550. Hooker's late 16th century plan of Exeter indicates none left within the city walls. All three towns were ports with relatively easy access to Devon and Cornish slate. Plymouth was particularly well-placed for access to South Hams slate quarries. In 1698 Celia Fiennes admired the slate roofs in both Plymouth and Plympton, then a port in its own right. After 1550 slate became a favoured townhouse material, not just for roofing but also for slate-hanging on houses with timber-framed fronts and stone side walls. This style of fashionable Devon town house, making the most of valuable urban plots by building tall and by ingenious internal planning, survives particularly well in Totnes. This style of late 16th and 17th century Devon town house appears never to have had thatched roofs and created a demand for slate in the bigger towns. They must also have made a contribution to the long process of thatched roofing disappearing from the Devon townscapes, rendering the material unfashionable by contrast with the newer buildings and contributing to a difference of status and identity between town and country. Other types of progressive 17th century urban development, whether the so-called 'Dutch' houses on the Strand at Topsham, or the speculative development of Bridgeland Street in Bideford, employed slate roofing from the outset.

As towns expanded in the shape of 17th century suburbs, earlier and formerly rural thatched houses might survive close to their newer neighbours. Outside Exeter's city walls 17th century or earlier thatched houses survived in St Thomas until the early 19th century, when a mixture of slate and thatch is shown in a print of 'old houses' in St Thomas. A single storey projection off the house in the background, possibly a little shop extension, judging from the size of the window, is slate-roofed. The rest of the house and its neighbour are thatched. The use of slate avoids what would have been a long, vulnerable junction with the wall of the house, if the extension had been thatched. The house in the foreground is evidently 17th century or earlier, judging from the windows and the turned post shown at the corner of the gabled wing. The drawing is detailed enough to show the system of rolls of straw at the verges of the gable, designed to give a kick to the thatch which is laid under tension. It also shows the gable slate-hung above the oriel window. This probably dates from the 17th century at least, contemporary with the oriel window and the whole of the front projecting wing.

By permission of Devon Library Services (West Country Studies Library).

A 17th century house in St Thomas, then close to, rather than part of Exeter, shown in an engraving c.1830 by F M Jenkins.

Two 1609 maps of Exe Island, a suburb of Exeter, drawn by Robert Sherwood show land leased by the City to a brewer, Nicholas Evans.[9] *(See colour page 10, plate 27)*. Sherwood uses two colours to represent roofs, thatch being shown both on service buildings (without chimneys) and on what appear to be occupied houses. Three dwellings and the gateway are shown slated.

The smaller towns present a rather different picture. Moretonhampstead is a rarity in preserving early 17th century thatched almshouses. These are exceptional, clearly well-funded and built of granite roofed with thatch. Their quality reflects the status of those that paid for them, rather than their occupants. The presence of thatch in two small Devon towns at least, was noted in 1669 by Count Magoletti, who accompanied the Grand Duke of Tuscany on a tour through England. Magoletti had an eye for building materials, noting, for example, that

Thatched roofing and granite ashlarare used in an ambitious and expensive design for these Moretonhampstead almshouses, rebuilt in this form in 1637.

houses on the Scillies were roofed with 'nothing but a simple mat spread over the rafters, drawn tight all round and fixed firmly to the top of the walls', a covering which needed annual renewal. He described Okehampton (a slate-roofed town today) as 'a place of little account: the houses are all built of earth and stone and thatched with straw'. This is an interesting comment as Okehampton is not particularly remote, as the crow flies, from sources of slate, but perhaps being 'of little account' the cost of transport put slate beyond the means of the inhabitants in 1669. Magoletti also commented that 'Axminster is a collection of two hundred houses, many of which are made with mud and thatched with straw'.[10] Axminster had been burned in the Civil War but clearly did not ban thatch in the subsequent rebuilding. Although a handful of thatched buildings survives in the town today, slate is the dominant roofing material.

Michael Laithwaite notes that recorded town fires are concentrated in the east of the county, presumably because slate was more readily available and used for roofing in the west of the county.[11] A town fire in the 16th or 17th centuries was not always motive enough to ban thatch when reconstruction followed. In some cases this may have been a matter of the cost and availability of less combustible alternatives. Bye-laws requiring replacement buildings to be covered in materials other than thatch may have had to wait until this was economically viable. Laithwaite records Tiverton reputedly losing 400 houses in the 1598 fire, 600 in the 1612 fire and another 298 in 1731.[12] Pevsner refers to additional fires in 1661 and 1730.[13] Thatch was not banned until after the 1731 fire, after which there were no more major fires in Tiverton. This loss of more than 1000 buildings in one town in less than 150 years, before insurance was commonplace, is one example of the economic disaster that thatch could represent to Devon town life in the period.

Another important map survives showing the market and wool manufacturing town of Crediton as it was before the fire of 14 August 1743 *(see colour page 10, plates 28 and 29)*. This beautiful map is a precious record of the appearance of a large Devon town in the early 18th century, comprising houses of several dates.[14] It shows that by 1743 the commercial centre of Crediton included a handful of late 17th century buildings with timber-framed fronts, including gabled projections probably added to earlier structures. There is also a smattering of early superior 18th century brick or rendered buildings with regular fenestration and straight eaves. The brick buildings are carefully coloured. Judging from the way the map-maker has drawn their roofs, all these (with a couple of exceptions) were slated. It was the smaller houses in Crediton that retained thatch, the map-maker showing the eaves as a wavy line rising round half dormers indicating that most were single storey with attic rooms. In the commercial centre of Crediton, flanking 'The Flesh Shambles' there was still a fair amount of thatch. The map also shows that the finest houses in town, including 'The Mansion', off the main street, were brick with slate roofs, although one large house with a classical porch, labelled 'late Mr Stone's' on the outskirts, appears to have been thatched.

The Crediton fire of 1743 was exceptionally catastrophic, but it is a vivid illustration of the potential scale of urban destruction when thatched buildings were side by side. The town consisted of two settlements, (now merged into one continuous development), East Town, round the parish church and West Town, both spreading along either side of a broad main street in which the cattle market was held. The houses along the north side of the high street were interrupted by only one major road and, on the south side, only by narrow cartways into long courtyards used by weavers. The lie of the land, which rises steeply behind the south side of the street, allows no escape out of the courtyards. The fire started in a baker's shop on the north side of the street in West Town, where there was a long row of continuous thatched roofs, and spread eastwards from building to building. There was no obstacle to its course, given a windy day and the wind that a fierce fire generates. After most of the houses in West Town had been consumed, the wind changed direction and the fire crossed the road and burnt down the south side of the street, travelling west. The method for dealing with thatch fires then, as today, was to pull of the burning thatch. Special hooks for this purpose used by fire fighters survive in the collection held in the Bicton Botanical Gardens, East Budleigh. At Crediton, the speed and ferocity of the fire meant that conventional methods were abandoned and houses were blown up to try to create a gap across which the fire could not spread. It was all to no avail, only causing more loss of life.

Eighteen people were killed and 460 dwellings were destroyed, as well as the market houses, wool chambers and other public buildings. The homeless were destitute of clothes, food and possessions, as well as the looms on which most of them depended to earn a living. Mr William Curtice, a London builder acting as surveyor to the Trustees of the Sun Fire Office, estimated that the cost of rebuilding the uninsured houses, 'in as plain a Manner and with the like Materials as before', would amount to at least £41 019, with £50 for the loss of uninsured goods and an additional £11 250 on the insured properties.

The list of smaller Devon towns that are particularly rich in pre-1750 town houses may not be just a matter of those that escaped comprehensive later redevelopment, but may represent those where prosperity or location meant that most of the housing stock was slated. Ashburton, for instance, was served by a local slate quarry, noted by the historian of Devon, Polwhele. Totnes and Dartmouth were both close to quarries, Dartmouth to the extent of exporting quantities of slate from the 16th century. Topsham was the entrepot for Exeter, where the demand for slate must have made the material a commonplace import. Moretonhampstead and Hatherleigh are the towns where early thatched town houses still survive, and Colyton retains some fine examples.

Thatchers' Accounts

The most readily available thatchers' accounts from the period are in the churchwardens' accounts and relate to the maintenance of church property.

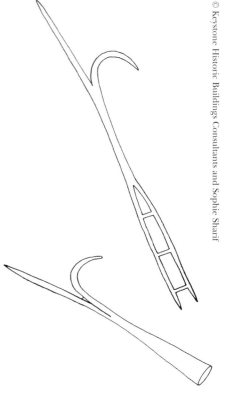

Tools used by the Sandford Fire Brigade for pulling thatch off a burning building to create a fire break. The hooks are metal, the wooden handles are missing. The longer hook is 1m (3ft 3½ins) long; the smaller is 685mm (2ft 3ins) long. From the Rural Life Collection at Bicton Botanical Gardens, East Budleigh.

Thatch as an acceptable roofing for two smart but very different early 18th century town houses in Colyton.

They often show little more than the date and common use of the term 'nitch' (sometimes spelled 'knitch 'knich', 'neech') for a bundle of combed straw and the common use of the term 'reed' or 'rede' for straw. Whether the weight of a nitch was always the same is unclear. It may have varied, as did other agricultural measures, from place to place and across time. Today a nitch weighs about 6 kilos (14lbs), although historically they were usually double that weight. One late 18th century reference describes bundles of reed for thatching (here they are called 'sheaves') as 36lbs each.[15] The modern term 'spar' for the twisted timber staple with sharpened ends, used to pin down the thatch, has a number of spellings: 'speres' 'speeres' 'spears' 'spares' 'spers' – these are sometimes referred to in 'bundles'. Needles are mentioned as 'neelds' 'neels'. 'Binders' and 'clifte stakes' are occasionally mentioned probably referring to the split hazel sways pegged down by the spars. The practice of watering the straw is sometimes itemised separately. Wetting combed straw before fitting is still common practice, although there are arguments about how much wetting was and is desirable. Sometimes the accounts include payment for an assistant to the thatcher, a 'tender' or the thatcher's 'boy' or 'man'. It is known from other counties that women sometimes assisted thatchers on the roof, but none have yet been identified from Devon documentation.

A good 17th century series of churchwardens' accounts at Colebrooke shows that several different thatchers were used, although there also seem to be thatching families too, Beer, and Adams (both spelt several different ways).[16] John Middleweek is recorded thatching with his son. In 1634 the account refers to 'mats for ye chancel and Rude' (the latter probably erected on the rood loft). It is not completely clear from the context but these may have been supplied by the thatcher and if so, are a nice reminder of one of the other uses to which straw might be put in 1634. There were regular payments for thatching the churchyard wall which seems to have been built (or rebuilt) in 1634 (cost £1 6s 6d), and thatched with 'Reade' at a cost of £1 2s. The thatch on the wall is next mentioned 25 years later, in 1659, when it received three days work and 'halfe a hundred of reeds'.

The frequency with which the church house is mentioned in the Colebrooke series shows that regular patching was the method of maintenance, rather than rethatching a whole roof. In some years the payment to the thatcher does not mention the building, but it is likely to be the church house; however the following is where the church house is mentioned by name.

1636   200 and 3 quarters of reed laid on the church house
1649   86 nitches of reed [this work also involved lathing; so it would seem that the church house roof had either got into such a bad state of repair that it had to be partly stripped and re-lathed, or perhaps was being extended].
1650   180 nitches of reed [these were supplied by two different people, not the thatcher].
1661   105 nitches [the account records that this took three days to lay using two people].
1673   20 nitches of reed.
1675   54 nitches of reed [supplied by two different people, the thatcher supplying four nitches only, probably for a quick repair and at a different time from using the fifty nitches, also paid for in this year and supplied by 'Agnis Prye'].

In the following two years the accounts show the thatcher being paid for 'stoping' the thatch on the church house. This was the technique, sometimes called 'stobbing' of thrusting bundles of straw into the thatch as a cheap repair. There is an early 17th century series of thatching accounts in the parish wardens' accounts for Zeal Monachorum.[17] The condition of the document and the binding order of the pages makes the exact dates uncertain. However some of the detail is rather fuller than most. The following may be c.1636:

paid for one hundred nitches of reed	*12s 0d*
paid for a days carriage of reed	*1s 2d*
paid for watering the reed	*4d*
paid for spars and for cleaving of the said spars & and for ... of them	*2s*
paid for three days work for thatching the parish house	*3s 4d*
and one to attend the thatcher	*2s 9d*

Payment for wetting straw before fitting it is also mentioned in an undated, but from the context, early 17th century account, at Yealmpton: 'paid unto Lavers the thatcher for thatching and for watering the reed for the beacon four shillings'. [18]

The cost of carriage at Zeal Monachorum corrects any assumption that combed straw was invariably found or acquired just round the corner. Another account in the Zeal Monachorum series c.1634, gives a single figure for carriage of spars (measured in 1658 in 'burdens', perhaps a packhorse load, of spars) and reed; perhaps the parish or the thatcher kept them both in the same store. The 'nitch' is not the measure employed in the c.1658 account when the church-wardens paid four shillings for 'a quarter hundred of reed'. If this quantity was 25 nitches (which is by no means certain) the price of a nitch had risen by a third since c.1636, having previously dropped from 13s for 104 nitches in c.1634, to 12s for a hundred nitches in 1636.

It is interesting to compare the Zeal Monachorum account with an unusually full one from 1637.[19] This was found written on a torn piece of paper among a collection of documents mostly relating to the manor of Sherford, near Stokenham in South West Devon. Coombes, who published the account in *Devon and Cornwall Notes and Queries* comments 'it is not possible to be certain whether the house was the demesne farm there or on another estate belonging to the same lord'. Stokenham is a coastal parish, not far from the area where water reed is known to have been cut for thatching from the late 19th century, but to date with no firm documentary evidence of having been exploited for thatch before. Is this a reference to the use of water reed for Devon roofing, rather than combed straw?

'A note what Charge is Disburst a boute the house 1637

for on hundred and three quarters of reed	*01-*	*04-*	*6*
for Charge of Carringe	*00-*	*06-*	*2*
for Carpenters wagges 16 dayes	*00-*	*18-*	*8*
for masons six dayes	*00-*	*07-*	*2*
for draing down the thach	*00-*	*01-*	*0*
for willwors and wadling	*00-*	*02-*	*6*
for williors and neels	*00-*	*03-*	*2*
for spures	*00-*	*02-*	*0*
for lasts	*00-*	*01-*	*0*
for helling stones	*00-*	*02-*	*2*
for pauers	*00-*	*02-*	*0*
for on truse of straw	*00-*	*01-*	*0*
for halfe hundred of nayles	*00-*	*00-*	*6*
for three spukes	*00-*	*00-*	*3*
for the thucher wagges	*00-*	*05*	*10*
for the tender	*00-*	*05-*	*0*
	4-	*2-*	*11*
Remaineth more then the years rent	*1s*		
with is to be allowed in the next	*1-*	*2-*	*0*

The 'reed' is measured in 'quarters' (which is the word used in one of the Colebrooke entries) not the more common 'nitches'. On the other hand, if a nitch was about 28lbs, this is also a quarter of a hundredweight and a 'quarter' might be an alternative term for a nitch. The cost of carriage is surprisingly high, although it is not clear that the transport costs are solely for the 'reed' rather than one of the heavier items, the 'pauers' (paving stones), or 'helling stones' (slates). The 'draing down the thach' is ambiguous but could refer to stripping the flag off uncleaned water reed. In East Anglia this was, and still is, traditionally done at the reed bed, but the system in Devon could have been different. It could also refer to a final combing technique applied to straw, although it seems unusual, from what we know about later practice, to open up bundles of threshed straw and comb them on site, rather than at the point of threshing and storage. The 'willwors and wadling' and 'williors and neels' are more difficult to interpret. Coombes suggests withies. 'Wadling' is probably wattling and 'neels' likely to be needles. 'Spures' are almost certainly spars. All these could apply equally well to fitting water reed or combed straw thatch. It is assumed that 'lasts' and 'nayles' are the laths and nails for the slates. They would not have been required for the thatch if it was laid on wattle. The one truss of straw could be for a ridge roll, or for twisting into straw rope for fixing the thatch.

It is a shame that the account cannot be definitively identified as referring to water reed thatch. The cost, if it has been understood aright of the 'reed', the proximity to Slapton Ley, and the reference to 'drawing' do however suggest that this is a possibility. But it would have to be assumed that the writer was comfortable using the term 'reed' for water reed, whereas 'reed' in other documentary sources means combed straw.

There is no doubt that water reed was used in Devon building in the late 17th and 18th centuries. It can be found as a backing for wall and ceiling plaster as a convenient substitute for laths. It is the kind of building detail most likely to be noticed by owners if they are repairing plasterwork and there are likely to be many more examples than those noted by archaeologists or historians of buildings. However, to date there are no known firm examples – apart from the Otterton example of water reed laid between the laths and used as a support for straw thatch – of water reed used for thatching before the late 19th century.

Leaving aside the type of material in use, the account does suggest a system in which thatch and slate were employed side by side for roofing 'a boute the house', although the only craftsman paid was the thatcher. Exactly how these two materials were used together at Stokenham is unclear. There are various options. Slate might have been used at the eaves and/or verges of the house – a method known from a handful of illustrations from the 18th and 19th centuries and from photographs. It might have been used for valleys – at least one slate valley has been found on a thatched house in Moretonhampstead. The slate may have been applied to a minor element, or even a detached portion of the house.

A 1734 account from Berry Pomeroy parish makes it plain that in this case the estate owner, Sir Edward Seymour, was supplying the thatching material to the thatcher himself, presumably from one of the estate farms, and paying for the thatcher's labour. Richard Randall was a thatcher of both industrial and agricultural buildings: the mill at Berry Pomeroy Castle, a shippon, a poundhouse (a cider-house), a linhay and a stack of wood, to keep it dry for use. The following year an account for work on the Barton of Berry Pomeroy covers thatching hay, wheat and wood ricks, as well as a calf house and the pentice over the barn door. Randall was obviously in the business of providing short-term seasonal thatches, as well as what one assumes were longer lasting thatches on Sir Edward Seymour's farm buildings and mill. Randall is likely to have been a relation of a Robert Randle who, in 1710, was charging 7s 6d for himself and a man

Left: *An example of an 18th century thatched industrial building. The lavish moss growth on the patched thatch of this mill at Hatherleigh, photographed c.1890, is probably associated with a constant damp atmosphere from the mill race.*

Below: *The wood rick, thatched by Randall and recorded in his account, was probably roofed with straw. This enormous wood rick, shown with members of the Parkhouse family at Homewell Farm, High Bickington, c.1900, is thatched with brushwood. It illustrates the labour and care traditionally devoted to storing wood for fuel and other purposes.*

for seven days at Weekaborough (another Berry Pomeroy farm owned by the Seymours) and 1s for cutting 'spar sticks'.[20]

Landlords did not invariably supply thatching materials. It was not uncommon for leases to require a tenant to supply straw (presumably growing and processing it himself on the farm) and sometimes spars. In 1735 George Domett, of Hawkchurch (then actually in Dorset, but now in Devon) conveyed his property to one of his sons. The conveyance includes a good list of crops, livestock and farm implements including 'some old reed and sparrs'.[21]

The two centuries from 1550–1750 were a prolonged golden age for Devon thatch. Economic growth saw the tradition extend over new buildings and extensions to existing ones. The limitations on transport meant that thatch remained acceptable as a roofing on new houses as well as existing. Progressive farming extended the arable acreage which supplied straw and generated additional demand as old farm buildings were rebuilt and enlarged and new farm buildings were erected. It is possible, however, to detect a threshold of status, variable from area to area and partly dependent on other roofing options, above which thatch was unlikely to found. There is also a pattern of thatch, slowly, by fits and starts and partly determined by urban fires, squeezed out of urban areas and becoming concentrated in rural Devon.

After 1740 the vigour of Devon agricultural improvement began to slacken off in parallel with the decline in the wool trade and, economically, the county would never rise to its former prosperity relative to the rest of the nation again.

Footnotes

[1] Thirsk, (ed.), *The Agrarian History of England & Wales*, Vol 5, 1640-1750, 1984, 23.

[2] Hooker's *Synopsis Chorographical of Devonshire'* (c.1600), quoted in Hoskins 1954, 95-96.

[3] Finberg (ed.), *The Agrarian History of England & Wales*, Vol 4, 1500-1640, 75.

[4] Moir and Letts, 1999, 204.

[5] *Calendar of State Papers Domestic 1547-1580* (1856) p449, vol 88 item 52; folio 149ff.

[6] Stanes, *TDA*, Vol. 96, 1964, 287.

[7] Cherry, 'The Devon Country House in the Late Seventeenth and Early Eighteenth Centuries', *PDAS* 46.

[8] See Thorp, 1990, 117-128.

[9] Ravenhill and Rowe, 2000, 34, 35.

[10] Count L Magalotti's 'The Travels of Cosmo III., Grand Duke of Tuscany, through England', 1669, in Pearse Chope (ed.), 1967, 104, 111.

[11] In Beacham, 1990, 95-96.

[12] *Ibid.*

[13] Cherry and Pevsner, 1989, 807.

[14] Devon RO, 2065m add.3/E332.

[15] Marshall, Vol I, 182.

[16] Devon RO, EDRO PW1 Colebrooke.

[17] Devon RO, PW1 Zeal Monachorum. Supplied by Ann Adams.

[18] Church Wardens Accounts, West Devon RO, 731/34, supplied by Todd Gray.

[19] Coombes, 1965, 117-118.

[20] Devon RO, 3799 Box 27, Seymour Duke of Somerset.

[21] Quoted in Chapman, 1988, 102.

TRADITION & FASHION
1750–1850

After 1750 Devon's population growth slowed down, relative both to its own past and to other counties, especially the North and the Midlands. Industrial development and new kinds of industrial organisation in expanding cities began to leave the county behind, especially by the early 19th century. Between 1750 and 1801 the Devon population grew by only four per cent, compared, say, with Cheshire, which increased by 66 per cent.[1] By comparison with Cornwall, especially in the mining area, the expansion in urban population in Devon was tiny.[2] Nevertheless, by 1801, Devon was still fourth in rank of the most populated counties in England, coming after Middlesex, Yorkshire and Lancashire.[3]

Rural Devon ceased to be noted as a region of progressive farming, compared with the national picture. Agriculture survived, sometimes quite comfortably, by consolidating trends apparent in the 17th century with increasing regional specialisation in production, reinforcing the south-east of the county as predominantly dairying and Mid and North Devon as livestock-producing areas. Dairy products and considerable quantities of cider were exported by coaster to London and the South East. Beef cattle were driven overland on the hoof.

By the end of the 18th century detailed accounts of regional farming practice were researched and produced by agricultural commentators. These exercises were not designed to be mere historical records of farming at a particular time, but had a propagandist purpose. They were intended to encourage efficiency in farming by spreading the news of improvements, whether to stock-breeding and management, machinery or rural housing, throughout England. In the comparisons of one county with another, Devon farming was regarded, for the most part, as backward and idiosyncratic compared with progress in other counties, a complete turnabout since the 17th century.

The reasons why Devon did not maintain the advanced approach to agriculture which had helped to create the demand for rural thatch in the 17th century, are complicated and have been reconsidered by Sarah Wilmot.[4] One factor was the relative absence of large estates run by land magnates actively seeking to maximise profits and efficiency. Such men were a requirement for investment in 'progressive' farming in the 18th century. Most Devon farms were tenanted and owned by the lower gentry or squire class. Landlords often simply let the tenant get on with farming without interference, or suggesting ways in which the farms might be made more profitable, leaving the management of the tenancy arrangements to attornies. Failing industries, out-competed by developments in other counties, meant that the capital to invest in radical improvements to farming was not available, either to the landlords, or to tenant farmers. There are many surviving new farm buildings from this period, but they are modest in scale compared with, say, the improved farmsteads of East Anglia, and cob or stone and thatch continued to be used.

Stagnation in the rural economy relative not only to the 17th century past but also to other areas of the country, had a significant impact on the thatching tradition. On the one hand it discouraged the spread of alternative materials. Roofing options remained thatch or West Country slate, with the possible exception of tiles from the Somerset tileries for parishes on the Devon/Somerset borders. Tiles had certainly appeared in Exeter by 1795 and by 1832 there were three tileries in the county producing over 100 000 tiles *per annum*. In the south-west of Devon expansion in the use of slate continued. Improved transport encouraged slate in small Devon towns along the Somerset border, which were close to Somerset slate quarries at Treborough and Huish Champfleur. However, thatch remained an obvious choice for most of rural Devon and slate was excluded from many parts of the eastern half of the county on grounds of cost. The use of slate in towns sharpened the definition of thatch as a 'country material' and one increasingly likely to be found on new buildings only below a certain level of status.

Roofing materials as a direct reflection of status in the early 19th century. An 1844 view of Chittlehampton with expensive lead on the church roof, West Country pegged slates on the church property that leads to the churchyard, and thatch elsewhere.

By and after William Spreat. By permission of Devon Library Services (West Country Studies Library)

Research into insurance records by James Moir suggests that in the South West overall there was not only a reduction in the demand for thatch but a staggering decline of 65 per cent in the number of thatched buildings between 1800 and 1862-3.[5] While insurance records are a valuable source of material, they are, as Letts and Moir indicate, a blunt instrument, 'becoming less reliable as the distance from London increases' and the decline may not have been quite so sharp as the policies indicate. Increasing premiums on thatch insurance may have encouraged some landlords to abandon insurance on thatched buildings of small value during the period and thus create an impression of a very high figure for decline. In *Small Talk at Wreyland*, Cecil Torr records after the 1845 fire in Moretonhampstead his grandfather wrote to his father: 'many houses not insured; their owners dropt it at Ladyday last, when the advance took place on thatched houses'.[6]

A pair of 18th century stone and cob cottages in Meshaw, photographed in the early 20th century.

Materials and Techniques

A questionnaire sent out between 1747 and 1756 to the local clergy by Jeremiah Milles, Precentor, and subseqently Dean of Exeter Cathedral, enquired into the farming methods of Devonshire. Just over half the incumbents replied and although not specifically asked about thatching, the incumbent of Plymtree noted that rye was grown for thatching only and at Witheridge it was said that a little rye was grown.[7] These are unlikely to have been the only parishes still producing rye in the mid 18th century and, as we have seen, pockets of rye were still being grown, specifically for thatch, on the Dartmoor fringes into the early 20th century. No doubt other materials were also used when wheat straw was difficult to come by.

County studies of Devon farming written by improvers include the first detailed first-hand accounts we have of the production of straw thatching. Wheat, not rye, is the material invariably noted in use. Like other writers of the late 18th and early 19th centuries, the improvers considered the combed straw tradition in Devon not only as distinct from crushed straw used in counties beyond the South West, but superior. The 20th century debate about the relative merits of West Country combed straw versus crushed straw thatching really starts here, with authors who identified, described and praised the West Country tradition.

The 1785 edition of Risdon's *Survey of Devon* (a general history rather than agricultural description of the county), as corrected and annotated by William Chapple, included the following comment on the neatness of combed straw thatch, compared with crushed straw:

> *These cob-built houses are generally covered with Thatch; in which our Thatchers only use combed Wheat-Straw, which we call* Reed, *consisting mostly of the stiff unbruis'd and unbroken Stalks, which are carefully separated from the Fodder-Straw by the Thresher, and bound in large Sheaves call'd* Nitches: *This enables the Thatcher to finish his Work much more neatly than can be done in the Counties where no Reed is made, but the Straw used as it comes tumbled together from the Barn, with very little Separation, except perhaps of the long from the short; being fastened on the Roof rough as it comes to Hand, and the Eves, etc, seldom so regularly shorn as by the Thatchers here'.*[8]

Chapple's comments were amplified by the agricultural writer, William Marshall, ten years later in his *Rural Economy of the West of England*, 1796. Marshall's account is particularly valuable coming from a man familiar with different regional farming systems and includes his grasp of how combed straw thatching in Devon related to other regions. In his section on the district he calls 'West Devon' (rather different from the modern administrative district) he says:

> *The COVERING MATERIALS of the District are* slate *and* thatch-prov. "reed," *namely, unbruised straw: the grain being separated from the straw without breaking it; in the manner which will be hereafter described: a practice common, I believe, to the WEST of ENGLAND. Straw thus preserved makes a neat and durable covering: and, when no other species of covering can be procured, it is certainly preferable to thrashed straw: which, being less durable, tends still more to the impoverishment of the lands that are robbed of it'.*[9]

It is clear from this that Marshall considered thatch inferior to any other type of roofing but, if nothing else was to hand, combed straw thatch was superior to crushed straw. Marshall's perception that thatch was a low status material is very evident throughout his two volumes. 'Mean' towns he passed through tend to be those that have thatch, although he does sometimes refer to 'bad slate'.

He is the earliest writer to provide a detailed description of how combed straw was produced in the wider context of cereal-growing in the county. It is worth remembering that this was written about five centuries later than the earliest evidence for the combed straw thatching technique that survives in Devon roofs.

He describes corn in Devon cut with a 'yowing hook', similar to a reaping hook, rather than using a scythe. The scythe was more economical in terms of labour but produced a scattered cut. The more carefully hand-controlled use of the reaping hook kept the corn lying in the same direction from the point of cutting. It could then be collected into bundles by the labour of women and children. Marshall was doubtful of the efficiency of the Devon method, which incorporated the green weeds, so common after a wet summer, into each bundle. After cutting, the corn was set into 'shocks' of nine sheaves, each with a tenth placed over the top, like a hat.

Vancouver, writing 12 years later, noted that the use of hooks (he refers to 'reaping-hooks') cut the crop so low that it left little in the way of stubble compared with other parts of England, where there was sometimes a second cut for 'haulm' or stubble, which might then be bundled up and used for thatching.[10]

A number of writers describe folk rituals that marked the end of harvest. The details differ from writer to writer but some elements are common to each description. The best ears of corn, or the last sheaf in the field was picked out. Sometimes the reapers stood in a circle and threw their hooks at it until it was struck. Sometimes it was elevated, either held up by hand or taken to a high place. The reapers then shouted a chorus. There are various different recorded versions of this. Mrs Bray, married to the incumbent at Tavistock, said the reapers used to 'holla the nack', shouting, 'arnack, arnack, arnack, wehaven, wehaven, wehaven, wehaven.'[11]

Marshall writes that small stacks of straw were sometimes erected in the fields for the corn to ripen for a few weeks before it was taken to the barn. The largest contained about a wagon load of sheaves, the smallest no more than about ten. These were a square pyramid in shape, made of a carefully constructed pile of inward leaning sheaves, rising to a point which was not thatched, but given a capping of an inverted sheaf. The design protected the ears from the rain. After drying out and ripening in these field stacks, the sheaves of corn were carried from the fields, either for storage in rickyards or in the barn, by packhorses, so heavily laden that the upper part of their load had to be piled on with a fork. The use of packhorses carrying their burdens in a kind of yoke, rather than bags or baskets, is frequently mentioned as a peculiarity of both Devon and Cornwall in the late 18th and early 19th century.

In the late 17th century Colepresse had stated that storing corn in rickyards was less common in Devon, where it was usually taken directly into the barn, than in Cornwall. Over a century later, Marshall's account proves that yards of ricks were clearly commonplace in the west of the county, perhaps prompted by an expansion in wheat production in the Napoleonic Wars. The construction of ricks was, and still is, a skilled business. The sheaves in a stack were laid butt ends outwards, the whole structure designed to ensure enough ventilation, preventing overheating and the risk of combustion. As the rick grew in height, the men on the ground had to toss the sheaves up to the individuals on top, who were laying them, without breaking the straw ties that bound them. When the rick was complete, it was thatched to keep the rain out. The base was either a layer of dry straw, if it were built directly off the ground as a field stacklet or, if it was in a mowhay (a local term for a rickyard), off timber laid on staddles.

Staddles are upright stones with a projecting cap (looking something like a toadstool). Nowadays most have been moved from their original positions and are used as garden ornaments. Some survive *in situ*, as at Yeo Farm, Chagford, where they are arranged to support square-plan ricks in the part of the orchard nearest the threshing barn. The raised base helped to ventilate the rick and the projecting caps of the staddles were designed to deter mice and rats. At Bullaton Farm, Bovey Tracey, there is a pair of large circular rickstands, built of granite, with a projecting ledge round the top. It is built uphill from the barn, but such solid rickstands are an unusual feature.

Marshall describes the usual design of the Devon rick as square and high:

> but the roof very flat, and hipped, or sloped on every side: so that the roof, which in many Districts contains nearly one third of the contents of the stack, does not here, perhaps, contain a sixth of it. The difficulty of pitching from the ground, and the excellency of 'reed' as a thatch, may have assisted in fixing this prevailing fashion. [12]

It seems from this that the slack pitches of Devon houses applied equally to the shape of ricks. This would have slowed down the drainage of water from the thatch on a stack. However, the quality of the straw used to roof the structure, according to Marshall, ensured that the thatch provided a waterproof covering for as long as it was needed. His reference to 'pitching from the ground' relates to his observation that in Devon, horse-drawn vehicles were not used for the men to stand on, to give extra height for building the upper parts of the rick. He admired the thatching of stacks as 'very judicious and effectual':

> The 'reed' is spread thinly and evenly over the roof, and is fastened with 'spars' of hazel rods, pegged down to the butts of the sheaves, and covered in the next course of reed, in the manner that reed roofs are laid, in Norfolk. [13]

In his eyes this was infinitely superior to the practice he noticed in Cornwall, where reed was fastened on to stacks with straw ropes, stretched horizontally, within a few inches of one another.

Marshall then turns to describe the method of threshing in the district he called 'West Devon' and 'throughout the West of England'. This was highly profitable when straw was used for thatching and 'too singular to be passed without notice', being one of several peculiarities he observed in Devon harvesting practices. The aim was to extract the grain 'with the least possible injury to the straw'. The flail was applied to the ears of grain only, or the ears were beaten across a cask, by hand. Threshing was followed by combing, which was sometimes undertaken by women:

> The next operation is to suspend the straw, in large double handfuls, in a short rope, fixed high above the head, with an iron hook at the loose end of it; which is put twice around the little sheaflet, just below the ears, and fastened with the hook's laying hold of the tight part of the rope. The left hand now being firmly placed upon the hook, and pulling downward, so as to twitch the straw hard, and prevent the ears from slipping through it, the butts are freed from short straw and weeds, by means of a small long-toothed rake or comb. This done, the rope is unhooked and the 'reed' laid evenly in a heap.

> A quantity of clean straight unbruised straw of 'reed', being thus obtained, it is formed into small sheaves, returned to the floor, and the ears thrashed again with the flail, or is again thrashed by hand over the cask, to free it effectually from any remaining grain, which the former beating might have missed.

> Lastly the reed is made up into large bundles – provincially "sheaves" – of 36 pound each; with all the ears at one end; the butts being repeatedly punched upon the floor, first in double handfuls, and then in the sheaf, until they are as even, as if they had been cut off smooth and level, with a sithe or other edgetool; while the straws lie as straight, and are almost as stout, as those of inferior reed, or stems of the Arundo. [14]

The Bicton collection includes combs which are probably of the type that Marshall describes, although likely to be later. They are wooden with metal teeth. Marshall's reference to 'Arundo' (water reed), shows that he regarded this as the exemplary material for thatch and judged combed straw as equivalent to inferior water reed. In his text he tends to put 'reed', meaning combed straw, in inverted commas, evidently regarding the West Country term as a quirky use of a word normally signifying East Anglian water reed with which he was clearly familiar. Neither of his volumes refer to any use of water reed for thatching in Devon.

In a footnote Marshall mentions another method of threshing, which he observed on one occasion. This involved the use of a frame:

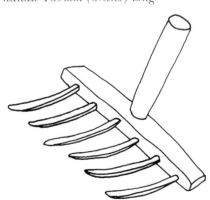

A Devon comb with metal teeth. This is probably the type of comb Marshall described in 1796 as a 'small long-toothed rake or combe', dragged through a tied-up bundle of wheat to comb out the short and broken straws and remove the leaf. One of two similar combs at the Rural Life Collection at Bicton Botanical Gardens, East Budleigh. The teeth are 150mm (6ins) long; the handle 165mm (6½ins) long

The construction somewhat resembling that of a very wide, short, crooked ladder, supported nearly horizontally, with its convex side upward; the crossbars being set edgeways, and a few inches from each other; and with an angular piece of wood running length way through the middle of the frame and rising above the cross bars, – to separate, and spread with greater ease, the ears of corn; and thereby to render the strokes the more effective.

The use of combed straw for roofing was not the only reason for a system of careful threshing to avoid bruising the plant stems, according to Marshall, but also provided more durable litter for bedding livestock.

Hand-combing was certainly assisted by the mid 19th century and very likely before, by simple devices without any moving parts, probably constructed by ingenious farmers or labourers. A number of reed combers consisting of a comb of iron spikes fixed to a trestle survive in museum collections. This type of reed comb was a device that could be used for threshing as well as combing. Handfuls of straw could be struck against it before being dragged by hand through the 'comb' component to clean off leaves and short straws.

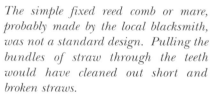

A frame for threshing of the kind Marshall noted, used experimentally at Blackawton. This was called a 'brishing horse', or 'whipping horse.'

The simple fixed reed comb or mare, probably made by the local blacksmith, was not a standard design. Pulling the bundles of straw through the teeth would have cleaned out short and broken straws.

The 'barn-comber' had probably been developed before 1850. Examples of these machines survive in several collections of agricultural machinery in Devon museums and private collections, but are sometimes mislabelled. The early examples were powered by a hand crank. Moir and Letts, helped by the knowledge of West Country thatchers, describe how the hand-operated versions worked:

Handfuls of straw were inserted into the comber where the flag leaf and grain was stripped off by a rotating drum with spikes (Ian Wright, Richard Wright and Arthur Hannabus, pers. comm.). The handful was then turned round and re-inserted to clear the butts of weeds and short straw. A final combing in the barn, and on the roof when being applied, ensured that the straw was free of contaminants that might lessen its longevity.[15]

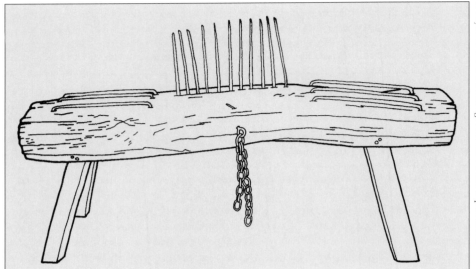

Another fixed reed comb of slightly dif-
ferent design, from the Rural Life
Collection at Bicton Botanical Gardens,
East Budleigh. Bundles of straw could
be threshed by knocking them against
the metal staples on either side of the
comb. This example has a double chain
so that it could be firmly fixed to a wall
against the pressure of the straw pulled
through the comb. The beam is 1.6m
(5ft 3ins) long; height (not including
comb) 685mm (2ft 3ins).

A hand-operated barn comber, probably
early/mid 19th century. The revolving
spiked drums cleaned out broken straws
and the leaf. The machine shown has a
maker's label, 'J Blackler, Kingsbridge'.
It was used at Lambside Farm, Newton
Ferrers. By 1966 (when mechanical
reed combers attached to threshing
machines and modern combine har-
vesters were both in general use in
Devon) one man on the farm still
remembered how to use it.

Speeding up the process of combing was obviously an advantage in reducing
the cost of labour. Developments in combing machinery benefited thatch.
Developments in threshing machinery did not. The thrust in the development
of threshing machines was to increase speed. A fully mechanised system that
crushed the straw along its stem proved to be the most rapid and efficient
method for extracting grain. This rendered the straw useless for combed straw
thatching. It was theoretically possible to thresh only the apex of the plant, as
Moir and Letts have explained, by pushing a handful of straw into some of the
machines and withdrawing it.[16] This was not only laborious but must have been
more than usually risky for the operator. A machine in Dorset in 1812 is
described as having a special pedal 'when it is desired to draw back the straw for
reed thatching'.[17] To date there is no evidence that this type of machine was at

all widespread. Fortunately for the survival of the combed straw tradition, threshing machines arrived late in Devon.

The first threshing machines were developed and pioneered in Scotland in the 1780s, powered by horse or water. By 1815 stationary threshing machines were commonplace on most large grain-growing farms in southern Scotland and northern England. Their use elswhere was more patchy, but between 1815 and 1830 they were taken up in the main grain-growing areas of England, notably East Anglia. It is not surprising that in a pastoral area like Devon, Marshall does not refer to any threshing machines in 1796. There may have been some in existence. On 23.2.1797 *The Exeter Flying Post* reported that 'Jubbs Patent Threshing Machine' manufactured in Yorkshire, had been installed in that year, both at Upton House near Brixham and Bystock, near Exmouth. Jubbs' machines cost 30 guineas, plus the cost of carriage and setting up, which must have put them beyond the pocket of most Devon farmers.

Vancouver, writing in 1808, refers to a handful of threshing machines in Devon in his *General View of the Agriculture of the County of Devon; with Observations of the Means of its Improvement*. Vancouver's account of horse-drawn threshing machines 'made by Baker of Exeter, and other wheel and millwrights in the country' describes their cost as 'about 40 guineas each'.[18] Six bushels (the average weight of a bushel of wheat was 63lbs) an hour could be thrashed, the machine needing to be tended by six people.[19] Vancouver was keen to stress advantages he judged the machines brought to rural employment. No doubt his comments on mopping up spare labour from failing Devon industry were prompted by machine-breaking in Dorset by agricultural labourers who saw that the mechanisation of threshing deprived them of wages. The water-powered machine belonging to the Honourable Newton Fellows employed:

> …only one man…to five women, and which together with the drill-husbandry introduced and practised by Mr Fellows, affords an opportunity of employing a large proportion of women and children; the work being so systematically arranged, that in its execution it becomes in a manner impossible for them to deviate or to go wrong. The men, in the mean time, are engaged in more arduous and laborious employments; and the whole of this society is thus, in a season of great dearth of labour from the failure of the neighbouring manufactures, actually employed to their own interest, the manifest relief of the parish burthens, and the general benefit of the community at large.[20]

Vancouver does not record where Fellows lived in Devon, but he was a respected agriculturist and owned land in Winkleigh parish. Oat and barley straw, which was not combed, could be pushed through the threshing machine for fodder particularly cheaply and the result was 'much softer and more pliant to the mouths of their cattle'. Vancouver also mentions threshing machines owned by Mr Vinn, at Payhembury, East Devon, (water-powered), and a horse-powered thrashing-mill owned by Lord Clifford of Ugbrooke, Chudleigh, which tenants on the estate could use for free.

Hand-threshing continued in the county later than in many other areas with more funds to invest in machinery and the motive of larger percentages of arable land relative to pasture. In Devon the use of the flail was a continuation, in spite of the machine age, of the laborious methods of producing combed straw thatch which can be traced back to the days of the open hall house. However, by the late 1830s the sheer speed of mechanical threshing was beginning to have some impact in the county. Devon had its own, low-key version of the anti-machinery protests that affected Dorset. In 1830 Miller Whiteway of Chudleigh, where Lord Clifford's threshing machine, noted by Vancouver, was probably set up, received an anonymous letter from a disaffected labourer threatening to destroy it, 'because I have had now work all oing to yor threshing machine'.[21] By 1831 Lord Clifford was writing, 'incendiaries are busy round Newton; two barns and threshing machines have been burnt... threatening letters are sent to the farmers and others who, notwithstanding all my exertions to the contrary, are taking down their machines'. This certainly suggests that protests about the threshing machine in Devon may have contributed to a reduction in their numbers, something known to have occurred in other counties.[22]

Nevertheless, in 1837 *The Exeter Flying Post* reported that Mr L Beare, machine maker of Meeth near Hatherleigh, had erected fixed threshing machines on several farms in Devon and Cornwall. One was demonstrated on the premises of William Holman, a Bideford butcher. Mr Tremlett of Hollocombe Barton, Crediton, was using his to turn out 34 bundles of threshed straw in ten minutes, using three horses. With four horses he was prepared to thrash '100 bundles of corn in one hour fit for Maltsters or for seed'.[23] In 1844 the same paper reported 'a newly-invented' portable threshing machine, also designed by Beare, set up at Powderham, the Earl of Devon's estate for the use of the tenants. On the same day Beare set up another similar machine for J B Swete of Oxton House in Kenton, one of Devon's major enthusiasts for Picturesque scenery.[24] While this shows that Devon was not backward in home-grown mechanical skills, there were few landlords or enterprising farmers with enough acreage of cereals to justify the purchase of a threshing machine before the mid 19th century.

Many Devon farms preserve horse engine houses, attached to barns. These provide a covered space for the driving wheel and horse, which supplied power to machinery in the barn via a drive shaft. Horse engine houses are plain structures and difficult to date, but unlikely to be earlier than the late 18th century. Some are shown on the tithe maps of the late 1830s and 1840s. Most, however, were not built until after the date of the tithe maps but arrived before the first edition Ordnance Survey maps of the 1880s. They could power a range of machinery, including apple crushers for cider-making and chaff-cutters for fodder, but some must have been used to power fixed threshing machines. The delay in adopting threshing machines in the county, including those associated with horse engine houses, meant that the traditional method of producing combed straw, by hand-flailing, survived. Straw that was not crushed by mechanical threshing continued to be available.

Vancouver provides some interesting detail about the costs of hand-threshing and combing. It took 'a common day's work' to thresh and comb six 28lb bundles of 'reed' (i.e. six nitches) which, in North Devon, cost 'in different parts of the country from 14d to 16d besides an allowance of three pints of cider'. An alternative was task work paying 3d a bundle, but with no allowance of beer or cider, or 4d per stook 'and a man with diligence will thrash six stooks per day'.

> In all cases, the man who thrashes, combs and secures with a double band the bundles of wheat-reed. This is generally laid by for thatching hay and corn, the roofs of farm-houses, cottages, barns and other buildings; and for bands for tyeing up sheaves of the ensuing harvest of both winter and spring grain.[25]

The 'bands' would have been bonds made of twisted straw.

Vancouver provides some interesting detail about the use of straw on building types that no longer survive. He refers to an improving farmer near Watermouth erecting yards with sheds in fields distant from the farmhouse, to reduce the labour of shifting livestock and fodder to the yard by the farmhouse. The sheds were temporary and could be dismantled and re-erected. They consisted of a framework usually of deal, 'covered with thatched hurdles'.[26] The light weight of straw made mobility possible. He also refers, in the South Hams, to a type of farmbuilding for storing sheaves of corn. This was a kind of permanent rick, with a light movable roof which could be raised or let down over a stack on staddles, presumably as the sheaves were removed for threshing. The design was said to have been borrowed from the Dutch. The roofing was almost certainly thatch, as are most of the Dutch examples.

© Jo Cox 1994

A storage building with an adjustable roof that can be raised or lowered to give maximum shelter. This is possible because thatch is such a light roof covering. This is an example from the building museum at Arnheim in the Netherlands, but there were buildings of this kind in Devon in the late 18th and early 19th centuries. None survives.

Thatch and Slate combined

Illustrations showing the combination of thatch with local slate at the eaves and verges, or in vulnerable places on the roof, are rather startling. This is not, so far as the authors of this book are aware, recorded in any of the 'antiquarian' descriptions of Devon thatching. It does appear in illustrations of the early 19th century by John Swete and Samuel Prout, and continued into the 20th century, recorded in photographs. It may be an early technique in a county with local sources of both materials in use from the medieval period. This combination of 'hard' and 'soft' roofing is also known in other counties from documentary references. The Board of Agriculture report for Derbyshire gives the reason for 'hard' eaves in association with thatch as a means of preventing of cattle pulling off thatch on low buildings and to protect the eaves from ladder damage.[27] Risk of damage by cattle can hardly have been the reason in most of the illustrated Devon examples. These show the eaves

Thatch with slate eaves and verges in a painting of a farm group at Meavy c.1808 by Samuel Prout. If the slates on the building in the foreground could be a repair, the house in the background has neat slate eaves and verges which have clearly been designed in combination with the thatch. Eaves and verges receive the run-off of all the rain that falls on a roof and are particularly vulnerable. However, the thatch overlapping the slate must have suffered from lack of ventilation from below. Prout may have over-emphasised the shabby condition of Dartmoor buildings in the early 19th century but his record of traditional thatch is in sharp contrast to thatch on the houses of the genteel.

well out of the reach of livestock. A similar combination is also known from the Netherlands, where thatch in some regions is combined with clay tiles. There is also archaeological evidence of the use of local small slates to form valleys, where today lead would be used. Awkward junctions that would now be managed with mortar fillets or lead might also be made or repaired with slate.

Right: *Slate used in conjunction with thatch at Rushlade, Ashburton in a photograph of 1962. Slate may always have been used here around the awkward junction of the chimney and the plane of the roof, or may be a repair.*

Below: *The Pilchard Inn, Burgh Island, in about 1900, showing thatch with slate eaves and verges. The thatch had been replaced by 1913.*

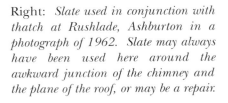

Rural Thatch

The slow-down in economic and population growth limited the demand for thatch (and any other roofing material) on new farmhouses. Farm tenancy agreements of the late 18th and early 19th centuries record the system of tenants providing the thatching material themselves, the landlord paying for the thatcher. An agreement of 30 November 1810 between James Buller of Downe, near Crediton and Robert Mead of Coffinswell Barton required Mead to provide yearly: 'three hundred nitches of good Redd and Spars to lay the same for and towards thatching the said Premises during the said term on having an allowance of 16s per hundred for such last mentioned Reed and five shillings and sixpence for Spars'.[28] One tenancy agreement quoted by Marshall prohibited the tenant from selling hay and straw but permitted the sale of thatching straw, indicating that it was a recognised cash crop for farmers.[29]

Insurance policies are a rich but overwhelming source of information on what was thatched where in the county from the 1790s – so long as it was insured. Sampling the records of the Sun Insurance Company, held at the Guildhall Library in London, it is clear that policies with this company in the late 18th century were more likely to be taken out on town buildings – with valuable goods as well as houses and warehouses to cover – than on rural buildings. The company also seems to have had better coverage in the south than the north of the county, which distorts the picture of distribution. However, the records show that in the villages – with exceptions – thatch was still commonplace and included numerous outbuildings as well as dwellings. John Bridle of Houlton village in Otterton, yeoman, for example, took out insurance in 1795 on his thatched house, offices, barn, cellars, poundhouse (including a 'pound engine' and cider press), stable and linhay. His ricks and stacks were also insured, but the terms excluded (as was common for Sun and, presumably, other insurance companies) 'such hay or corn as shall be damaged by its natural heating'.[30] This is a reference to the risk of combustion from the build-up of internal heat if ricks or stacks were not correctly ventilated when built.

Differences in the pattern of thatch to slate between the west of the county and the east were quite sharply defined by 1800. This is a judgement that has to be made partly on contemporary sources, partly on survival. The lists of buildings with statutory protection can only ever be a rough guide to historic roof coverings, since they represent only a selection judged to be of special historic or architectural interest, and that is only a selection of what has survived. Nevertheless they are the best resource to hand that covers parishes at approximately the same level and are a valuable, if imperfect, source of information on roofing.

Looking through the lists it is possible to compare a block of parishes in Mid Devon (Cheriton Bishop list) where thatch was the obvious choice of roof covering [31], with one in West Devon where there was access to South Hams slate (Bradstone list).[32] The Mid Devon block includes fifty thatched or formerly thatched domestic buildings, identified as having '18th century' or '18th to early 19th century' origins. Type varies from substantial farmhouses to small cottages. The fifty thatched buildings compare with only four slate roofs on houses of the same period, one of those being a small mansion and another a large villa. This shows substantial quantities of new thatched buildings in part of Mid Devon in the period.

In a block of West Devon parishes (Bradstone list) there are far fewer domestic buildings identified as having 18th century origins – only 13 in all. Eight have slate roofs and only five have thatch. The difference in the roofing of agricultural buildings built in the same approximate period is also in sharp contrast to the Mid Devon area with only a single slated 18th century farmbuilding and eight thatched farm buildings or mills. The West Devon parishes have five thatched agricultural buildings and nine with slate roofs.

The comparisons are never perfectly balanced, of course. The West Devon block of parishes includes two superior houses with 18th century outbuildings. These are a cut above the vernacular and may have had slate roofs for reasons of status. These distortions, however (which give a glimpse into the diverse pattern of new building across the county in the period), reinforce the view that thatch continued to be used on new 18th century buildings in rural parishes in the east of the county, with a distinct cut-off point at a high level of status, whereas in the west, new buildings, including some ancillary buildings, were far more likely to receive a slate roof.

Richard Polwhele's *The History of Devonshire*, 1793-1806, has occasional, but unfortunately patchy, comments on roofing materials. In a note on Ugborough, a parish in the South Hams which has some slate outcrops, he writes:

> *82 cottages, mostly in a woeful plight; 2 mills, 5 public & 74 farm-houses (in all 81) of which about a score or so are tolerably neat & compact; the rest make but a paltry figure. The dwellings are generally slated, the out-houses thatcht. Paupers between 60 & 70… Manufactures none.*[33]

This is a vivid record of commonplace poverty in one parish as well as showing that, where slate was to hand, thatch had disappeared from most dwellings, however 'paltry' but survived on outbuildings.

Early 19th century images by Samuel Prout showing thatched Devon buildings are a good index to the range of rural buildings that were still thatched: mills; simple cottages and farmstead groups. As a general rule he shows the condition of the buildings, including the thatch, in a state of decay. This may be exaggerated for effect in some cases, but the record of thatch held down with stones or rotted away to expose roof timbers is surely a record of the rural poverty of the time, also noted by contemporary writers.

Above: *Tor Bridge Mill drawn by Samuel Prout c.1811.*

Right: *A 'Moor Cottage' drawn by Samuel Prout c.1811. Prout shows loose stones holding down the thatch on a simple single-storey cottage.*

'Moevy', a 17th century or earlier building drawn by Samuel Prout c.1812 with a thatched roof shown in a state of disrepair and combined with a slate pentice on brackets.

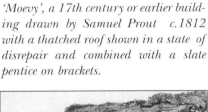

Domestic Buildings

In the 18th century changes to the plan and general design of new buildings played a part in excluding thatch from fashionable buildings of the 'middling sort'. Georgian architecture was a national style, disseminated through pattern books from London and fashionable towns. Georgian houses were often built two rooms deep and were box-like in form. The depth of the houses allowed for a central entrance hall combined with a staircase on a generous scale. These houses were most economically covered with a shallow hipped roof, ideal for slate. The run-off of rainwater was just too slow for thatch to perform effectively on a roof of this design which would have needed massive height to produce a suitably steep pitch.

The aesthetics of the Georgian house, where external symmetry was part of an aesthetic of smooth, urbane, even surfaces was in sharp contrast to the organic,

variable textures of thatch. This is not to say that no Georgian houses of pretension were thatched, but this was usually done by sacrificing the advantages of the two-room, two-storey, deep plan, and designing them with a single depth main range, with a symmetrical arrangment of windows and a central front door, and one or two rear wings. The majority of the modest Georgian houses found throughout Devon, were slated from the outset. They are found in the expanding urban areas of the larger towns – free-standing, in pairs or in rows and terraces – and in country parishes. Some were farmhouses, others were occupied by the clergy, retired sea captains, army officers and the like. When the houses were thatched, plastering to conceal the underside of the thatch in the first floor rooms was ubiquitous. A flat ceiling would be inserted across the width of the room, if there was enough height, or the ceiling might follow the pitch of the roof. At Ford Street, in Moretonhampstead, plaster was applied directly to the thatch between the battens.

If the numbers of new thatched buildings grew smaller, combed straw roofs held up on the stock of well-built single-depth farmhouses inherited from the 16th and 17th centuries, and on new cottages and small village houses outside the South Hams. In other regions the 18th century saw new Georgian style farmhouses built on newly-enclosed land, roofed with slate and tile. As a county of early enclosure, there is little of this to be seen in Devon and few new enclosure farmhouses were built in the 18th century. The old farmhouses were relatively large and robust and could be adapted in accordance with new tastes in comfort and fashion. They could be updated on the show front with the insertion of regularly-positioned sash windows in place of casements or mullioned windows, and the rooms that visitors were likely to see could be made fashionable by superficial modernisation. A massive 17th century fireplace could be reduced in size and refined by the addition of an applied timber or marble chimney-piece. New doors might be added on the ground floor and perhaps a corner cupboard introduced to display china in the parlour. However, what survives in Devon suggests that there was neither the need for drastic enlargement, nor the funds available to go in for re-roofing and abandoning thatch. Many of the farmhouses did become two rooms deep,

A cluster of thatched buildings at Torbryan, drawn by Samuel Prout c.1812. Agricultural and domestic elements exist side-by-side. Ladders, including a thatcher's ladder, are available for repairs. The cruck construction of the right hand building, visible through a hole in the roof, has been propped up with a cider barrel.

Park Cottages, The Green, Whimple. Thatch is not the ideal roofing for this kind of tight valley between two adjoining ranges, but in thatching there are always exceptions to the rule. Although there are two dwellings here the photograph illustrates the practical obstacles to thatching a house plan that was two rooms deep and two storeys high throughout.

Village thatch made urbane in associa-tion with sash windows and classical detail on an up-to-date c.1820 house in Coleford.

Right top: *A smart thatched Georgian house, Cross Park, at Manaton on Dartmoor, photographed in 1910.*

Right middle: *Higher House, an early 19th century village house at Payhembury.*

Right bottom: *Thatch associated with smart 18th detail in Alphington, on the road out of Exeter. A Tuscan porch, sash windows – including a first floor triple sash in a bow – and original attic dormers with horizontal sliding sashes.*

Below: *Thatch seen from inside a late 18th century extension to a medieval town house, at 2–4 Ford Street, Moretonhampstead. The method of tying the base coat on to the laths with tarcord can clearly be seen. Plastering directly on to the thatch between the laths would have kept the dust out of the first floor rooms but, if the thatch ever needed stripping back to the timbers, the plaster would have had to be sacrificed too.*

but only on the ground floor, with a lean-to roof added against the main house which did not affect the pitch or line of thatch over the main range.

Cottages

Vancouver, writing in 1808, records that the shell of rented cottages in some parts of the county was maintained by the landlord, 'the tenants drawing the materials, and finding reed for thatch in return for the tops and bark of any trees cut down for repairing their farms'. He gives the cost of thatching as 8s per square of 10 feet (thatch was measured, like slate, in 10 foot 'squares'). '100 sheaves of wheat-straw, weighing 25lbs each, are supposed equal to the making of one square of thatch'. He also comments on shortage of housing for labourers, some areas having a 'want of cottages' and cottages going to ruin and having fallen down.

The Devon tithe maps of the late 1830s and early 1840s record numerous small cottages, probably 18th century in date, built within isolated farmsteads or villages. Most of these had disappeared by the 1880s as shown on late 19th and early 20th century Ordnance Survey maps. Photography from the late 19th century and between the wars shows some of the survivors, but there have been enormous losses to this class of thatched building in Devon and relatively unaltered examples are now extremely rare, often being too small to suit modern housing requirements.

Existing 18th and early 19th century cottages in villages, built for farm labourers or rural craftsmen, were usually two storeys high with a one- or two-room plan and with one heated room. These are plain vernacular buildings and, outside the South Hams, were generally thatched. Some are conversions from

Lower Ingley Farm, Broadwood Kelly, showing probably early 19th century sash windows introduced into a substantial 17th century or earlier farmhouse to keep in step with fashion, without altering the basic structure. Layers of thatch show that the roof structure has not been changed as earlier sections of earlier thatch can be seen. The farm burned down in 1929.

A small cob and thatch estate house, probably 18th century, at Waddington Green, Stoke Gabriel.

2–8 Cob Row, Broadclyst. A piecemeal development of mid 19th century cottages.

larger, earlier houses built in settlements that lost status from the 17th century. A good example is the row of 15th century houses in Silverton, East Devon, Nos 2–12 Fore Street, divided into smaller units in the 18th century. Newton Poppleford illustrates the same process, although later modernisations often hide the true age of the buildings. Nevertheless the layout and features on the inside show that several pairs of cottages along the main road from Exeter to Lyme Regis were created in the late 18th and early 19th centuries by dividing up older houses and at the same time filling the space between them with new cottages. This process can be observed in most of the smaller towns and villages of Devon. There are similar examples in Morchard Bishop but this village is more famous for the row of 18th century cottages, Nos 1–13 Fore Street, reputed to be the longest run of thatched buildings in England. Spanishlake Cottage in Doddiscombsleigh (now converted into a single house) was a rare example of an agricultural labourer's cottage in a farmstead. It had a thatched roof and a cob stack with one heated ground floor room which probably served as both kitchen and parlour. A simple winder stair in the corner led to the first floor which was divided into two unheated bedrooms. The cottage, sited in a farmyard and built off one end of a barn, dated 1771, represents a class of humble thatched domestic buildings in farmyards for which little physical evidence now survives.

Part of the Morchard Bishop row of cottages in Fore Street, said to be the longest row of thatched houses in England, photographed in 1992.

Farm Buildings

Surviving examples of farmyards rebuilt and thatched in the 18th and early 19th centuries, can be drawn from most of rural Devon. The rebuilding and enlargement of barns in Devon in the 18th century suggests that 17th century barns were either too small or too inconveniently-arranged to accommodate increased cereal production and, in some cases, enlarged farm sizes. The numbers and size of linhays, the distinctive West Country form of open-fronted cattle shed with a hay loft over increased in the period, reflecting regional specialisation and improved accommodation for cattle rearing.

A very modest thatched outbuilding at East Park, Iddesleigh. This is an ashhouse for storing ash from the wood fire in the farmhouse before spreading it on the fields. It is square on plan rather than round, as some were. They were sometimes combined with hen-houses or pigsties, to mix the ash with manure. The child is Philip Bale, wearing petticoats as children of both sexes did in the early years of the 20th century.

Left above: *A c.1815 cattleshed at Dulcis Farm, Kilmington, designed for thatch but roofed over with corrugated iron.*

Left: *Inside the same cattleshed the base coat of the earlier thatch survives, supported on skimpy laths on a slender oak roof construction. In some 18th century farmbuildings there were no purlins or common rafters. The trusses were relatively closely-spaced with only sturdy thatching laths between them.*

The farmhouse at Broomham, King's Nympton, North Devon, has medieval origins and has retained thatch throughout. It has a much-altered medieval barn but in the 18th century acquired a second barn, a linhay and shippon, all thatched. In East Devon, the 16th century farmhouse at Upton Farm, Clyst St Lawrence, has a three-sided courtyard of 18th century thatched buildings, comprising shippon, linhay and barn. Beetor Farm, in North Bovey on Dartmoor has the ruins of a medieval longhouse, originally thatched. By the mid 18th century the early barn had been enlarged and a generous-sized shippon and a detached bakehouse built in the yard. Later, in an ambitious scheme of 1816, a water leat was brought around the tor to supply two stockyards. The new buildings associated with this phase, reflecting an increase in cattle-rearing, were all

A thatched farmhouse and Linhay at Seaton from Francis Stevens' Views of Cottages and Farmhouses in England and Wales (1815).

thatched. Only a bank barn (with shippon) and a pigsty, which were not added until the late 19th century, were slated from the outset. At Beetor, all the thatch on the farm buildings was later replaced with corrugated iron, reflecting the pattern for most Devon farm buildings *(see colour page 9, plate 26)*.

In the South Hams it is more difficult to find 18th and early 19th century thatched farm buildings. This was not only a matter of easier access to the Devon slate quarries but also because specialisation in cereals meant that the South Hams farmers were more likely to have invested in the threshing machinery that could not produce combed straw. It is also noticeable that the South Hams has far less evidence for pre-1550 farmhouses than North, East or Mid Devon. The surviving farmhouses have been far more comprehensively rebuilt in the 18th and early 19th century. No doubt this reflects a more buoyant economy in Devon's main cereal-producing area than on pastoral farms, and the capital to invest in slate, seen as a more progressive roofing material than thatch.

The use of brick, referred to in the previous chapter, was extended, particularly in East Devon where the soil type was suitable for local brick-making. Using brick for farm buildings may have been progressive, by comparison with cob or stone, but many brick buildings continued to be roofed with thatch. One example is the early 18th century brick and thatch courtyard at Woodbeer Court in Plymtree, containing a cider house and cellar, a stable, barn and shippon. A thatched brick granary at Lower House, Payhembury, has a date plaque of 1780 and there is a probably early 19th century timber-framed granary, the frame infilled with brick, at Higher House, Atherington.

Urban Thatch

The Sun Insurance records indicate that little thatch survived in the larger towns by the late 18th century. By 1795 town buildings, including warehouses, workshops and 'offices' (outhouses) are usually described as 'plaister and slated'. Insurance policies for Plymouth and Plymouth Dock taken out in that year refer to no thatched buildings at all, although of course there may have been some, either insured with a different company or not insured at all. In Exeter, where 'tile' is mentioned as well as slate, there are exceptions, but usually on the ouskirts. For example, William Cuttyfort took out insurance on The Red Cow in St Davids, comprising a 'dwelling house, brewhouse and cellar adjoining', all thatched. Little Silver, too, a square of houses off St David's Hill in Exeter, included several thatched houses. Richard Pinn had a thatched malthouse in Magdalen Street, close to the centre of the city, but outside the city walls.

The picture from the Sun Insurance records for 1795 is more mixed in the middling-sized towns. No thatch appears in policies taken out in that year in Dartmouth, as one would expect for a town close to Devon slate sources, as well as with easy sea access to Cornish slate. In Cullompton, however, two serge-makers insured their dwelling house, workshop, warerooms, yarn shop, warping chamber, offices, pound house and barn. These were all thatched and either adjoining or near one another. Tiverton, surprisingly, retained some thatch in the town centre, after no less than four town fires before 1732. Edward Boyce, a builder, insured 'a college of tenements call'd Luggs Court situate in Peter Street', all thatched. Colyton preserves some superior thatched town houses with fashionable doorcases and sash windows.

© John R L Thorp 2001

A combination of smart 18th century detail and thatch at 1 and 2 Court House, Colyton. The moulded cornice is used to give a kick for the thatch at the eaves. The gutter, though not strictly necessary, is a courtesy to pedestrians and is supported on simple but elegant brackets.

Urban thatch fires continue to be recorded, with less than ideal fire-fighting arrangements. Moretonhampstead, for example, suffered a number of early 19th century fires and had a fire engine in the town. However, when a particularly bad fire broke out on 11 September 1839 at about one in the morning, it was soon realised that outside help was needed. An express messenger was sent to Exeter to request horse-drawn engines, owned by the companies with whom the Moretonhampstead properties were insured: The West of England, the Sun, and the Norwich Union. As F D Gentry describes in *Take Care of Your Fire and Candle* the logistics of this arrangement were painfully slow. The brigades of three engines, each manned by six men, had to be found, as well as horses hired before the journey to Moretonhampstead could begin. The first engine arrived five hours after the fire first broke out. The damage was extensive with 14 families left homeless. *The Exeter & Plymouth Gazette* of 15 September reported that the spread of the blaze was stopped by a house with a slated roof.

Cecil Torr's *Small Talk at Wreyland* records an additional problem. The town fire engine was owned by the West of England office, and therefore houses insured by that company had been given priority in the first efforts to put out the blaze:

> '*my father writes in his diary:- "The Moreton engine poured on the thatch in front of Mrs Heyward's house, and kept the fire in the back premises. But, as the fire was extending towards the White Hart, which was insured in the 'West of England,' the engine (which belonged to that office) was removed there to endeavour to preserve the inn. As soon as the engine was removed, the fire came into the front of Mrs Heyward's house, and extended on in Pound Street… There ought to be two engines in the place; and, as the 'Sun' lost so much, perhaps they will send one there."* [34]

Genteel thatching

The Picturesque movement of the late 18th and early 19th centuries encouraged a national revival of 'rustic' building materials for owners of fashionable architectural taste. With this came a new perception of thatched roofing, used self-consciously as part of an aesthetic that referred to a notion of the rural architectural past, filtered through the lens of Romanticism. The Picturesque was the style of gentlefolk rather than tenant farmers: cottages for lords and ladies in a version of the past that was rather different from the standing realities of local vernacular farmhouses. The Picturesque was neither agriculturally rural, nor was it urban. Using thatch on these houses expressed an attachment to the local scene or, at least, suffcent funds for a garden, but the attachment was visual, rather than a working relationship. It is something of a rarity to find the style associated with a working farm.

Marshall Farm, Ide. Picturesque principles applied to a working farmhouse of medieval origins. This was remodelled c.1820 and given two-storey bows glazed with Gothick windows under a thatched roof. The arched motif is used on all the walls overlooking the garden, including blind arches applied to the rear wall of a farm building. Photograph of 1948. The house was demolished in the 1960s.

Plate 1

Plate 2

Above: *Devon thatch at East Coombe, Chagford, in a pasture landscape and wet climate.*

Left: *Whelmstone Barton at Colebrooke, a superior and very well-preserved early 17th century house.*

Below: *An example of village thatch in Coleford, Colebrooke.*

Plate 3

Plate 4

Plate 5

Plate 6

Anti-clockwise from top:

Thatch roofing plastered cob at Greenaway Cottages, Stockleigh Pomeroy.

Thatch roofing a stone rubble house at Lower Ridge, Chardstock.

Thatch roofing a fashionable brick house of 1687, Harris's Farm, Talaton.

Thatch roofing granite at Great Ensworthy, Gidleigh.

Plate 7

Plate 8

Moorstone Barton, Halberton, a grand medieval house shown on the 1603–1689 map with a surrounding wall. The map-maker shows it slated. This is confirmed by surviving evidence for a former phase of slating in the roof under the thatch. The replacement with thatch suggests a downgrading from the original covering by an owner without the means to replace slate with slate.

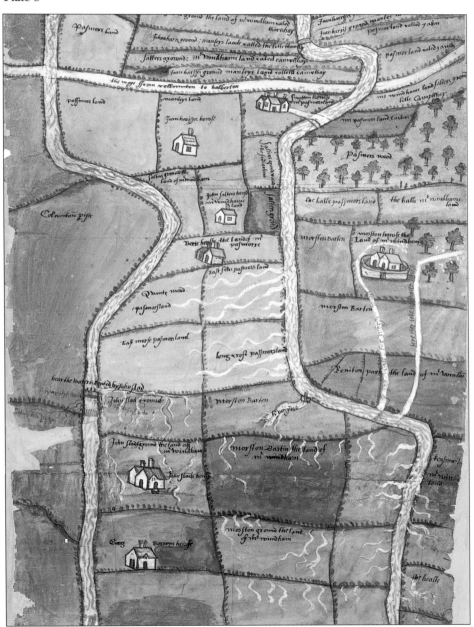

Plate 9

An extract from a 1603–1608 map of Halberton. The brownish colour of the roofs of the smaller houses probably indicates thatch, contrasted with the blue slate roofs which are shown on the larger ones.

Right: *Lower Chilverton, Coldridge, is a particularly good example of a Mid Devon farmhouse originating as an open hall house built in the late 15th century.*

Plate 10

Below: *The roof over the former open hall at Lower Chilverton preserves not only the late medieval roof timbers but also thatching laths, ties and a neatly-presented base coat of the straw, all heavily-sooted from the smoke from the original open hearth fire.*

Plate 11

Tytherleigh Cott, Chardstock. As with many other Devon buildings the exterior gives few clues to the age of the house, which is probably 15th century.

Plate 12

Left and below: *Inside Tytherleigh Cott there is an unusually elaborate (for Devon) medieval open hall roof with cusped windbraces, seen here after fire damage.*

Plate 13

Plate 14

Right: *Broomham, King's Nympton, built as an open hall house by the Furse family in the late 15th century and enlarged in 1634. The same family occupied the farm until 1832 and then rented it out until 1912 when it was sold for the first time. The present farmer, Graham Clements, remembers that the overcoat thatch shown here was a variety of wheat called Squareheads Master especially grown for the roof on the farm.*

Plate 15

Plate 16

Plate 17

Plate 18

Above: *Over Broomham's open hall the inserted ceiling creating an attic can be seen as well as the neatness of the underside of the carpentry and thatch, designed to be seen.*

Top left: *Looking at the roof over the agricultural end of Broomham from the inside, the timbers and thatch are smoke-blackened from the open hearth fire, the smoke having been carried over low partitions which divided this end from the open hall. This roof gives a good picture of just how large and impressive the blackened roofs of open halls must have been. The clean sections of rafter below the purlins are the result of 19th century repairs which involved jacking up one of the trusses.*

Bottom left: *The layered straw thatch at Broomham was excavated prior to rethatching in 1997. The house had then been unoccupied for some years and the thatch was in poor condition. The smoke-blackened layer can be seen where the excavation has extended to the base coat over the roof timbers. The medieval thatch at this house was carefully preserved by building a second layer of rafters, made from oak grown on the farm, over the medieval roof to carry the new thatch.*

Picturesque use of thatch for an aristocrat's 'cottage' with accessories ranging from peacocks to a grotto and fountain. Knowle Cottage, Sidmouth, built for Lord Despencer in the 1820s. The building was widely known, not only from visits, but was extensively illustrated, with images circulated as prints.

Plate 19

Thatch was an acceptable roofing for large, high quality 16th century buildings in Devon as at Spence Combe, near Crediton. A thatched roof has been retained through several phases of modernisation and extension to the house, and continues to be used to cap the garden walls.

Plate 20

Knowle Lake, a small late 17th or early 18th century cottage just outside Copplestone.

Plate 21

Hayne, Zeal Monachorum. A substantial house built in the second half of the 17th century with an up-to-date lobby entrance plan, photographed in 1985.

Plate 22

An early 18th century farmyard cottage at Lower Netherton, Stoke-in-Teignhead. This is a building type that is now extremely rare in Devon.

Plate 23

Plate 24

Above: *A c.1700 double barn at Dira, Sandford, unusual not only for its large size and pair of threshing floors but also for retaining a thatched roof.*

Right: *Thatch used on a probably early 19th century cob ash house at Middle Henstill, Sandford. Such a simple building is hard to date but is probably early 19th century.*

Below: *An 1816 double shippon at Beetor Farm, North Bovey, part of a major scheme of new farmbuildings at that date. All were thatched but all had their roofs replaced with corrugated in the 20th century.*

Plate 25

Plate 26

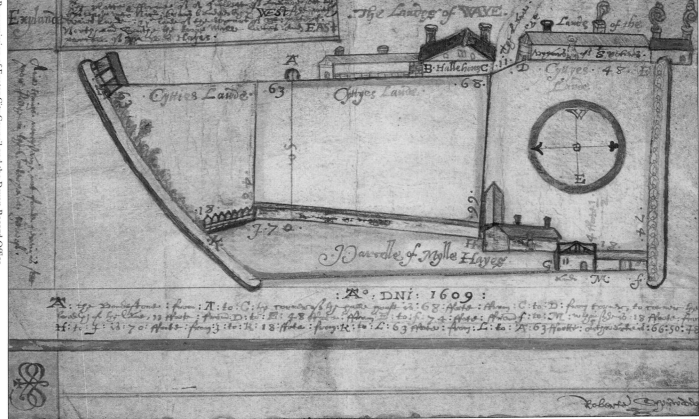

Plate 27

Above: *1609 map by Robert Sherwood of a property on Exe Island, Exeter, showing a mixture of thatch and slate at that date.*

Below: *Two extracts from the 1743 map of Crediton, showing the outbreak of the fire.. The extract on the left shows the centre of Crediton with a mixture of brick houses with slate roofs, timber-fronted houses with gables to the fronts, also slated, and smaller thatched houses. The extract on the right shows the outbreak of the fire.*

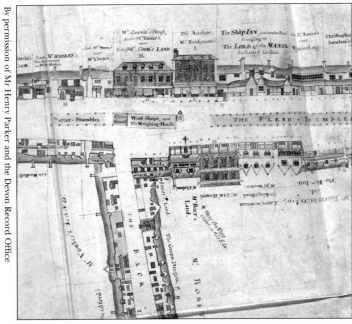

Plate 28

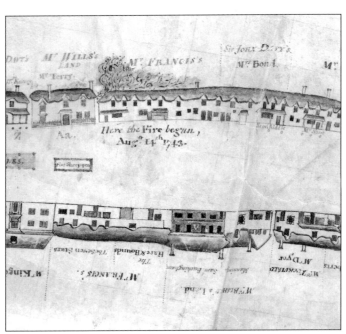

Plate 29

Plate 31

Plate 32

Plate 33

Left top: *Building a properly ventilated stack of the right size to contain the crop, especially on sloping Devon ground, requires art and judgement.*

Left middle: *A thatcher's team reed combing at Nymet Rowland in 1994. Bundles are passed to the man on the back who feeds them into the comber.*

Left bottom: *People and landscape connected to produce traditional thatch in Devon in the 20th century. Tristan Johnson, thatcher, and a team of helpers ricking straw for thatching at Nymet Rowland in 1994.*

Below: *Wheat destined for thatching straw has to be harvested and processed without using a combine harvester. The bundles cut by a reaper-binder are left in the field to dry out as stooks.*

Plate 30

Top right: *A Devon house divided into two. The left-hand half is combed straw, the right-hand water reed. The visual differences are slight. The water reed is slightly thinner in colour. As a longer material it requires more of a kick at the eaves and this can be seen by looking closely at the eaves line, which changes at the porch.*

Middle right: *The same building viewed from the rear. Water reed to the left, combed straw to right.*

Bottom right: *A water reed roof in Gittisham.*

Below: *A consignment of water reed arriving from abroad at the headquarters of a large thatching firm in 1994.*

Bottom: *Overcoating with water reed at Croyde.*

© Jo Cox 1994

Plate 34

© Jo Cox 1994

Plate 35

© Jo Cox 1994

Plate 36

© Peter Child 2000

Plate 38

© Jo Cox 1994

Plate 37

Plate 39

Plate 40

Above: *Roofs of old houses in Dean Street, Crediton, showing the variety of materials that the transport revolution has brought to a town that was once slate and thatched.*

Above: *New and old village building in Whimple. Timber-frame, brick and tile are materials characteristic of the South East.*

Below: *Hedgehog Cottage, Talaton, designed and built in the 1990s as a reinterpretation of the Devon vernacular tradition, rendered and thatched.*

Plate 41

Above: *A traditional cob and thatch extension to an old house in Down St Mary by Mr Alfred Howard, a leading light in the revival of cob in Devon.*

Plate 42

Most thatched roofs today look far tidier than the roofs shown in late 19th century and early 20th century photographs. Typical of a highly-maintained appearance familiar today is Spencer Cottage, Coleford, Colebrooke, a house of medieval origins with a fine two-storey porch.

Plate 43

Scribbles at Lamerton. A formerly thatched masonry rubble longhouse in a state of disrepair in 1991 after a long period of use as a farmbuilding and having lost its thatch in a storm in the 1980s. It is now re-thatched and has been restored as a house.

Plate 44

Scribbles at Lamerton in 2001, restored, rethatched and re-occupied.

Plate 45

Plate 46

Plate 47

Plate 48

Above: *Membury Court. A photograph taken c.1900. The L-plan house, of medieval origins, is thatched, so is a medieval chapel at the rear of the house, downgraded to use as a farm building by this date. All the farm buildings are thatched too. Note the stooks in the field behind.*

Left: *Membury Court, the same view in 1993. All the thatch has gone, not only on the farmbuildings, but also on the house, replaced by a wide choice of materials available in the 20th century: tile, slate, corrugated iron and corrugated asbestos.*

Below left: *Membury Court in 2000. After the place changed hands it was repaired and the roof of the house was returned to thatch.*

Plate 49

Above: *Outer Marsh Farm, Clyst Hydon, waiting for a rethatch in 1987. There may be a long wait for the funds, or for the thatcher to be available, but thatched roofs on Devon houses are now unlikely to be replaced with other materials.*

Below left: *Thatchers at Gittisham. Gittisham is an estate village and the estate grows wheat for thatching straw.*

Below right: *A house in Gittisham being rethatched in combed straw.*

Plate 50

Above: *Straw bond used during rethatching with combed straw in Gittisham.*

Plate 51

Plate 52

The Picturesque was less strong in Devon than in some other counties, but was important in raising the status of thatch in the county at the end of a period in which it had increasingly been downgraded. Thatch on psicturesque buildings was to be found especially in South Devon, where the climate and landscape attracted superior leisured society at the end of the 18th century.

The Reverend John Swete, who lived in Oxton House, Kenton, produced volumes of his own amateur watercolours and gushing descriptions of Devon scenery written between 1792 and 1801. He also designed himself a tiny two-storey, one-room plan garden house, sited in the grounds of Oxton to give views of the rugged Devon landscape. Squeezed into the small compass of this rustic retreat were all the accessories that any Picturesque enthusiast might need: access to scenery, references to English Gothic in the shape of painted glass, a touch of Tudor in the canted oriel window, a Latin inscription in the antiquarian manner, and thatch. Inside, the marble chimneypiece and coved plaster ceiling were hardly rustic, but provided gentlemanly comfort and refinement where Swete could display his collections and paintings. Outside, the building was ostentatiously thatched, including a thatched pentice to the external staircase and gallery that led to the first floor room.

The Reverend John Swete's cottage in Oxton Woods in a c.1812 etching by and after T H Williams. This shows thatch as one of the accessories of an enthusiast for the Picturesque.

Thatch was employed for modest rural villas and for lodges to rather grander houses. On a larger scale than Swete's retreat, but no less charming and eccentric, the rustic cottage, A La Ronde, in Summer Lane, near Exmouth was erected in 1798 for two spinster cousins, Mary and Jane Parminter. The house, probably to the designs of John Lowder, was sixteen-sided and top-lit, the walls stone and the roof thatched.[35] Outside and in, it represented a refinement of rustic charm which was as much like the 'paltry' thatched cottages of Devon as chalk to cheese. The garden and pleasure ground contained an obelisk, fountain, shell-house, sundial and ornamental seats. The interior provided the kind of canvas on which ladies of leisure could apply decorative finishes of shells and feathers. Unfortunately the thatch was later replaced by tile.

A La Ronde, built in 1798 and originally thatched. The dormers, and especially the complex junctions at the peak of the roof, would have been fiddly for the thatcher.

In 1797 the diary of John Skinner records thatch used for a pleasure building for the better sort to use in Sidmouth in bad weather. He noted that many bathers had been attracted to Sidmouth because of its pleasant situation, but complained of only four bathing machines. The inhabitants, he reported: 'have formed a gravel walk nearly a quarter of a mile in length, facing the sea, which is the usual resort for the company ; and also a thatched building to shelter them in bad weather, & a billiard table'.[36]

As Sidmouth developed it acquired a large collection of modest thatched villas, many illustrated in the c.1826 *Forty-Eight Views of Cottages and Scenery at Sidmouth Devon*. Most had Picturesque elements: Gothick windows, verandahs or balconies and plenty of trellis. Some examples show the thatch extended over substantial conservatories, as at Myrtle Cottage, owned by a Miss Campbell, where one of the thatched garden buildings seems to have a glazed panel cut into the thatched roof.

Vignettes from Forty-Eight Views of Cottages and Scenery at Sidmouth Devon *(n.d. c.1826).*

Myrtle Cottage.

Lodge to the Marino.

Clifton Cottage.

Further vignettes from Forty-Eight Views of Cottages and Scenery at Sidmouth Devon *(n.d. c.1826).*

Right: *Temple Cottage.*

Below: *Woodbine Cottage.*

One of the most expensive versions of the Picturesque in Sidmouth was Knowle Cottage built by Lord Despencer in 1810 *(see colour page 7, plate 19)*. This was much visited by genteel tourists, in the style of visiting large mansions, when Despencer was not at home. 'Cottage' was something of a misnomer for a single-storey and attic building with 30 rooms and a verandah 96m (315 ft) long. Outside there were elaborate gardens, conservatories and choice specimens of foreign birds and animals, and inside 'an unparalled variety of the most rare and costly articles of taste'. The house was thatched, including the dormer windows in the attic where, judging from George Rowe's view published in 1826, the thatch was swept right down over the cheeks of the windows. The Rowe engraving is revealing because it shows that this very expensive and extensive version of the Picturesque in Devon did not merit ornamental detail on the thatching itself. Both the main roof and dormers have plain ridges in the local fashion and there is no sign of the elaborate external patterning or block-cut ridges that characterised Picturesque cottages in other counties.

Amongst all the Temple, Woodland and Woodbine Cottages, owned by single ladies, Esquires and Rear Admirals at Sidmouth, the engravings show only one, the Hermitage, Elysian Fields, with any kind of fancy detail on the thatch. This is either a simple pattern of lozenges on the flush ridge or it may be a curious ridge detail of a crest of upstanding spars which was also found between World Wars One and Two in Devon.

Thatch was also applied self-consciously to the parsonage (now divided as the Chantry and Elmfield) in Teignmouth. This was designed for Thomas Whipham by John Rendle of Teignmouth in 1815. It is an ingeniously-planned

A futher vignette from Forty-Eight Views of Cottages and Scenery at Sidmouth Devon *(n.d. c.1826).*

Woodland Cottage.

101

A futher vignette from Forty-Eight Views of Cottages and Scenery at Sidmouth Devon *(n.d. c.1826).*

The Hermitage.

gentleman's house, providing dainty oval rooms and refined Gothick detail inside. Externally, in addition to the roof, it had a thatched verandah on rustic posts across the undulating garden front.

Devon's finest and most carefully-designed contribution to the Picturesque, Endsleigh Cottage and grounds, near Milton Abbot was erected for the Duke of Bedford in 1810, with Humphry Repton contributing to the garden design. Here, the main house or 'cottage' was slated from the outset. This reflects the proximity of the local Mill Hill slate quarries on land owned by the Duke and in which he had a financial interest. A couple of the garden buildings were designed for thatch: the salmon larder and ice house (now shingled) were both thatched. No doubt, the insulating qualities of thatch tipped the balance here. The Swiss Cottage, appropriately sited overlooking the steep wooded valley to the Tamar, was thatched too, in recognition of the Swiss vernacular tradition known to English gentlemen wealthy enough to do the Grand Tour, taking in the Alps.

Thatchers' Accounts

An account of 1814 makes it clear that new houses were being thatched at Ilsington. Documentation shows that the thatcher, Richard Perryman, was also involved in a property transaction, selling the remainder of a lease on the three 'cott houses' to George Wills. Perryman probably did not write the account, as he confirms payment only with his mark, not a signature.

Account of Work Done uppon the new houses at Brimbley by me Rich'd Perryman

The 57 Nitch Reed for laying 7 square & 4 feet at

2 per hundred comes to	*3.3.0*
to laying the same at 12s per Hundred	*0.19.0*
to Sparsticks for the same	*0.6.0*

1814 April ye 12th rec'd the above bill by me.
The mark of Rich'd Perriman.[37]

Some accounts of the 1840s show the mixture of agricultural (hay stacks) and house thatching (some probably repair) that was undertaken on the Kennaway Estate in East Devon.

1840 Account of Sir John Kennaway Work What was Don to Mr Eveliegh at Ottery West Hill Mills

3 of July	*Began to laid the some of 25 Square and 75 feet of thatch at 2s 6d per square*	*3.4.4?*
	and 15pound of tarcord	*0.7.6*
16 of Dec	*One Days Work*	
1841		
2 of Feb	*Began to laid the some of 3 Square and 75 feet of thatch at 2s 6d per square*	*0.9.4?*
	3 punds of tarcord youse	*0.1.6*
	to Larkpare cott house	
17 of June	*thatching one haye Reek to Escot*	*1.9*
8 of July	*thatchird one haye Reek*	*3.6*
9 of July	*One Days Work to Mr Trobridge house*	*2.6*
	thatching one haye Reek	*4.6*[38]

Footnotes

1. Mingay (ed.), *The Agrarian History of England & Wales*, Vol 6, 1989, 863.
2. Barry, in Kain and Ravenhill, 1999, Maps 53.2 & 43.3, 415, 416.
3. Hoskins *Devon*, 1954, 174.
4. 'Land ownership, farm structure and agrarian change in South West England 1800-1900: regional experience and national ideals', PhD Thesis, University of Exeter, 1988.
5. Letts and Moir, 1999, 18.
6. Torr, f.p. 1918, 1979 edn., 47-48.
7. Stanes, 1969, 54.
8. Chapple, *A Review of part of Risdon's Survey of Devon*; 1785, 1970 reprint, 50-51.
9. Marshall, Vol 1, 1796, 1970 reprint, 64-65.
10. Letts & Moir, 1999, 70-92.
11. Mrs Bray, 'Letter to Southey from The Vicarage, Tavistock, September 7th 1832', 1879, new edn., Vol 1, 286-287.
12. Marshall, Vol 1, 1796, 178.
13. Marshall, Vol 1, 1796, 179.
14. Marshall, Vol 1, 1796, 181-183.
15. Moir and Letts, 1999, 84.
16. Moir and Letts, 1999, 83.
17. Stevenson, 1812, cited in Moir and Letts, 83
18. Baker may be the same individual recorded in the *Exeter Flying Post* in 1816 as an Exeter innkeeper & 'machine-maker', 9.05.1816.
19. *General View of the Agriculture of the County of Devon; with Observations of the Means of its Improvement*, 1808, 121.
20. *Ibid.*, 122-24.

[21] In the correspondence of Charles, sixth Lord Clifford at Ugbrooke. Reproduced in Sellman, *D & C N & Q,* Vol 35, part III, Spring 1983, 116.

[22] Collins, *in Tools & Tillage, Vol 2,* 1972-1975,17-18.

[23] *The Exeter Flying Post,* 26.10.1837.

[24] *The Exeter Flying Post,* 26.10.1837.

[25] Vancouver, 1808, 149.

[26] *Ibid.,* 87.

[27] Farey, J., *A General View of the Agriculture and Minerals of Derbyshire,* Vol 2, 14. Reference supplied by Terry Hughes.

[28] Devon RO 2065M/Buller of Crediton.

[29] Marshall, Vol.1, 1796, 82.

[30] Sun Insurance Records, Guildhall Library, 1795, Vol 10, 11937/10, 57.

[31] The parishes are Cheriton Bishop; Crediton Hamlets; Hittisleigh; Sandford and Upton Hellions.

[32] The parishes are Bradstone; Brentor; Coryton; Dunterton; Kelly; Lewtrenchard; Lifton; Marystow; Milton Abbot; Stowford; Sydenham Damerel and Thrushelton.

[33] Polwhele, 1977 reprint, Vol 3, 458.

[34] *Small Talk at Wrayland,* f.p. 1918, 1979 edn., 47-48

[35] Hugh Meller, *Devon Buildings Group Newsletter* Number 11, Feb 1992, 10.

[36] Skinner, 1985, 28.

[37] Wills family of Ilsington, Devon RO 2644 M/E6.

[38] Devon RO 961.add M /E57 E8.

5

DECLINE 1850–1945

Before 1850 Devon farming had played the key role both in the production of, and the market for thatch. The wheat (and rye) harvest had produced straw for roofing and the changing pattern of farming, associated with changes in the demand for housing, had created a strong and developing market for thatching in the 17th century. After the mid 18th century, the plight of farming and more general plight of the economy of the county cut two ways for the thatching tradition. On the one hand, the depopulation of rural parishes since the 1820s reduced the demand for thatch and saw losses of many thatched dwellings and their associated buildings, which simply fell into ruination. Some smaller parishes lost up to 60 per cent of their population between 1861 and 1901.[1] Small cottages continued to disappear. On the other hand, economic decline discouraged 'improvement' and the use of alternative roofing materials, which were costly to obtain. This meant that where thatched rural buildings survived, thatch continued as a major roofing tradition in the county, although corrugated iron began to present a cheaper and commonplace substitute for over-coating. A map showing the distribution of thatchers in England and Wales in 1851 shows that, however great the losses to thatch in the county, Devon, along with Somerset, was showing the greatest density of thatchers by comparison with other counties. The estimated total number of thatchers in England and Wales was then 5 946. By 1881, the total number of thatchers in England and Wales had reduced to 3 719.

The importance of mainstream farming to thatch continued until well after 1945 but, by the late 19th century, there is evidence of a gradual parting of the ways between the normal processing of the wheat harvest and the production of straw for thatching. After 1850, in addition to farming, the developing tourist industry also began to influence the survival of thatch. Public perceptions of the beauty of the Devon landscape began to be voiced by people who, rather than living under thatch, saw it from the outside. This was a perspective that emphasised the visual charm and 'artistry' of thatched roofs, noted losses of thatch with anxiety, and the arrival of corrugated iron as a cheap substitute covering with undisguised dislike. This was a change of outlook helped along by the late 19th century architectural interest in reviving vernacular forms and materials for new buildings from the 1880s to the 1930s. As with Picturesque thatching in the late 18th and early 19th centuries, the patrons of new thatched houses in the Arts & Crafts style were small in number in Devon, but exercised considerable authority in giving thatch respectability.

Worries about the disappearance of thatch in the county are most evident between 1918 and 1939, but they also appear before World War One. They were well-founded. Between 1850 and c.1870, a general upturn in agriculture made Devon farmers wealthier and gave them the impetus to improve farm buildings. The extension of the railway network across the county from 1844 onwards opened up new markets for farmers and shrank the distance between

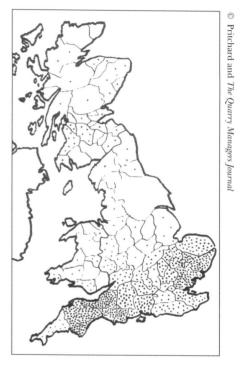

The distribution of thatchers in England in 1851, showing a heavy concentration in the South West, the combed straw areas. Map by Dylan Pritchard from 'Aspects of the Slate Industry: The Expansionist Period. IV', The Quarry Managers' Journal *(June 1944). The source for the map is probably the Census Returns, raising the question of how many men who thatched, but had other occupations too, would have described themselves as thatchers to the census-taker.*

A c.mid 19th century improved, compact farmyard at Bearscove, Buckland, most of the buildings slated.

farms and sources of slate. The Devon slate industry died out in the last quarter of the 19th century. It was squeezed out of business by Welsh and, to a lesser extent, Cornish slate which both became more economical as transport improved. By the 1850s the Welsh quarries supplied slate in standard sizes which made fitting it less laborious and quicker than the smaller and usually thicker local slates. When Devon farm buildings were improved or rebuilt in the period 1850-1870 (and afterwards) they were likely to be roofed with Welsh slate and not thatch.

Writing in 1919 T J Joce, recommending a revival of cob cottages, listed possible roofing materials, which included a number of non-vernacular alternatives, clearly already in evidence on modest rural buildings in Devon by that date. Thatch came first 'for snug appearance, but with remembrance of damaging storms and all-devouring fire'. Slate laid in graduated courses would provide 'a good and tasteful roof', but there were other options – various forms of bitumen felt including 'the excellent green Rhuberoid, which harmonizes perfectly in the landscape', tiles, which 'belong by rights to other districts' or red asbestos slates, these last criticised for their 'unpleasant meaty appearance'. Corrugated iron was not mentioned. Presumably Joce regarded this as beyond the pale for domestic buildings.[2]

The transport revolution changed everything. The pattern of farming in the Blackdown Hills on the Devon Somerset border, for example, was affected by the arrival of the Culm Valley Light Railway in Hemyock in 1874. This made it practical to establish the Culm Valley Dairy Company in 1886, manufacturing butter, which could then be sent via Tiverton Junction to Birmingham and London. The dairy gave the small farms in the Blackdown Hills an expanded market for their milk. It is striking to see how many farm buildings were rebuilt in the late 1880s and 1890s using slate, rather than thatch.

The transport revolution brought new materials for roofing to Devon, contributing to the downturn in the use of thatch A thatched house that escaped clearance for the railway, precariously close to the line at South Brent railway bridge.

Slate began to look like a 'better' material than thatch because the world around, and the terms on which the materials were judged, had changed. As we have seen, there had been a slow but steady increase in the use of West Country slate before 1850. Before then, on mixed farms, where most of the labour had been handwork and straw was bound to be found close by, thatching with combed straw had been a completely natural solution to roofing. Increased mechanisation, particularly the use of threshing machines, and increased specialisation on farms meant that in the second half of the 19th century suitable thatching straw was not always available as a by-product of the grain harvest.

Owners began to count the cost of the attention that a thatched roof required: re-ridging every 10 to 15 fifteen years and recoating at intervals that contemporary commentators usually put at 20 to 25 years.

Insurance

Insurance premiums played a major part in the disappearance of thatch. There is no doubt that some individuals abused the insurance system and used it to get rid of thatch. As Cecil Torr says:

> Writing to my father about a small estate that was for sale, my grandfather remarks quite placidly, 13 June 1864: "The premises are all but new, for ***** took care to burn down the whole at different times – so all new and well built and slated. No office would continue the insurance for him, but being all slated it did not much require it." I have heard the same thing said of other small estates. [3]

The cost of insurance crept up. Moir and Letts note that the classification system proposed by the Sun Insurance Company in 1727 had identified thatch as 'Doubly Hazardous', meaning that an annual premium of 5s was paid on a thatched building worth £300 compared to 2s on a slated building insured for the same.[4] By the late 19th century insurance premiums are regularly given as a reason for the expense of thatch and its replacement. The Revd. Baring-Gould, the owner of a small estate in Lewtrenchard, West Devon, wrote in 1898 in *An Old English Home and its Dependencies*:

> That which is destroying the old cottage is not the tooth of time, but the insurance office, which imposes heavy rates on thatched buildings, and when the thatch goes and its place is taken by slate, the beauty of the cottage is gone. But generally, if a cottage that was thatched has to be slated, it is found that the timbers were not put up to bear the weight of slate, so have to be renewed, and then it is said by the agent, "Pull the whole thing down, it is not worth re-roofing. Build it afresh from the foundation.[5]

The main timbers of the over-engineered roofs of substantial late medieval and 16th and 17th century Devon houses were quite capable of bearing the weight of slate as an alternative to thatch, but the roof construction of more humble, later cottages could not be adapted so successfully. By 1920 the disparity in insurance premiums between slate and thatch, quoted in an article in the *Report and Transaction of the Devonshire Association*, was breathtaking:

> But undoubtedly one of the chief reasons which deters many country people, the present writer amongst them, from retaining old thatch or putting on new, is the outrageous premium demanded by the fire-insurance companies from the owners of thatched houses, who may wish to insure their property, 15s per cent I believe it is, as against about 1s 6d for a slated roof! This fact, added to the very high wages asked by the few thatchers still available, has unfortunately caused this once universal, and most picturesque, art of thatching to become, except in the case of repairs to old buildings, a mere luxury for the rich to indulge in. [6]

The cost of insurance generated some sensible debate about the excessive fear of thatch fires and how they might be prevented. Several writers pointed out (now confirmed by careful testing) that it is rare for a stray spark from a chimney on to a roof to cause a thatch fire and most fires start under or within the roof (leaky chimneys were, and still are, a common cause) and not outside. Techniques for preventing fire were offered in letters to the newspapers. Whitewashing was reputed to be effective, though it was acknowledged that it spoiled the appearance of a roof. Soaking the straw in a mixture of alum and copper of sulphate was also recommended. [7]

Materials & Techniques

Wheat Production

The acreage of land under arable in the county fluctuated considerably in the period. It rose between 1850 to about 1870, with Mid Devon, in particular, switching from pasture, although some of the grassland ploughed was for root crops rather than corn. The agricultural depression of the 1870s and 1880s saw a return to pasture. By 1900 the balance between pastoral and arable farming was much as it had been in the 1830s. Acreages of cereal increased again between 1914 and 1918 in the push to make Britain self-sufficient in food production during World War One, but this was only temporary. By 1927 Devon's wheat acreage as a percentage of arable land (7.6 per cent) was less than half the average for England and Wales (15.9 per cent).[8] Relative to other counties, the Devon climate continued to ensure that wheat yields were poor. The pattern, already established in the 18th century, was of low investment in, and slow take-up of harvesting machinery. This was critical to the survival of the combed straw tradition as it allowed time for the development of mechanisation designed specifically for combing straw. Machinery included hand-powered devices for combing straw and, by the late 19th century, the first mechanical reed comber that could be attached to a standard threshing machine. Progress from one device for combing straw to another was not even. Some farms were still hand-flailing and hand-combing at the same time as a neighbouring farm may have been up-to-date with the latest technology. By the late 19th century there was a wide span of methods for combing straw in use in the county ranging from the use of simple hand tools probably little changed since the medieval period, through the fixed combs to a range of hand-operated barn-combers with moving parts. At the top end of the range was machinery powered by horses or steam-powered traction engines.

Wheat varieties

Mechanical means of cutting the corn harvest, the horse-drawn reaper binder, were developed from the late 18th century, but did not arrive in numbers in pastoral Devon until the late 19th century. Mechanical cutting went hand-in-hand with developments in wheat-breeding to reduce the length of cereal straw and ensure that the crop ripened simultaneously, which was more convenient for a swifter, mechanical harvest. Most of the reaper binders and threshing machines devised in the late 19th century could only handle crops about 1.4m in height [9] and mechanisation led to a desire for a reduction in the height of cereals. Some wheats grown in the third quarter of the 19th century were still over six feet tall, as Henry Stephens notes in his *Book of the Farm*, published in 1876. This book of practical advice for farmers was based on the author's experience in Scotland, where thatching had been vigorously replaced by slate. Nevertheless, Stephens' section on wheat-straw shows that Devon was already noted for its thatch, compared with other English counties:

> *The strength and length of wheat-straw render it useful for thatching, whether houses or stacks. It is much employed in England for thatching houses, and perhaps the most beautifully thatched roofs are in the county of Devon.*[10]

As the potential for greater grain yields was realised, wheat-breeding, which was entirely motivated by the needs of the grain-producer and not the thatcher, aimed to produce varieties where the energy of the plant was given over to the ear of grain, and as little as necessary went into the stem. The development of pure-bred varieties of wheat and the reduction in the height of straw were not a major concern to thatchers before World War One and it was not until after World War Two that seriously shortened straw and constraints on growing taller varieties of wheat began to make it difficult for thatchers to find straw of a minimum length suitable for roofing.

© Halsgrove

Harvesting at Cornishes Farm, Gillbrook, Woodbury, in 1912, with eight men, two boys, a girl and two dogs, the latter for catching any rats or mice disturbed by the reaping. The wheat crop is tall by today's standards.

Threshing & Combing

Threshing machinery became more widespread in the county. Reports in the local press show a pattern of increased use of increasingly powerful machines. In 1856 a 'Portable Steam Engine and Threshing Machine Co.' was established in Devon 'for the purpose of introducing the advantages of steam power to agriculture in Devon'.[11] The cost of setting up the company was £2 000, raised as shares, with H Seaman of Gerston House, Totnes, as the prime mover in the project. By the time the funding for the limited company had been raised, it was already operating three steam threshing machines, one in North Devon, one in the South and one in the neighbourhood of Exeter. Where ten shareholders lived in one place they could hire the machine for 5s an hour. One of the machines, with an eight horsepower engine manufactured by Hornsby & Son of Grantham, Lincs, was demonstrated in the Ide valley in September 1856. The novelty and noise attracted a crowd of farmers. By 1863 a twelve horsepower machine was being demonstrated near the Copplestone Inn.[12]

Before the end of the 19th century, the use of mechanised threshing had begun to create apartheid between the treatment of the wheat crop for grain, and its treatment if thatching straw was required. The Revd. Baring-Gould, in *An Old English Home and its Dependencies* (1898) described the harvest rituals he remembered as a boy, and went on to write:

> *...All this is of the past, as is the throb of the flail. There are not many labourers now who understand how to wield the flail. The steam thrasher travels from farm to farm and thrashes and winnows, relieving man of the labour. The flail is only employed for the making of 'reed', i.e. straw for thatching the rick.*[13]

The mechanisation of combing straw was slower to develop than threshing. It had only a West Country market and was therefore not going to attract the attention of the developers and producers of standard agricultural machinery. The relatively primitive methods of combing described in the previous chapter continued but the 'barn comber' evolved. The hand-cranked version developed into a belt-driven machine powered by horse, water or even tractor power.[14] An article in the *Transactions of the Devonshire Association* describes combers powered either by horses or engines. Machines at Lower Rocombe Farm, near Stoke-in-Teignhead, and at Aller Farm, near Kingskerswell, consisted mainly of two spiked wooden drums, and were worked by a horse-wheel in the roundhouse, while at Downe Farm, Denbury, an old wooden reed-comber was driven by an engine. Derelict and broken

A barn comber, now part of a museum display of thatching equipment at the Bicton Botanical Gardens, East Budleigh. This version was belt-driven. It is dated c.1825 but may be later.

horse winches and reed combers were found at Court Farm, Maidencombe, and in Barton, Daccombe, and at Kingskerswell.[15]

The barn comber, whether hand-, horse-, or engine-operated, bridged the gap between hand-flailing and the development of a comber that could be attached to a standard threshing machine. The first mechanical comber used in conjunction with a threshing machine is said to have been built in 1894 by Richard Hancock of Knowle, near Braunton, although Messrs Isaac had patented a machine earlier.[16] Hancock described himself as a carpenter in *Kelly's Directory* of 1883. The comber was called a 'reed comber'.

The reed comber attachment to the threshing machine, in fact, effectively threshed the straw as well as combed it, using the power of the thresher to rotate the spiked drums over which the cereal was passed on a belted conveyor system. In theory it could be removed if combed straw was not required, and the threshing machine used as standard. Removing the reed comber was not an easy task, however, and once fitted, they tended to remain. There were grumbles about the introduction of this novel reed comber. Some thatchers insisting that the straw it produced was inferior to the hand-flailed material. The complaints do not mention an important aspect of the comber, noted by Moir and Letts. The combing box could not handle straw much taller than 47ins (120cm).[17] Little by little, machinery, even that designed specifically to produce combed straw, was ensuring that taller wheat varieties were becoming impractical, even for machinery especially developed for combed straw thatching.

A Modbury thatcher, from a long line of thatchers, recollects the first reed comber he saw in Devon in 1906, when he and his father thatched a barn and cottage in Kenton parish. By World War One reed combers attached to threshing machines were commonplace in Devon. Cecil Torr, writing c.1918 and pleased to have, as he estimated, 12 000 square feet of thatched roofing in his ownership, grumbled both about the reed comber and changing methods of cultivation:

> *There is also a machine now to prepare wheat straw for thatching; and this bruises the reed, and renders it less durable than when it was prepared by hand. And now they never grow wheat early enough for the straw to gather strength. The*

© John R L Thorp 2001

result is that the thatch decays, and landlords and farmers both get tired of patching it, and put up slate or iron instead, thereby helping to destroy the market for one of their own products. I have known a field of wheat pay rent and rates and every outlay with the straw for thatching, and the grain was all clear profit.[18]

Hand-flailing survived in pockets in the county. It is mentioned in an article of 1920 in the *Transactions of the Devonshire Association*, where the author states:

An old thatcher tells me that the best reed is obtained from wheat reaped in the old-fashioned way by hand, with the sickle or reap-hook; as reaping-machines and self-binders tend to a certain extent to bruise the straw, and at the same time longer straw is obtained by hand-reaping, as the machines do not cut it off so close to the ground.[19]

Combing is noted using either the same kind of hand comb traceable back to the early 19th century or before, or by 'a machine called a *reed-comber* or *reed-maker*'. From the context this was probably a barn comber.

Hand-flailing was recorded by Marjory Feilden on a handful of farms as late as 1934.[20] Several were on Dartmoor. The technique was used not only for threshing but for beating dust from fleeces of wool. Feilden notes flails used at: Bullhornstone, South Brent; Lake, Higher Tor; Sherwell, Poundsgate; North Creaber and Scorhill, Chagford: Southway and Rowden, Widecombe in the Moor and occasionally at Haywood Farm, Netherton, near Newton Abbot, and Skerraton, Dean Prior. At Higher Tor and Sherwell flails were still made, as well as used by the farmers:

…these Dartmoor farmers go chiefly for stock-raising, and grow only sufficient corn for their own use. It would not, therefore, be worth their while to hire a

Combing straw in 1942 at St Giles in the Wood using a reed comber attachment on the top of a standard threshing machine. The first comber of this type was patented and built in Devon in the late 19th century. The machine is powered by a tractor here, but would originally have been powered by a traction engine. Alfred Copp, in the foreground, is making up a nitch of combed straw by banging it against a board, called a spot-board.

threshing machine, as their small crop of corn can be threshed out with the thrashel in the barn at odd times or in bad weather in the winter.

The handles were made either of hawthorn a light wood or, more frequently, holly, which is described as a heavy, durable wood that wears to the colour and polish of old ivory. The two parts of the tool were united by a hide thong linking flail and handle with a universal joint.

The actual practice of hand-flailing required both dexterity and a good sense of rhythm:

A skilful thresher will change over the fall or beat of his flail from left to right, and right to left, without losing his rhythm, and two men threshing together, standing opposite each other and whirling the thrashels round their heads before each blow will work in perfect harmony, one thrashel being up while the other is down. "two vlails an' a gookoo" (cuckoo) is the rustic's beau ideal of a musical concert!

Freda Wilkinson records the flail used as late as 1947 on one farm in Widecombe in the Moor. While this was only being used at that time for threshing dredge corn for feeding fowls, it does show that the tool, and the ability to use it, had a very long survival in the county.[21]

Feilden also referred to the curved wooden frame with horizontal iron or wooden bars across it, the 'brishing' or 'whipping' horse, if the wheat was required for thatching. The various elements of one of the processes to produce combed straw, described to her by Mr Meade of Bullhornstone Farm, were laborious:

'The Whipper'…is only used before threshing when the straw is intended for reed for thatching. In that case 'wads' are taken from the sheaves, whipped, tied for combing, threshed (with the thrashel) and then combed.

Water Reed

Water reed was available in Devon in the late 19th century, but apparently with only a limited use for thatching. In 1936 a writer referred to water reed from near Dartmouth: 'an abundance of reeds used in thatching grows in marsh behind the beach'. This was described as being cut and used by an old thatcher who had been working there since the 1890s, but no other thatcher was expected to replace him when he died.[22] This may have been the same thatcher sought out to thatch the Arts & Crafts house, 'The Barn' near Exmouth, described later in this chapter. Slapton Ley and Norfolk were the sources of water reed used by John Rogers, a Modbury thatcher, whose career spanned 1910 to the 1950s, but it is not clear at what period he started using it. Alan Prince of the Devon Master Thatchers' Association reports finding layers of coarse water reed, less fine than Norfolk reed, which had not been stripped off, on some South Hams houses he has rethatched. The layers were difficult to date but could have been 19th or early 20th century. References to Slapton Ley as a source for water reed for thatching are confusing. A photograph in the Museum of English Rural Life shows water reed being cut at Slapton in 1939. Slapton Ley was mined by the US Army during World War Two and, according to the *South Devon Journal*, was finished as a source by 1959.[23] An article in *The Field* in 1960 describes it as a supply that had only been tapped 'recently',[24] so perhaps it was revived after mine clearance.

Water reed from Norfolk was brought into the county in the 1930s. There may have been isolated examples before this. By the 1930s a couple of large, enterprising East Anglian firms were travelling long distances to thatching jobs by train, bringing water reed from Norfolk with them. In 1939 there is a reference

Harvesting water reed at Slapton Ley in 1939.

in *Country Life* to Norfolk reed thatchers working on the Dorset/Devon border. Interestingly enough they are described as having been brought in by newcomers having new houses built for them.[25]

Techniques that can be Established from the Photographic Record

The photographic record from the late 19th century onwards establishes some useful information about distribution and techniques in the second half of the period. Late 19th century photographs frequently show, especially on farm buildings, but also on some cottages and houses, a thin coat of thatch fixed with external sways. This method was a relatively short-lived, cheap thatch and can still sometimes be seen today. The exposed fixings interrupt the flow of water down the roof and this shortens the life of the material. It is essentially the same method used for a thin and short-lived roof over stacks and ricks. The photographs may represent the work of the farmer, rather than a 'professional' thatcher, or a two-tier system where a farmer or owner could opt for an inexpensive thatch instead of the more common overcoat where the fixings were concealed and protected.

It is clear from the photographic record that this method was commonplace. This corrects the image that all 'traditional' Devon thatch is composed of multiple layers adding up to a considerable depth, and is perhaps an indication of more stripping off of old thatch in the late 19th century than we might imagine.

Photographs also show how commonplace patching was before 1945. Straw thatchers all over the country who recollect thatching before World War Two emphasise that a large percentage of their work was then made up of patching, rather than rethatching. This reflects a 'little and often' attitude to maintenance, keeping costs manageable.

Above: *Foxworthy, Manaton, on Dartmoor in the 1880s. The granite rubble barn (later converted to a cottage) has a neat rick-thatched hip. A sledge, widely used on Dartmoor then, is being used to move stone.*

A rick-thatched farmbuilding near Hatherleigh, c.1900, recently re-ridged and patched. The house beyond is also patched, but has a superior overcoat with the fixings concealed.

Ridges

A photograph of c.1885 outside Jolly Lane Cottage, Widecombe in the Moor shows a narrow block-cut ridge with a scallop pattern and is the earliest example known to date of a cut pattern in a Devon ridge. The fancy treatment on what is reputed to be an 1830s squatters' cottage, contrasts sharply with the adjacent rick-thatched barn, where the sways are exposed for a short-lived thatch. It is an isolated example in the late 19th century photographic record. A similar ridge is shown in a 1916 wedding photograph posed outside Clannaborough Farm, Throwleigh.[26] Given the proximity of date and location, the buildings may have been the work of the same thatcher, or thatching family. Both ridges are very different from the proportions of the deep block-cut ridges with cut patterns,

Jolly Lane Cottage c.1885. The earliest example of a photograph of a block-cut patterned ridge found by the authors. The smart roof on this single-storey house contrasts with the rick-thatched farmbuilding.

lavishly ornamented with patterns made from lozenges and scallops, that have appeared frequently in the county since about 1980, in imitation of the increasingly elaborate ridges in East Anglia. They are sometimes regarded as the thatcher's 'signature'.

Between the wars narrow block-cut ridges with cut patterns began to appear on renovated cottages. One photographed example has been found of an eaves course with a cut pattern just above the eaves. Dartmoor seems to have been in the forefront of the fashion, perhaps because of its community of 'artistic' incomers. In 1937 the *Western Independent & Daily Gazette* printed a photograph of 'the new and scientific rope scalloped ridge on Miss Beatrice Chase's house at Widecombe in the Moor'. Historic photographs also show that from at least the 1930s and into the 1940s some Devon thatchers provided a two-dimensional openwork cresting along the top of the ridge, made from upstanding spars, each spar twisted at the apex. Although there are not many photographic examples of this technique, they are quite widespread, suggesting that this was a form of ornament favoured by several different thatchers. Other photographs show that the tradition of plain ridges persisted in most rural areas.

John Rogers of Modbury, who started thatching in 1910, described various kinds of ridges he employed. Judging from the photographic evidence only two are traditional, the others arriving between the wars. This is a nice example of the speed of change to regional tradition in the 20th century, and the transmission of change to the next generation:

> *The ridge on the roof can be put on in different patterns. You can cut out diamond shapes on the ridge. Or what thatchers call snail creeping. You can have*

This house at Broadhembury, photographed before 1945, has a cresting detail on the ridge that seems to have been popular between the wars and was widespread in Devon, judging from the photographic record. It consisted of a row of spars, each one twisted at the top and driven into the ridge but left upstanding.

a lap ridge, for that sort of ridge you must have fairly long reed and very tough. With a lap ridge, the reed is bent in, the one half of the reed is on one side of the roof and the other half is on the other side. To do this style the ridge has to be very even and level.

Another pattern is a rope ridge, which consists of reed made in a twist which spans both sides of the roof. Then there is the upright ridge, sheared off nice and tidy. Lastly there is what thatchers call a mock ridge, reed bent and out on one side only with a little cross stitching of spars and rods. It can be done, and you would hardly tell it from the original lap ridge. I have done all these and trained my son to be able to do all these different styles.[27]

Pre-war traditional thatch in the countryside. A mossy roof in Netherton, Stoke-in-Teignhead with what appears to be a mud ridge or a cement ridge repair.

Rogers' 'lap' ridge, with handfuls of straw bent over the ridge is sometimes called a 'wrapover' ridge today. It is not possible in water reed, as the material is too stiff to be bent over the ridge without damaging the water reed. His 'upright' ridge, sometimes called a 'butts up' ridge today is also probably traditional, with the upper course on each side of the ridge butted together, the join on the non-weather side of the building. It is rarely used outside Devon and many thatchers in other regions consider it a less durable finish than the wrapover.

Thatchers

After 1850, thatchers themselves begin to emerge in more detail from the records. The enthusiasm for 'folk' Devon, particularly between the wars, is evident in articles in the *Transactions of the Devonshire Association*. The authors clearly went out and interviewed farmers and thatchers, often noting down dialect words which were included in articles. Tools and practices that were falling into disuse were carefully described.

There must have been a good many men from the late 19th century to 1945 who would never have given their occupation as 'thatcher' but who were capable of patching a barn roof or hay rick, although not thatching houses. In many Devon

Thatching on the lower road at Galmpton, South Huish, c.1900 with an assistant supplying the thatcher on the roof with a nitch of combed straw.

A young Devon thatcher poses for the camera in about 1910, wearing knee pads and holding a bundle of spars and a measuring stick.

parishes, people remembering the inter-war period will say that 'almost every-one' in the parish could thatch then, from the postman to the rabbit catcher, although some of this may have been agricultural thatching.

John Rogers' biography, published by the Modbury History Society, gives a glimpse into the life of a skilled craftsman who thatched houses, a career that started by thatching with his father in 1910 when he was aged twelve. He began by wetting the reed and carrying it up the ladder to his father: 'It was hard work for a little boy'. He came from a family that produced 16 thatchers in five generations. All the family mixed thatching with other occupations. His great uncle

Mixed occupations. Jim and Dick Joy, hedgers, working in Acland Wood before World War One. One was also a thatcher. Thatching was closely connected with the underwood industry that produced spars and sways for fixings.

John was a smallholder, keeping a few cows and mixing his enthusiasm for Devon wrestling (and refereeing it), with thatching, as well as being parish constable. This must have been back in the 1860s. John Rogers, the author of the biography, and his older brother Charlie, thatched together sometimes, but they also did sheep shearing. There was a seasonal pattern to thatching and their other occupations:

> *The cottages and barns we usually thatched in the winter. All the summer after shearing we would be thatching hayricks, then cornricks, and then the strawricks. It was all in rotation.*[28]

This fits in with all we know to date about most thatchers mixing thatching with other occupations as late as World War Two. Even skilled thatchers mixed house-thatching with agricultural thatching and usually undertook other farm work, too. Those who were capable of house-thatching had better wages than, and a status above that of an ordinary farm labourer. Rogers was clearly a respected man in Modbury (as were other thatching members of his family), and was special constable, town crier, volunteer fireman and lay preacher for the Methodist church. This is a case of unusual dedication to the community, but is also suggestive of the independence of thatchers and status that came from that independence. Although they may have thatched on estates (Rogers thatched on both the Flete and Kitley estates) in Devon, they were employed mostly as independent craftsmen, not as estate employees. Mostly work would be within walking distance (the owner supplying the straw and a ladder), but the railways meant that a man of reputation might get work elsewhere, staying for as long as the job took.

Rogers' experience during World War One is interesting. Thatching was a sheltered occupation. This was not to ensure that thatched roofs were well-maintained, but to keep thatchers roofing ricks on the increased acreage of home-grown cereals when food imports were at risk from submarine attack. During the First World War Rogers and his brother did agricultural thatching as far afield as Coffinswell (about twenty miles from Modbury), staying in farmhouses and inns. In 1917 they thatched 200 corn ricks.[29]

Thatch on New Houses

After 1850, thatch on new farmhouses and cottages is very unusual, so far as we have been able to discover, but this may reflect the greater interest shown by historians of Devon buildings, in earlier traditional houses. There are likely to be some built in the mid 19th century but fewer at the end of the century. Late 19th century and early 20th century thatch on new buildings appears to be found exclusively on architect-designed houses. The best-known of these are close to the East Devon coast, designed by individuals with national reputations: Edward Prior at The Barn, Exmouth, which was finished in 1897, Ernest Gimson at Coxen, Budleigh Salterton, built in 1910, and Oliver Hill at Cock Rock, Croyde, in the 1920s. None of these architects sought to imitate the Devon vernacular, and the use of thatch on these houses was more a matter of a broader national interest in organic and natural materials amongst Arts & Crafts architects.

The Barn at Exmouth was built for Major Weatherall on land that originally had been owned by the Rolle Estate. This was not a typical local job in any way. The house had a novel butterfly plan. Prior depended on the Rolle Estate agent, Mr Chaumier, to help him obtain materials, with many ups and downs in the process. There were problems with the use of thatch. To begin with the local council recommended that the plans were turned down as the use of thatch was contrary to the local bye-laws. There was also the worry of fire risk:

> *From Mr Prior as to the speargrass roof, proposed to be put on Major Weatherall's house saying that he would cover it with an incombustible solution and hoped that as the house is so far from others the Council will give special leave to that being done.*

The 'treatment' was a condition of permission to build the house, and was probably the mixture of alum and copper sulphate that was sometimes recommended in articles. As it turned out, it failed to prevent a disastrous fire of 1905, after which the building was re-roofed in slate.

With an architect involved, the process of thatching was decidedly non-traditional. The roof was battened before a thatcher was settled on. The thatch battens were sappy and caused problems. Prior was eventually reimbursed for their cost. A local thatcher told Prior's Clerk of Works, Mr Emms, 'that tile battens were better'. Prior found that obtaining battens from the estate was a seasonal affair: 'we supply sticks after the shooting season but don't usually cut the underwood until after then'. There was also a problem with the thatch. Looking at the design of the roof with deep valleys between the main range and

Architect's thatch at The Barn, Exmouth, c.1898. The thatch was water reed, the curious banding is unexplained.

Traditional thatch, c.1920 and roughly contemporary with the architects' thatch at The Barn and Coxen. The photograph shows Stafford Beer, Broadwood Kelly, a house of at least 17th century origins and a thatched barn, probably 18th century or earlier, with a horse engine house, probably mid 19th century. There is a small outbreak of corrugated iron on the farmbuilding to left of the house.

the wings, and small dormers cut into the roof, one suspects that the architect did not ask any advice from a thatcher when he was producing the design.

The term 'spear grass' in the documents suggests that Prior, who had Dorset connections, may have intended to use 'Abbotsbury Spear', the local name for the water reed grown on the Ilsham Estate, rather than the abundant local combed straw. Neither water reed, nor a thatcher to fit it, could be found in the Exmouth area or via the Rolle Estate. Chaumier wrote to Major Weatherall on 26 August 1897, stating that the best man about the Dartmouth area, 'and the one accustomed to SLAPTON REEDS is J Burgoyne, Strawberry Valley'. Burgoyne may have been the old thatcher recorded who was still cutting water reed 'near Dartmouth' in 1936. The problems were overcome and the house was thatched.

A pre-fire photograph of The Barn, shows a startling deep band of lighter coloured thatched material along the ridge, eaves and round the dormers. This may have been the result of shearing for ornamental effect, although the striking difference in colour is difficult to explain.

At Coxen, where the owner was an Arts & Crafts blacksmith who had worked with the architect, Gimson, who also designed furniture, the materials were more local. Cob was used for the walling and the local combed straw roof was fitted by

Mr Caseley of Otterton. This had a plain ridge but untraditional (and unnecessary) wooden box gutters on brackets. When first built with this plain ridge the roof was immensely attractive, its thatch undulating over not only half dormers, but also dormers in the roof, and all offset by a summerhouse with a steep peaked thatched roof. By the 1980s, rethatching with a deep patterned ridge and sharp angles had effectively wrecked the original beauty of the roof, but could be remedied if it were rethatched with more sensitivity to the intended simplicity of the profile of the house. Hand-made ironwork to the windows, internal carpentry of elm and chestnut and simple, solid furniture to the designs of Gimson, provided an interior that was a model of the Arts & Crafts movement. The 'cottage' as it was called on the plans, was closer in status to Lord Despencer's Knowle Cottage of 1810 than anything from Devon's vernacular past, but was a reminder that there was a place for Devon thatch on the houses of people of 'artistic' taste.

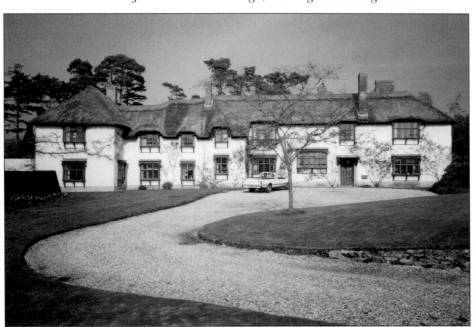

Coxen, Budleigh Salterton, a photograph probably taken shortly after completion in 1910.

Cock Rock, Croyde, was built for two authors, Brenda Girvin and Monica Cosens. It burnt down comprehensively in the 1940s. Its replacement for the same clients and also to the designs of Oliver Hill was built in the 1950s but did not have a thatched roof.

Less well-known than any of these, architects working in Devon designed a handful of large thatched houses for gentleman owners. Broadhembury House was an early 20th century enlargement and complete refurbishment of an early 17th century house. Little evidence of the original was left in the process, but the building incorporated re-sited panelling and a re-used Jacobean chimney-piece. It was designed some time between 1903 and 1914 by a Devon architect, Harbottle Reed, the Exeter Diocesan surveyor. The client was Mr Cedric Drewe, the owner of the Broadhembury estate and later MP for Honiton. Julius Drewe, his father, was the founder of Home & Colonial Stores. He had worked hard at establishing an 18th century family connection with Broadhembury before he had Castle Drogo built for himself at Drewsteignton to the designs of Lutyens in 1910–1930. In 1900 he bought most of Broadhembury village; unfortunately the big house in the parish, 'Grange', the seat of the branch of the old Drewe family with which he claimed to be connected, was not for sale. Broadhembury House was built for Julius Drewe's family and is a nice example of money carefully spent to establish an apparently well-rooted 'squire's home' in the village. Harbottle Reed produced a spacious house, one of the largest thatched houses in Devon, designed to harmonise with the adjacent thatched village, with a good-sized garden.

Broadhembury House, thoroughly rebuilt and extended some time between 1903 and 1914 by Harbottle Reed for Mr Cedric Drewe, later MP for Honiton.

Bruce Oliver, the president of the Devonshire Association, was a Barnstaple architect known to have designed several thatched houses in North Devon in the 1920s/1930s, using Mr H Gratton, a Barnstaple and North Devon thatcher.

Mr H Gratton, a North Devon thatcher who worked with Bruce Oliver on new thatched houses, displaying a model of a thatched building he used to illustrate a lecture to the Devonshire Association at the North Devon Athenaeum in 1937. The cresting detail on his model was popular on thatched houses in Devon between the wars.

Thatch on Recreational Buildings

Responsiveness to surviving thatch also influenced the design of the Drum Inn, by Sir Edwin Lutyens, at Cockington, near Torquay. Cockington developed into a Devon village thatched beauty spot in the 19th century, largely because of proximity to the holiday trade in Torquay. In the 20th century it became curiously fossilised as a living picture postcard of what Devon was supposed to be like. In the 1930s the Cockington Trust was formed and there were plans to extend the settlement with a model village centred on a village green, flanked by thatched estate cottages, all to the designs of Lutyens. The Drum Inn was the only part of the scheme to be erected and was thatched. Pubs in holiday areas were quick to appreciate thatch as an attraction to tourist custom.

Other buildings associated with entertainment and the tourist industry also appeared. There was a thatched bandstand on Paignton Green by the 1930s. Thatched boat houses appeared on the South Hams coast. At Hope Cove,

Left: *The Drum Inn, Cockington, designed by Edwin Lutyens in 1934.*

Above: *A municipal authority in a seaside town recognises the appeal of thatch to tourists. A thatched bandstand on Paignton Green in the 1930s.*

Below: *A thatched cricket pavilion of 1935 at Bampton, one of several in Devon, in a photograph of 1959.*

holiday makers were entertained in a thatched farm building converted to a cinema. The roof made a comfortable home for spiders who had a habit of dangling between projector and screen, treating the audience to unexpected monstrous images projected on to the screen in front of the film.[30] Bampton was one of several villages which acquired a thatched cricket pavilion.

Rural Buildings

Documentary sources for understanding the pattern of rural roofing materials in contrasting parts of the county are far richer in the post-1850 period than they are before.

Between 1910 and 1915 a valuation survey of all land in the United Kingdom was carried out to levy a tax, 'increment value duty'. The survey results were produced in two forms. Bound volumes sometimes called the 'Domesday Books' after the post-conquest survey of 1086, were kept locally. The valuers' 'Field Books' were kept centrally and are now held by the Public Record Office. Different valuers provided different levels of information in their field books, but the most detailed included descriptions of the building materials, including roof coverings, and can provide a detailed picture of the distribution of thatch at the time.

It is plain from a sample of these that by 1915 there was a general pattern of farm buildings being slated on the larger holdings (which had more farm buildings). Detail on the second edition Ordnance Survey maps shows that this was especially so where the farmyards had been 'improved' by rebuilding and reorganisation into more neatly-planned courtyards. The slate-roofed buildings were assigned a higher value than thatched buildings. On the smaller farms thatch predominated, although galvanised iron was already in use in quantity, indicating that this material was proving cheaper and more easily available than keeping combed straw thatch in repair.

In Morchard Bishop, for example, where the surveyor identified 567 agricultural buildings in 1915, there were 166 farm buildings overall in the parish covered in corrugated iron. This was slightly more than the 163 that were covered in thatch. We can assume from this that thatch on more than 50 per cent of farm buildings in the parish had been replaced with corrugated iron since the 1820s, when corrugated iron was first available. The change is more likely to have occurred since about 1850. There were 173 slated farmbuilding roofs in the parish. No doubt many of these were on buildings erected after 1850. The rest were accounted for by 48 tiled roofs and various mixtures of roofing.

Slate for improvements to an old thatched house. The slated dormers and porch suggest that Pizwell House, Widecombe, had been recently up-graded when this photograph was taken c.1892. The dormers would have created a relatively well-lit space in the roof of what was probably a medieval open hall house. The porch was an extra barrier against the weather.

If this shows thatch pushed into third place by slate and corrugated iron on farm buildings, the picture for dwellings is rather different. Either farmers were prepared to spend money keeping thatch on the farmhouse if they could afford to, or farm buildings were more subject to change than houses, either graded 'down' to corrugated iron as thatch became more expensive, or liable to improvement, rebuilding and covering in slate. Of the 77 houses, cottages and the mill in the parish, just over half (39) were still thatched when surveyed. No roofs of dwellings had been completely replaced with corrugated iron, although four were a mixture of thatch and corrugated iron and nine a mixture of thatch and slate; 23 had slate roofs and two were tiled. The photographic record confirms that even when the old thatched roof was maintained, alterations and extensions were often slated, reflecting a domestic version of improvement.

Cottages

Fires continued to cause losses. The Broadclyst fire of 1875 merited engravings in contemporary journals. Rural depopulation saw the continuation of the loss of rural cottages noted in the previous chapter. There was, however, a counter-movement between the wars. Between 1926 and 1939 a national housing scheme saw a number of rural dwellings renovated in Devon. The scheme was described, 40 years later, in *The Conservation of Devonshire Cottages* 1968, by R T Shears, who had been a leading member of the administrative committee. Although the figures were small, relative to the numbers of poorly-maintained rural houses, the photographic evidence of what was done gives a snapshot of what 'renovation' meant to the appearance of labourers' dwellings in the period.

The aftermath of the fire along the main road through Broadclyst in 1875. The rebuilding used tile for the roofs.

In 1926 Neville Chamberlain, Minister of Health, visited Devon to discuss forthcoming changes to the administration of Poor Relief. During his visit the question of housing conditions for agricultural workers was raised and the Minister spent a day visiting derelict village houses. Low agricultural prices and low wages between the wars meant that many dwellings were in a poor state of repair and sanitation was primitive. This had been pointed out in the reports of the Medical Officers of Health who identified defects in rural housing but the funds for remedying those defects were just not available. The Housing (Rural Workers) Act was passed in

1926 photographs showing 17th century or earlier houses that had dropped in status to agricultural labourers' cottages. Their location in Devon is not identified in R T Shears' book. It is not only the thatch that has been neglected. Both houses were reconditioned under a scheme to provide better housing for rural workers.

1926 and allowed reconditioning grants of up to £100 provided the value of the property was not more than £400 after works had been completed. The objective was to keep rural workers properly housed in country areas, discouraging migration to urban areas. Restrictions meant that owners could not sell the cottages on without repaying the grant, and rents were tied to agricultural rates.

Devon was in the lead in implementing the terms of the Act: 2 082 buildings in the county were refurbished between 1926 and 1939, when the outbreak of war brought the scheme to an end. It is clear from the photographic evidence that the poor condition of thatch was frequently one of the reasons why owners applied to be part of the scheme. It is also interesting that thatch was by no means always abandoned in the renovations, although it was sometimes replaced with slate. There were protests in the late 1920s that Medical Officers of Health were inclined to condemn thatch as verminous and insanitary. One particularly irritable letter to the *Express & Echo* accused them of being 'bent on having cob and thatch cottages down' and argued for the healthiness of Devon's traditional buildings and natives: 'You very rarely hear of a consumptive person living in a cob cottage (if so it is a newcomer)'.[31]

On the whole, however, it seems that the committee administering the renovation grants became increasingly sensitive to the idea that thatch should be kept.

Mixed messages about the status of thatch between the wars in the scheme to provide improved accommodation for rural workers. The barn loses its traditional thatch to slate (right), whereas the blacksmith's shop (over) gains thatch. The location of these buildings is not identified in R T Shears' book.

By permission of Colin Shears

This was in sharp contrast to 'improvement' applied to farm buildings, which seems usually to have meant the abandonment of thatch in favour of slate. The committee's stated objectives were not only to provide proper sanitation, ventilation, and bedroom space for labourers, but to retain what they saw as the 'artistic interest' of Devon cottages:

> *care was taken to make requirements which would prevent the disfigurement of such buildings so as to secure, as far as possible, that the special character and beauty of these dwellings and fitness for their surroundings as maintained.*[32]

A strong appreciation of the distinctiveness of thatch as part of the local scene meant that it was sometimes kept, even in examples where the roof structure was clearly completely replaced. Letters to the press about the appearance of recon-

In contrast to the previous barn's loss, the blacksmith's shop gains thatch with ubntraditional fancy detailing – not only a patterned block cut ridge but also a block cut pattern at the eaves. The location of this building is not identified in R T Shears' book.

ditioned cottages may have had their impact on the committee. One to the *Western Morning News* in 1935 complained that cottages renovated under the scheme looked like public lavatories and reminded readers that the Act did not prevent rethatching, although there were worries about fire risk.[33]

The photographs of 'before and after' reconditioning in Shears' publication are an instructive reminder that changes to the thatch tradition in the county this century are only one aspect of more radical alterations to vernacular building. Pre-reconditioning, all the thatched buildings illustrated in Shears' publication have plain ridges. After renovation, ridges cut into patterns appear on some, and there is even one example of patterned eaves. Far more dramatic changes occurred to the shape and character of walls and roofs, where enlarged and brand new windows were inserted, providing full first

Improvement on Exmoor, better light and ventilation and the replacement of a rick-thatched roof with slates of uniform size sourced from outside the South West.

floors to some buildings that had previously been single-storey and attic. The conversion of agricultural and industrial buildings represented an even greater transformation.

The Movement to Save Thatch

Corrugated iron had been used in England since the 1820s and patented by 1829. Judging from the photographic record it did not become a familiar part of the rural scene in Devon until the late 19th century but, unlike thatch, it was not material that photographers sought out. By the early 20th century it was common enough as a cover over thatch to be a cause of outrage to the kind of 'lovers of the countryside' who campaigned and wrote to the papers. From a farmer's perspective it was light, easy to fit, cheap, available and, unlike thatch, did not need maintenance. Its use was a symptom of an increasing shortage of thatchers between the wars, and the increasing cost of thatch.

Most of the early campaigns in support of Devon thatch started by referring to the ugliness of corrugated iron. In c.1914, L Mark Kennaway, a Teignmouth solicitor, wrote a pamphlet 'To Lovers of English Rural Scenery, Landowers, Stockbreeders, and Others', making a nice distinction in the title between those who looked at thatch and those who actually lived and worked under it. He began by describing the corrugated iron roof as 'frankly hideous'. He then went on:

> The present appeal is directed, primarily by Westcountry-men to the West Country, for the West, it is to be feared, is unworthily pre-eminent in harbouring the offence. All who traverse our country-roads with a seeing eye will know of many a village, and scores of cottages and farms, the beauty of which has been ruined or is being marred, by the iron roof. We may instance Hennock and Ashton, in the Teign Valley, as examples of exquisitely picturesque villages, the charm of which has been completely destroyed by unsightly roofs on many of the beautiful old houses they comprise.[34]

Kennaway acknowledged that thatch was expensive and that it was unreasonable to expect the small freeholder to go to the extra cost of the renewal and insurance of thatch or recognise that: 'a cheaper substitute is an outrage to an artistic sense which he probably does not possess'. However, he appealed to farmers not to 'sacrifice everything to the utilitarian spirit of the times' and to landlords to preserve thatched roofs by insisting that tenant farmers should find the combed straw to keep roofs in good repair, even at the sacrifice of a little rent. It seems from this that the old system of agreements requiring tenants to provide combed straw for repairs disappeared in the 19th century, or was no longer observed. The 21st century reader may judge that Kennaway's appeal sounds remote from the realities of farming life, and the list of his supporters was heavily weighted on the 'artistic' side. As well as clerics and a surgeon it included the artist and illustrator, Walter Crane; the Secretary of the National Trust for Places of Historic Interest and Natural Beauty, various members of the Scapa Society 'for Prevention of Disfigurement in Town and Country' and staff from the School of Science and Art at Torquay.

However, Kennaway made two shrewd points. Firstly he pointed out that the views of incomers and travellers deserved attention because they made a contribution to the rural economy:

> And in cases where all things must be weighed in the banker's scales, it may be pointed out that, in these days when so many seek residence or change in the country for its charm's sake, the destruction of rural beauty must soon affect the rural purse by diverting the traveller to less disfigured spots.

Secondly he made a persuasive case (still made by some farmers today) of the advantages of thatch over iron for farm buildings. It was a good insulating material over livestock, keeping them in an even temperature and free from the drips that form on iron roofs. A long letter of support from a Member of the Land Agents Society, G W Hinton, claimed never to have seen 'stock do so well, as when brought up under the thatch-roof'.

It is not clear what happened to Kennaway's campaign. During World War One many more thatched roofs fell into disrepair, thatchers concentrating on rick and barn thatching. It seems that Devon even tried to encourage thatching skills in formal classes. These may have started during World War One, to provide enough manpower for the increased acreage of arable crops.

A rope and spar-making competition in Devon. This might be during World War One to encourage the skills needed for agricultural thatching.

Wonderful photographs in the Beaford Archive show spar and rope-making competitons in the open air, one with supervisors including the vicar. This is rare evidence of collective training before World War Two and was probably directed solely to agricultural thatching at the time. After World War Two, a

This is probably a class or competition associated with agricultural thatching in the early 20th century, perhaps during the 1914-1918 war or the inter-war depression. The vicar was in attendance, at the back on the left, leaning against an enormous wood pile. The exact location in Devon is not known.

more widespread debate about the loss of thatched roofs in Devon appeared in the national and local press. This concern about Devon was part of a national anxiety that perceived the rural scene as disappearing in the face of change, particularly in the increased use of the car, new road-building, pylons and 'tasteless' suburban expansion. One essayist in 1937 graphically summed up the sense of horror: 'A gimcrack civilisation crawls like a gigantic slug over the country, leaving a foul trail of slime behind it'.[35]

In 1936 Sir Evelyn Wrench began a correspondence in *The Times* about the decline of Devon thatch. A response from Plymouth identified the reasons:

...several causes have contributed to the replacement of thatch by slates or unsightly corrugated iron. In the first place, modern roofings, if less lovely, are more durable, a thatched roof generally needing repair every 10 or 12 years. Fire risks also enter into the financial side. Thatchers, too are a disappearing race. A thatching family was living until recently at Thurlestone, where the craft was handed down in the old fashion from father to son. In the past families of thatchers were common, but they are slowly dying out.

...Landlords may be partly blamed for the disappearance of thatch. In many country districts local authorities have condemned thatched cottages on the grounds of bad ventilation or sanitation, and the owners of the property have preferred to see them demolished rather than face the bill for repairs[36].

One Devon landlord, J G Cornish of Salcombe House, Sidmouth, defended himself:

If any kindly organization will help me to pay my bills for thatching, I shall be grateful. They are unpleasantly large now, for the time is past when each farmer grew some wheat and was bound by his lease to provide 'reed' at a low price. Now the landlord has to purchase it and 'reed' is costly'.[37]

The inter-war depression affected the thatching trade, as it did most occupations. Low wages encouraged men to look for better-paid work in towns and the old pattern of training from father to son (or another young relation) seems to have broken down. By 1937 the general shortage of thatchers (which was particularly acute in the Midlands) prompted a national survey of house thatchers for the Rural Industries Bureau.[38] The results were not encouraging: 517 house thatchers using straw were identified in England. One third of the thatching workforce was aged over 60 with only ten apprentices and seven other workers under the age of 30. Plans to intervene and bring new blood into the thatching trade had to be shelved until after World War Two.

During World War Two a 'Report of the Committee on Land Utilization in Rural Areas', commonly known as *The Scott Report,* was published. This tried to answer some of the anxieties expressed by critics of new development in rural areas. It also developed the theme of improving housing conditions in projects such as the reconditioning of labourer's cottages between the wars. *The Scott Report* shied away from matters of detailed design for new buildings in rural areas, but did make a good case for keeping them long and low, with soft outlines and sited away from sky-line ridges where they dominated their surroundings.

The report had received comment that argued that new buildings should be constructed only of 'traditional' or 'local' materials, but was not persuaded that this was possible. However, it went so far as to say that new buildings should be required to be: 'in good material that is sympathetic in colour with the traditional colourings of the landscape in which it is situated'. There was an optimism that the future of architecture did not lie in:

the easy direction of mere preservation and narrow conservatism. It lies in the imaginative use of new opportunities... new materials and new methods of construction which are available to us.

It was a shame for Devon thatching, and thatching on new houses everywhere, that *The Scott Report* did not encourage the continuation of local materials on new houses in rural areas. This would have given a wider market for thatch after 1945 which would not only have kept the price down, but provided farmers with an assured market for growing a sustainable building material.

During World War Two most thatchers found themselves identified as agricultural workers and therefore key workers in food production. While some managed to join up, those left at home found themselves, as in World War One, preoccupied with rick thatching, or keeping farm buildings used for food storage in repair. The Devon County War Agricultural Executive Committee demonstrated a thatching machine, suitable for the speedy thatching of ricks. Rick-thatching championships were held and a rick-thatching needle was invented to speed up the process. Land Army girls were trained to supplement home-grown thatching skills for agricultural thatching.

Right: *The Devon County War Agricultural Executive Committee watching a demonstration of a thatching machine for agricultural thatch by Mr Hill. The machine was described as being able to do 'a day's work for one man in a few minutes'. A stitching machine for thatch on ricks was nothing new. One was advertised in a catalogue of c.1897, made by J W Titt of the Woodcock Iron Works, Warminster, Wiltshire.*

Below right: *A thatching competition (for rick thatching) at Cheriton Bishop organised by the local War Agricultural Executive Committee in 1944.*

A Land Army girl from Lancashire thatching a rick near Sidmouth in 1940.

A thatching needle patented for thatching ricks during World War Two. It is made of steel. The straight part of the needle could be pushed down to pick up the thread from an 'eye' in the curved section. From the Rural Life Collection at Bicton Botanical gardens. 560mm (1ft 10ins) long.

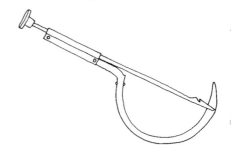

Any other thatching was deemed non-essential and put on hold. Given that there had been a problem of finding thatchers in the 1930s, the period of complete neglect to houses and cottages during the war left a massive backlog of work to be tackled after 1945.

Footnotes

1. Hoskins, *Devon*, 1954, 175.
2. Joce, *TDA*, 1919, 172-3.
3. *Small Talk at Wreyland*, f.p.1918-1923, 1970, 1979 edn., 47.
4. Moir and Letts, 1999, 9.
5. *An Old English Home*, 1898, 217.
6. Laycock, 1920, 158-181.
7. *Devon & Exeter Gazette*, 29.08.29.
8. Currie and Long, 1929, 9.
9. Cox and Letts, 2000, 18.
10. Stephens, 1876, Vol.1, 348.
11. *Exeter Flying Post*, 3.07.1856.
12. *Exeter Flying Post*, 21.10.1863.

[13] *An Old English Home*, 1898, 209.

[14] Moir and Letts, 1999, 84.

[15] Fielden, *TDA*, 66, 1934, 357-373.

[16] Ellacott, *Braunton Farms and Farmers*, 1981, 61. Ellacott gives his source as James Dennis, historian of Knowle, whose father was apprenticed to Hancock and worked on the second comber made there. Farmer Billy Johns, of Nethercott, financed the project.

[17] Moir and Letts, 1999, 84.

[18] Torr, f.p. 1918-1923, 1979 edn., 1918, 46.

[19] Laycock, 1920, 158-181.

[20] Fielden, *TDA*, 66, 1934, 357-373.

[21] Wilkinson, quoted in Woods, 2000, 83.

[22] *The Times*, 29.08.1936.

[23] *South Devon Journal*, 29.04.1959.

[24] 'Thatch as Thatch Can', *The Field*, 2.06.1960.

[25] 'Some Thatched Roofs', *Country Life*, 21.10.1939.

[26] Supplied by Val Harrison.

[27] Rogers, 1976, 25.

[28] Rogers, 1976, 23.

[29] Rogers, 1976, 2-3.

[30] Information from a lecture given by Gordon Chapman of the Cinema Research Project.

[31] *Express & Echo*, 4.05.1928.

[32] R T Shears, *The Conservation of Devonshire Cottages* 1968.

[33] *Western Morning News*, 5.07.1935.

[34] The authors are grateful to James Moir for supplying a copy of this document, which was found amongst the deposited papers of an East Anglian thatching firm. We are not aware of a copy in Devon.

[35] Howard Marshall in Williams-Ellis, 1937, 164.

[36] 'Thatched Roofs of Devon: Causes of Decline', *The Times*, 29.08.1936.

[37] *The Times*, 28.9.1936.

[38] PRO, MAF 33/770 6510, 60-62.

6

REVIVAL AND LOSS 1945–2001

There have been dramatic changes to Devon thatching since 1945. Before 1945 it is possible to understand the combed straw tradition in relation to the ups and downs of the county's wealth, to the pattern of Devon farming, and the variations and changes to the local building tradition. World War Two and its aftermath had an enormous impact on thatching, as it did on all aspects of life. As John Rogers, a Modbury thatcher, writes simply in his biography:

> *The last war upset everything and the whole pattern of our country changed, in some ways were for good but in other ways not so good.*[1]

After 1945 changes to Devon thatching cannot be understood without more reference to the world outside the county. The development of house thatching into an identifiable 'industry' affected all thatchers, not only those in Devon. It was a nation-wide transformation and part of the pattern of regulation and officialdom that accompanied the post-war modernisation of the whole country. The transport revolution made all thatchers more mobile and their territories extended as they acquired motor transport. Transport also created changes to the demand of thatching materials and turned supply, first into a national and, finally, also an international trade. This was associated with a period of erosion of the pre-war regional variations in thatching methods and materials between about 1950 and the late 1980s, until efforts to promote a conscious revival began with local authority conservation departments in the Midlands and then with English Heritage.

In the 1940s, from the point of view of a farm labourer, thatch was likely to be associated with unimproved housing, having no electricity and poor sanitation. A writer in 1947 commented:

> *Thatch is the material which townspeople sentimentalize over, but do not use themselves. Most country people loathe thatch – rats' nest they call it – and at the slightest chance they will rip it off and put galvanised iron or asbestos sheets to replace it.*[2]

But population change in the county meant that townspeople continued, not only to find romance in thatch, but became 'country people' and proved very ready to enjoy it as material to live under.

Widening car ownership opened up the whole county to tourists, most of whom had previously been restricted to the routes taken by charabancs, trains, or the tourist steamers that brought trippers from Bristol and Wales to Devon in the late 19th century. Devon thatching, like clotted cream, became a well-known symbol of the county to holiday-makers. It was admired, photographed, and made familiar on postcards. A new kind of thatch owner appeared, not only in Devon, but in all rural areas. They had not always lived in rural areas, often arrived from outside the county and had little or no direct connection with Devon farming.   They were ready and willing to pay to renovate rural houses and were prepared to pay higher prices for thatched property than for cottages and houses with any other kind of roofing.   A thatched roof seemed to sum up all that was idealised about Devon country life and some house hunters would look at nothing else.   Thatching, which had become a poor man's material by the late 19th century, rose in status and gradually became a roofing that could be afforded only by the well-off.

Mother Hubbard's Cottage, Yealmpton, following rethatching in 1962.   The occupier had just started a hand-weaving business, an attraction for visitors passing by on the main road. The thatching method was the economical one of rick-thatching and, in this case, the eaves were not stripped out. The rick thatch, however, has been made artistic perhaps to match the owner, the external sways following the contours of the roof, and patterned at the eaves and verges.

Between the wars the county was still, relatively speaking, remote from much of the rest of the United Kingdom. After 1945, as the bends in the main routes across the county were straightened out and national arterial roads reached Devon, distances were shortened.   Road improvements in the 1950s and 1960s made retirement to a picturesque thatched house in a Devon village seem practical, even if the rest of the family lived far away.   The M5 was built from the mid 1960s and officially opened in 1977. This, along with the North Devon Link Road, built in the 1980s, made it feasible, for the first time, to live in rural Devon and to work almost anywhere, with the accessories of the fax and the IT industry.   This change to the social make-up of rural Devon was possible as a result of changes to farming.

Compared with other counties, farm sizes had not increased.   In 1881 Devon had exactly the national average of farms under 100 acres.   By 1941 it had turned into a place of small farms by comparison with the enlargement of farms elsewhere: 70 per cent of farms were under a hundred acres.   This pattern began to change again before 2000 and especially in the late 1980s, as land prices fell. Small family farms became uneconomic and many were swallowed up in larger units.   Following ownership changes to village houses, changes to farming left old farmhouses for sale to comparatively wealthy incomers who could exchange a modest-sized house in London or the Home Counties for a generous-sized historic farmhouse with a few acres in Devon.   These owners could afford a tidy

Car ownership brought new money into the county for keeping thatch on Devon roofs. Road improvements also led to localised losses of thatch. This convex row of thatched houses in Newton St Cyres was demolished in the 1970s as part of a road-improvement scheme through the middle of the village.

sum for thatching and it proved a good investment. By 1990, after the boom years of the late 1980s, a chartered surveyor could state that the value of a thatched house in the county had doubled over the 'last few years' with the cost of thatching only increasing by 50per cent.[3] Thatch insurance dropped to levels that were a closer reflection of fire risk than the outrageous premiums of the late 19th century. In 1990 insuring a thatched house was about double the cost of a 'conventional' property at about £4 per £1000. In 2001 it is possible to find rates that are actually cheaper than properties with standard roofs.[4]

Non-farming owners buying thatched houses had no obvious access to supplies of combed straw, no storage space to keep nitches for patching and re-ridging, no long ladders on hand to make the odd repair themselves and no familiar access to local thatchers. Thatching ceased to be part of an intimate neighbourhood of thatchers and farmers where labour might be exchanged for materials and the younger members of the thatchers' family could be expected to cut spars for father in the evening. It became more, although never quite, like any other building work, a series of commercial transactions including estimating, selecting a thatcher in the manner of choosing any other contractor, the purchase of materials, invoices and receipts. It also became much smarter. The culture of house restoration dictated that a thatched roof should not merely be watertight, but should also look pristine and as though care and money had been lavished on it. There was not the same pressing economic need to stretch out the life of a roof as long as possible. Tatty, patched, moss-covered roofs became a thing of the past, except on some farmhouses. Extensive patching became less frequent and wholesale rethatching, both pitches at once, far more common.

The 'performance' or effectiveness and cost of thatch became a major issue after World War Two. This had happened to some extent before 1945. By the first decade of the 20th century, the substitution of corrugated iron for a new coat of straw on many farm buildings and some farmhouses was an indirect comment on the comparative performance of the two materials and the non-availability of thatchers. Corrugated iron was inexpensive and could be fitted without professional help. Being lightweight it could be applied to a thatched roof without interfering with the timbers and could even be fixed without stripping off all the remaining thatch. It lasted longer than thatch and did not require maintenance at ten to fifteen year intervals. While there are still divided opinions about the appearance of corrugated iron (which has enthusiastic advocates as well as detractors) it can be credited with saving the old roof timbers of many Devon farm buildings and farmhouses both when thatchers were hard to come by, and then as thatch became more expensive.

Right: *Rethatching a large house had become a costly business by 1971 and small farmers made do and mended as best they could. The roof at Kipscott Barton Farm, Bishop's Nympton, with a corrugated iron repair where run-off from the chimney flashing had caused a problem.*

Below: *Survival of thatch in Newton St Cyres. A village house within easy commuting distance of Exeter being rethatched in the 1950s by a two-man thatching team. The photograph shows a milk delivery by horse and cart. The concrete mixer indicates building work as well as rethatching.*

After World War Two there were far more alternative roof coverings from which an owner could choose. Options included not only corrugated iron but also corrugated asbestos, natural slate from Wales (and other sources) as well as artificial slate and concrete tiles. None required the same level of maintenance as thatch. Natural blue slate (rather than the stone slates of the Cotswold type) had acquired a British Standard in 1944, regulating its quality.[5] If thatch was to compete as a 'modern' roofing material the questions of how it was regulated, how quality could be judged and how long it lasted were bound to become increasingly important.

The story of Devon house thatching after World War Two, kick-started by the back-log on maintenance inherited from 1939–1945, has been a striking, but qualified success. While it has been a period of 'revival' by comparison with the high level of losses in the late 19th century and inter-war period, losses continued after 1945. If thatch was retained on many houses, and sometimes even reinstated on houses that had been covered with corrugated iron, the trend of its disappearance from farm buildings was not stemmed. By no means all houses that were still thatched in 1945 escaped re-roofing with other materials afterwards. The drive to 'improve' farms and remove thatch in the process continued.

Roxford Farm, Sandford, showing most of the buildings thatched in 1954. The agent, Mr Trumper, described it as 'A typical problem farm, with buildings which are inconvenient and unhygienic for modern livestock production methods'. He planned to re-equip it 'almost completely' believing that this was cheaper than adaptation in the long run. There is no thatch left at the farm today.

Another kind of loss, which was part of the revival, was that of the combed straw tradition when buildings were rethatched. From the late 1950s onwards, thatchers and owners of thatched buildings in Devon were presented with an alternative thatching material. Water reed, mostly imported from foreign sources, became an option for many owners, and began to replace combed wheat straw. By 2000 perhaps as much as 75 per cent of thatching in Devon used water reed.

There are a variety of reasons for the change to water reed. One was a shortage of combed straw in the county, explained below, but another important reason was the widely-held assumption that water reed has a significantly longer lifespan on a Devon roof than combed straw. This made it particularly attractive to owners who wanted to do the 'best' for their house and could afford the slightly higher cost of water reed. The assumption that water reed consistently lasts longer than combed straw in Devon has yet to be proved and is described in more detail below.

Thatchers and their Organisation

We know that from after about 1850, combed straw thatching of houses was employment that was mixed, according to the season, not only with agricultural thatching, but also with other farm-based work, even for the most skilled craftsmen. While we know less about thatchers before the mid 19th century, it seems highly likely that this was always the case. There is no evidence of any craft guild for straw thatchers or any formal organisation of thatchers, whether they used straw or water reed, before World War Two. This indicates that thatchers never had the craft status that was afforded to carpenters, masons, or many of the specialist trades outside building. Before 1945 it is not really possible to identify a thatching 'industry' of the kind that exists today. This is an industry in which thatchers have a clearly-defined 'market' that is now exclusively house-thatching, 'customers' (who may have no connection with farming), and some measure of trade organisation represented by two national thatching bodies as well as county groups. The only indication before 1945 of how thatching would develop into an industry was the previously mentioned East Anglian firms using water reed who had built up wide-ranging businesses between the wars.

Bill Hammond, thatcher, thatching a rick at Westacott, Riddlecombe in 1986.

The development of the modern thatching industry and the organisation of some (though by no means all) thatchers into county groups is closely connected with a government organisation called the Rural Industries Bureau. The Bureau was established before World War Two to support and encourage existing industries in rural areas in a bid to slow down the pattern of people moving to the towns in search of employment. This migration to the towns has subsequently been reversed. The Bureau aimed to assist the rural economy by offering technical, promotional and administrative advice to businesses that had become run-down, for whatever reason, or where research showed that there was a market that was not being fully exploited. Bureau staff took an interest in a number of different types of rural business, including saddlery, basket-making and agricultural engineering.

As we saw in the previous chapter, the Bureau conducted a national survey of thatchers in 1937–8. Fact-finding then, and in the 1940s and 1950s, was haphazard by the standards of the 21st century, so figures must be treated with some caution. The figures for most of the Bureau's surveys were probably collected from questionnaires sent out to Parish Councils and Women's Institutes, always a valuable source of information about rural areas. This was the usual method the Bureau used to gather information and if only a few questionnaires were returned, figures for whole counties would be based on samples only. The surviving results of the 1937–8 survey are not split up into counties so the details for Devon are not known, but the overall picture, especially the age profile of thatchers, was worrying for the future of thatching. The Bureau was keen to intervene and help, particularly by encouraging training, but was unable to do anything until after 1945.

After World War Two, the Bureau did all it could to promote thatch nationally, not only on old buildings, but also as a roofing for new housing. Thatchers and thatching, as the organisation was to discover, did not fit easily into the regulated compartments of the post-war world. Was thatching really a craft, not an industry? If it was an industry, did it belong, given that it used grown materials, with Agriculture and Horticulture, or was it part of the Construction Industry? How could the training of thatchers, traditionally undertaken by an experienced man teaching a young relation for perhaps as long as seven years, be rationalised to bring new blood into thatching without compromising quality? How could standards be established and maintained? How could quality of workmanship or value for money be compared and judged when there was so much variety in thatching from region to region and even from parish to parish? Were there any prospects for modernisation and increasing efficiency when, once the thatcher was on the roof with his materials, he used only simple hand tools? Were thatchers too independent by tradition and nature to combine with another? None of these questions, which the Bureau's staff (including employees who had been working thatchers) confronted directly or indirectly after 1945, has completely gone away in 2001.

By 1945 there was an even greater need for thatchers than the survey of 1937–8 had shown. This was exacerbated by the war, which saw a reduction in the number of thatchers, some of whom found opportunities for other kinds of employment. This was a gap in the manpower of the trade that could best be filled, the Bureau thought, by a Vocational Training Scheme. This was given impetus by the national need to find work for ex-servicemen.

Vocational Training Schemes were not available for seasonal occupations and for this reason the Bureau argued that 'house-thatching' was not seasonal, but could be carried on throughout the year. As it happened, the market for rethatching houses neglected during the war, along with the gradual replacement of stacks with Dutch barns and corn dryers, made full-time 'house-thatching' a realistic prospect after 1945. In Devon it was estimated that there were only 42 working thatchers in 1945. By 1954 the numbers had risen to 126, an increase of over 200 per cent, to deal with the glut of work, most of which was on domestic buildings, rather than farmyard and field stacks and ricks. It is not clear where all the additional thatchers came from, or how many of them were trained in the Bureau's Vocational Scheme which, in 1946, was only expected to produce 30 additional house thatchers in Devon.[6] The Bureau's training scheme nation-wide had only limited success, as it was discovered that experienced thatchers preferred young boys as trainees rather than ex-servicemen. Devon seems to have had a particularly advanced level of co-operation between local officialdom and the Bureau and for a time, the County Council had its own thatching instructor, supplementing the advice and training offered by the Bureau's staff.[7]

In the roundabout fashion of bureaucracy, the procedures for setting up a Vocational Training Scheme for thatching required a trade organisation to

Bill Hammond, thatcher, using a 'wink' to make twine for thatching a rick at Westacott, Riddlecombe in 1986.

Above and right: The Rural Industries Bureau advertising thatch as a modern roofing material on a pair of pavilions at the Royal Show of 1950. The differences between regional thatches were ironed out in their promotion. Both the combed straw (right) and the crushed straw pavilions are shown with fancy block-cut ridges, expected to appeal to modern architects and new owners of the period.

prove to the Ministry of Labour that such a scheme was needed. As there was no trade organisation in existence for thatching, the Bureau took on this task itself. However, it resolved to create a trade organisation for thatching by forming a national Master Thatchers' Association. The term 'master' meant then (as it means now) an experienced thatcher. It was not a qualification for which there was then any established form of training and there was (and is) no practical or legal obstacle to anyone at all calling themselves a 'master thatcher'. This was, and remains, a grievance amongst experienced thatchers who merit the title.

The Bureau's ideal of a national trade body was ambitious, given that there were no existing formal links of any kind between thatchers, apart from family ties within thatching families. Outside the family, the skilled thatcher's sense of territory meant little or no contact with 'competitors'. Regional differences in thatching were also a major obstacle to the task the Bureau set itself. It was hard to find common national ground and a national trade voice for thatching, given the differences between, for example, crushed straw (long straw) thatching and water reed thatching in East Anglia, or between the combed straw thatchers of the South West and crushed straw thatchers of the Midlands and the South East.

The ideal of a national body was approached gradually. To begin with the Bureau encouraged thatchers to form themselves into county or regional associations. Most of these were first established in the late 1940s.

The Devon Master Thatchers' Association (MTA) was formed in 1947. Unfortunately the early papers of the organisation have been lost (*pers. comm.* Alan Prince), but the initial meeting probably followed the pattern of Somerset. Here, thatchers who had been identified locally by Rural Industries Organisers were invited to a preliminary meeting, attended by members of the Bureau's staff as well as various county officials. There was no obligation for thatchers to attend. There were nine objectives to the proposed organisation and presumably these were the same for all the county associations. They reflect some preoccupations that have remained the same over fifty years on, and others that have changed. The first objective was to 'establish the proper status of the thatching trade'. Others related to the control of training, the negotiation of wage rates and collaboration in the working for the improvement of materials.

By 1954 the Devon Master Thatchers' Association (MTA) had about 25 members, less than a fifth of the 126 house-thatchers reckoned to be working in the county at that date. As with some of the other county associations, there were real difficulties in keeping the Devon MTA effective given that there was no obligation to join. Deciding not to join was not necessarily an indication that the thatcher was not a good craftsman. As the Bureau itself noted:

> *The Devon Thatchers' Association is having difficulty in increasing membership, partly due to their independence and family feuds; many of the best thatchers in this county are not members of the Association.*[8]

The thatching families that had survived in Devon until the 1950s also attracted comment from W M Williams, a writer on the modernisation of Devon rural industries in the 1950s and a critic of the Bureau:

> *In Devon there are several families of thatchers whose members are scattered over a large area of the county. The same surnames occur again and again in the list of thatchers and can be traced back in the various Directories well into the last century. These men are bound together into small highly cohesive groups by the sharing of special skills and techniques, immeasurably reinforced by ties of blood... It is not, therefore, surprising, that the Master Thatchers' Association met with considerable difficulties from its inception. What appears to have happened is that families either joined as a whole or not at all. Those that joined early were in a powerful position and seemed to have become dominant very quickly.*

In the first few years of the Devon MTA, it was difficult for thatchers to see how they benefited from membership.

The Bureau hoped that, for the good of the trade, county MTAs would adopt a standard schedule of prices and fix standards. They saw standard prices as a means to upgrading the status of thatching which, in turn, would attract young men into the trade. From the Bureau's point of view, only a standard specification could make thatch comparable with other roofing materials. This would make it competitive as a roof covering and opened up prospects for encouraging architects and builders to use it for roofing new houses as well as assuring its continued use on older buildings.

Standard prices and standard specifications meant changing established ways of operating with competitors. This did not always work to the advantage of MTA members. When a member gave a standard price for work, he was liable to find himself undercut by thatchers who did not belong. Williams describes how

Devon thatchers he interviewed in the 1950s had developed their own independent arrangements with competitors, which they felt were compromised by membership of the Devon MTA. They might preserve a sense of thatchers' 'territories' by refusing to price up competitively for work when they knew that another good thatcher was competing. On the other hand they were happy enough to compete against another thatcher if he had a reputation for not making a 'proper job' of thatching. This meant that good craftsmen saw themselves gradually squeezing out poor workmanship over time on the basis of reputation, which could be proved by how long thatch lasted. This system was most effective when property stayed in the same hands over a long period and when owners and tenants had an intimate knowledge of thatch and the reputation of local thatchers. The Bureau's officers, who worked with thatchers all over southern England, were in a better position than Devon thatchers to see that all this was likely to change in Devon. The change had already taken place in other regions, in which thatched cottages and farmhouses were sold to non-farming incomers who had limited, if any, knowledge of thatching territories and reputations and might not know how long the thatch had been on their roof.

Territories could extend across several parishes, as Williams discovered, with a ten-mile radius being about the furthest extent of travel in the 1950s, although in exceptional cases we know from other sources that thatchers might travel further and stay away while the job was in hand.

Map showing the working range of thatchers based in Lustleigh and Morchard Bishop in 1958, produced by W M Williams.

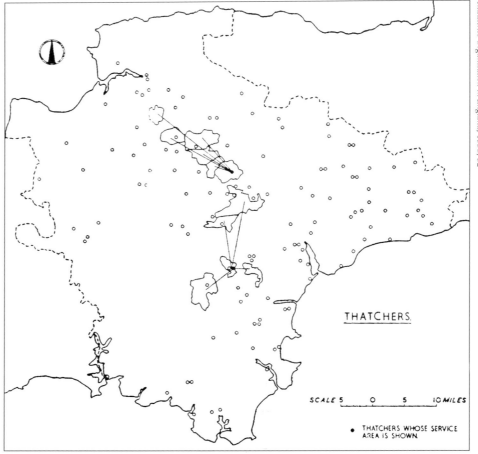

© Routledge & Kegan Paul. From *A Study of some Rural Crafts and the Rural Industries Organisation in England*, 1958, 32

THATCHERS.

SCALE 5   0   5   10 MILES

• THATCHERS WHOSE SERVICE AREA IS SHOWN.

Some of the Devon thatchers reluctant to join the MTA clearly mistook 'standards' for 'standardisation'. They feared that the Bureau's attempt to protect customers from poor workmanship (and by doing so, maintain the wider reputation of thatch as an effective roofing material) was the same thing as an insistence that the work of all thatchers should be 'the same'. It was a subtle difference and it was inevitable that the introduction of 'standards' would involve some loss of diversity. Thatchers in Devon interviewed by Williams argued that the superiority of Devon thatch – and the Bureau had no doubt that the quality of thatching in Devon was high – lay in its variety. The comments that Williams quotes from some of the thatchers who did not join the Devon MTA also reflect a keen sense of offence that an 'outside' organisation should be implying any criticism of the state of thatching in the county or imposing restrictions on the way an individual worked.

One of the key elements of a standard specification was a minimum depth of thatch over fixings. As a rule of thumb, the more depth of thatching material laid, the longer the thatch is likely to last before decay exposes the fixings and makes the roof vulnerable to leaks. It is clear from the photographic record of old combed straw roofs in Devon that there was, traditionally, a good deal of variety to Devon thatching. Eaves and verges, for example, were not always stripped out, as they are today. Depth of thatch laid over fixings included the 'rick-thatching' method described in the previous chapter, with the fixings exposed. Photographs show that thin-coated thatch was usually found on agricultural buildings where a few leaks could be tolerated, but it is also occasionally shown on houses. Well-informed customers, who understood how thatch worked, may have been perfectly content either with a thin thatch with concealed fixings, or one with the fixings exposed, knowing that they would pay less for less material. When thatchers and straw were easy to find, but finding large sums of cash was a problem, the possibility of a cheap thatch suited many landlords and tenants. As John Rogers wrote:

> *Regarding the amount of reed you use, to a certain degree that is governed by how long it is to last and the cost a person is prepared to pay.*[9]

Layers of old thatch showing at the eaves of this house in Ilsington indicate that a succession of thatchers did not strip them back to the roof timbers, as would be done today.

As it turned out, thin overcoats of thatch, along with frequent patching to stretch out the life of a roof, became less and less common after World War Two. This reflected the elevated status of thatch owners who were more able than their patch-and-mend predecessors to pay out once for a comprehensive rethatch.

Devon thatchers interviewed by Williams in the 1950s told him that they used, variously, ten to fifteen nitches of combed straw to a 'square' (10ft by 10ft) of thatch. This was partly determined by the condition of the roof when they arrived. More straw would be needed if parts of the roof were too rotten for sparring a new coat into an old one. A couple of good craftsmen criticised another thatcher who had done well for himself by charging high prices for only eight nitches a square 'just enough to last a couple of years' as they said.[10] It is clear that there was a natural understanding of 'standards' and fair pricing at work in Devon amongst most good thatchers, whether or not they belonged to the MTA. What some objected to was the idea that this sense of value for money could only be policed through a formal organisation.

The Dorset MTA was more successful in the early years, perhaps because of the stronger history of estate thatchers in that county. Many had been forced into independence when estates were split up after World War One and must have welcomed the Bureau's advice on business management and the opportunity to share problems with other thatchers. Devon, by comparison, had nothing like the same pattern of estate thatchers. When Williams pointed out how success-ful the Dorset MTA was, including adopting a standard specification, Devon thatchers forgot their territorial differences and united in formidable county pride with, as Williams reports:

> … condescension and scorn… Why should they give away the secrets of their skill? 'It's all very well for Dorset, us can tell they a thing or two'.[11]

In spite of the reluctance of the county's thatchers to join the MTA, the Bureau, on the whole, shared their confidence in their work and was hugely impressed by the quality of thatching in Devon in the 1950s, relative to other counties. In 1957 it was reported that their officer had visited 35 thatchers in North Devon and 54 in South Devon. Many of the North Devon thatchers had the Bureau's certificate of proficiency (an attempt to regulate the status of 'master thatcher') and most in South Devon were said to deserve it.

There is a hint in the records that the Bureau disapproved of overcoating and their early efforts in the county may have been responsible for a period of strip-ping combed straw back to the timbers. This may have contributed to the dis-parity between the survival of smoke-blackened thatch in the county and the far more common survival of smoke-blackened roof timbers. A book published in 1949, describing the Bureau's work in Devon, stated:

> There are many ways in which thatching practices need improvement; in some places thatchers have lost the art of 'thatching naked' which means putting new thatch to the timber supports, and making these supports, as the best thatchers do. All that some thatchers can do is to cover up old thatch with a new layer. Therefore much thatch , falling to pieces with age, which ought to have been stripped and burned, has been given a new coat.[12]

The Bureau's perception of the high quality of Devon thatching, relative to crushed straw thatching in the Midlands and Hampshire in the 1950s and 1960s, may be traceable back to the unbroken history of thatchers in the county over-coming the local obstacles to good performance roofs. The relative scarcity of straw, the wet climate and the slack pitches of Devon roofs were all impediments to thatching and, since at least the 14th century, had been powerful motives for developing techniques that made straw last as long as possible.

In 1959, the Bureau undertook a national survey of thatched buildings, the results put together in 1960. The number in Devon was judged to be 6 324. Nearly half the number of thatched houses was considered to be in poor condition. A 1965 national survey of English thatchers by the Bureau identified 96 Devon thatchers, more than in any other county. Hampshire came second for numbers with 68. A total of 83 of the 96 Devon thatchers were 'mastermen', experienced thatchers. The age profile was as follows:

CENSUS OF THATCHERS

County	Total Nos	Long Straw	Combed Wheat Reed	Norfolk Reed	Age Gp 15 - 20	Age Gp 21 - 35	Age Gp 36 - 50	Age Gp 51-65	Age Gp Over 65	Mastermen	Apprentices	Trainees	Employees
Bedfordshire	16	15	7	3	2	1	3	6	-	11	2	-	3
Berkshire	17	16	10	9	3	4	4	5	1	15	1	1	-
Buckinghamshire	9	8	4	3	1	6	1	1	-	9	-	-	-
Cambridge	22	22	-	10	1	-	2	7	6	15	1	-	6
Cheshire	1	1	-	-	-	-	-	-	-	1	-	-	-
Cornwall	6	-	6	-	-	-	1	4	1	6	-	-	-
Derbyshire	4	4	1	-	-	1	2	1	-	4	-	-	-
Devonshire	96	-	96	32	6	8	25	40	17	83	3	5	5
Dorset	58	58	57	20	4	11	8	21	14	41	1	2	14
Essex	40	38	8	9	2	3	10	16	-	34	2	-	4
Glamorgan	3	3	2	2	-	1	1	1	-	3	-	-	-
Gloucestershire	8	8	3	5	2	2	1	2	1	6	1	1	-
Hampshire	68	68	38	24	4	7	18	21	17	57	1	3	7
Hertfordshire	5	4	1	1	-	-	1	2	1	4	-	-	1
Huntingdonshire	15	15	12	15	-	1	1	4	-	6	-	-	9
Isle of Ely	5	4	-	4	-	-	-	4	-	4	-	-	1
Kent	6	4	1	1	1	-	-	4	-	5	-	-	1
Kesteven	1	1	-	-	-	-	-	-	-	1	-	-	-
Lancashire	1	1	-	1	-	-	1	-	-	1	-	-	-
Leicestershire	2	2	-	-	-	-	1	1	-	2	-	-	-
Lindsay	1	-	-	1	-	-	-	-	-	1	-	-	-
Middlesex	1	-	1	1	-	-	1	-	-	1	-	-	-
Norfolk	45	20	2	35	-	3	3	9	4	17	-	-	28
Northamptonshire	27	27	13	13	2	2	4	10	2	19	2	-	6
Nottinghamshire	1	1	-	-	-	-	-	-	1	1	-	-	-
Oxfordshire	25	25	11	4	1	4	8	11	1	22	-	3	-
Rutland	3	2	-	2	1	-	2	-	-	2	1	-	-
Shropshire	1	1	-	-	-	-	-	1	-	1	-	-	-
Somerset	27	-	27	8	4	4	4	10	5	21	-	5	1
Staffordshire	1	1	-	-	-	-	-	-	-	1	-	-	-
Suffolk	56	52	10	22	3	-	13	20	7	44	2	-	10
Surrey	1	-	-	1	-	-	1	-	-	1	-	-	-
Sussex	16	16	2	10	-	4	3	8	1	16	-	-	-
Warwickshire	11	10	8	3	-	5	1	4	1	11	-	-	-
Wiltshire	57	57	46	8	5	8	13	26	5	40	1	6	10
Worcestershire	8	8	3	3	-	2	4	2	-	8	-	-	-
TOTALS	**664**	**492**	**369**	**250**	**42**	**77**	**137**	**241**	**85**	**514**	**18**	**26**	**106**

A national trade body for thatching, the National Society of Master Thatchers' Associations, was not set up until the late 1960s. In the late 1970s it changed its constitution to personal membership, rather than a membership that represented the county associations and its name became the National Society of Master Thatchers. The idea of a body that would represent the county associations was revived in 1987 and the National Council of Master Thatchers Associations was formed. Relations between the two national organisations have not always been easy and the existence of two bodies has been confusing to outsiders. Fortunately there is now an industry lead body on which members of both bodies are represented.

The Devon MTA is a very valuable organisation. It continues to represent only about one-third of the thatchers working in the county and includes membership of thatching straw growers. It has often been said that thatchers who are not members can be as good craftsmen as Association members. This continues to be true. What can be more important for many owners is that employing a thatcher who is a member of the Devon MTA guarantees, both as a craftsman whose quality of work has been vetted by his peers as a requirement of member-

Figures from the Rural Industries Bureau survey of thatched buildings, information gathered in 1959. As well as the age of thatchers, the census identified how many thatchers in different counties could thatch in combed straw ('combed wheat reed'), crushed straw ('long straw') and water reed ('Norfolk Reed'). This is shown in columns two to four.

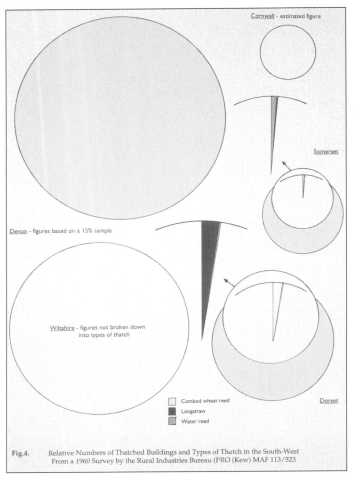

Fig.4.   Relative Numbers of Thatched Buildings and Types of Thatch in the South-West
From a 1960 Survey by the Rural Industries Bureau (PRO (Kew) MAF 113/523

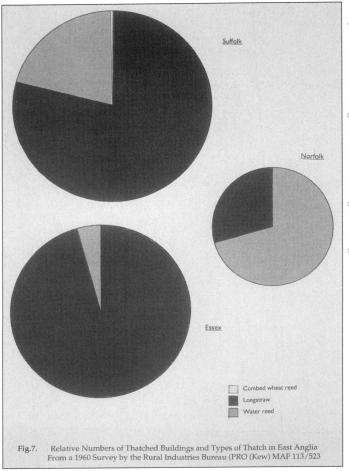

Fig.7.   Relative Numbers of Thatched Buildings and Types of Thatch in East Anglia
From a 1960 Survey by the Rural Industries Bureau (PRO (Kew) MAF 113/523

Pie charts based on selected counties from the Bureau's survey of 1959, indicating relative numbers of thatched buildings (size of pie) and regional types of thatching in different areas. The Devon figures, based on a 15 per cent sample, show that Devon had more thatched buildings than any other county and was exclusively combed straw (light grey, Fig.4). In fact there was almost certainly a handful of water reed roofs in the county by then. Norfolk was the only county in England which had more water reed (dark grey, Fig.7) than any other kind of thatching. Essex was primarily a crushed straw (black) county. Regional patterns of thatching types, all of which had a long history, were dramatically altered after 1950. A good percentage of Devon today would be shown dark grey.

ship, and arbitration by the MTA if there are any complaints about the work of a member. For thatchers themselves it is a forum where they can discuss local and national issues, from the quality of materials they can obtain to conservation issues. For outsiders, who may wish to find out what thatchers think about local and general issues, it is the only local collective of thatchers.

Materials

Combed Straw

After 1945 there were major developments in the efficiency and profitability of grain growing. Wheat-breeding programmes, changes in growing methods and the use of new types of harvesting machinery all contributed. Each new step that favoured the grain-farmer had an equivalent downside for the production of thatching straw. Looking back on the second half of the 20th century it seems a wonder that straw thatching survived at all. It did so partly because farmers and specialist 'growers' began to grow wheat specifically for thatching straw. This reversed the assumption that straw was a useful by-product of the grain harvest, straw growers regarding the grain as a by-product of straw. This specialised industry could only function by side-stepping, as far as it could, much of the post-war 'progress' made in cereal farming. It produced a crop, as it still does in 2001, using methods, manpower and machinery of the late 19th century *(see colour page 11)*. Perhaps there were historical precedents in Devon for growing grain specifically for thatching straw. We have a hint, though no more, in Colepresse's list of Devon-grown wheats of a type known to have limited value to the baker, but apparently used for thatch. We know from Crossing that rye continued to be grown on the edge of Dartmoor for use in thatching, more than a century after it had been replaced with wheat elsewhere in the county.

An old fashioned scene, but this is 1972. Harvesting technology, notably the combine harvester, consigned rick-making to the past. Only specialised growers of thatching straw continued to make ricks as part of the old-fashioned technology still used for harvesting and combing straw for thatch. These ricks at Middle Hollacombe Farm, Crediton, contained 10 acres of the wheat varieties Chalk and Maris Widgeon, grown especially for thatchers and ricked to allow them to ripen fully before threshing and combing.

Wheat Varieties

The way in which wheat varieties and the regulation of wheat growing has affected thatchers has been thoroughly researched by John Letts and the following is no more than a summary based on his work.[13] The old mixtures and selections of wheat that were grown in the early 20th century were gradually reduced, after 1945, to a smaller number of named varieties. This was part of a national trend in agriculture in the 20th century designed to rationalise cereal-growing by matching the characteristics of unique and clearly-named varieties to soil type. Farmers were encouraged to grow varieties that would produce the highest yields on their land. Some argued that the use of pedigree varieties lost the advantages of the old mixtures, which had less refined characteristics and tended to perform more consistently across a broad range of conditions and soil types.[14] Mixtures, as opposed to refined pure-bred crops, would always include some failures in a field, but overall, there was a better chance of achieving a percentage of success every season.

Most of the named varieties of wheat available in the late 1940s and 1950s could be used for thatching, but thatchers had their preferences, always looking out for tall, strong, straight, evenly-tapered straw. Devon farmers who supplied thatchers needed to ensure that what they were growing would suit their thatching customers: 'Some farmers grow special varieties of wheat to obtain good grain as well as good reed'.[15] Squareheads Master, also known as Red Standard, is often mentioned by older Devon thatchers as a good thatching variety. It was selected and named in the 1880s and had a straw approximately 1.1m (40ins) tall. It was the most popular winter wheat in Britain until the late 1930s, meaning that a wheat variety suitable for thatching was widely available. Some continued to be grown after 1945, but it had a soft grain that was not ideal for bread-baking.[16] It is the breeding ancestor of most of the varieties that are favoured by thatchers today.

By 1957 the contacts with Devon thatchers by the Bureau identified a worrying shortage of suitable thatching straw. Reading between the lines of the documentation, this seems to have meant that Squareheads Master was becoming uncommon. The Rural Industries Organiser for Devon decided to approach the Ministry of Agriculture, Fisheries and Food (MAFF) to try to encourage farmers to grow winter wheat varieties suitable for thatching on the basis that it was needed to support a rural industry.[17] In 1961–62 this led to what was probably the very first experimental trial in the country to try to identify scientifically what were the 'best' varieties of wheat for thatching so that farmers might be encouraged to grow them. Six commonly-grown varieties of winter wheat were planted on the Broadhembury Estate of Mr Cedric Drewe, MP for Honiton, in East Devon. These were then fitted to an old barn, laid so that differences in the way they performed could be identified. It was not until 1974 that slight differences between the varieties began to be visible, although it was suspected that these would rapidly become more pronounced. The barn chosen was not in good condition and partly collapsed after 1974, bringing the experiment to an end. However, there was a more important reason for the failure of the trial. By 1974, not one of the varieties commonly grown in 1961 was still commercially available, so the results would have been of academic interest only and of no practical use to thatchers.

The Broadhembury experiment underlines the difficulties that wheat-breeding has presented to thatchers since 1945. Varieties are succeeded by new varieties that are bred for grain yield and the convenience of modern harvesting technology, often at the expense of length of straw. Japanese dwarfing genes were incorporated into European wheats in the 1950s and 1960s. By 1977 a small sample (72 thatchers) indicated that the most common varieties grown in the South West for thatching straw were Maris Widgeon (bred 1964) and Maris Huntsman (bred 1972). Maris Huntsman, the most widely grown winter wheat in the country in 1977, has an ancestry that includes a Japanese dwarf wheat. 'When grown without nitrogen fertiliser, Maris Huntsman rarely exceeds 36in (0.9m), which is close to the minimum height needed for thatching. All of the wheats developed since the 1970s have even shorter straw than Huntsman and are not suitable for thatching'.[18] There is a now a twenty-year gap since a new wheat variety suitable for thatching has been bred and made available.

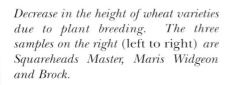

Decrease in the height of wheat varieties due to plant breeding. The three samples on the right (left to right) *are Squareheads Master, Maris Widgeon and Brock.*

Wheat-breeding is beset by complex legislation intended both to boost grain production and protect the rights of plant-breeders. John Letts describes this in detail in 'Thatching Straw' in Cox and Letts, *Thatching in England 1940–1994.*[19] While the roots of this legislation can be traced back to the beginning of the 20th century, the most significant controls in place today date from 1974. All member states of the European Union are required to maintain a 'National List' of wheat varieties. Only varieties on the National List can be traded legally within the Union. It is illegal to sell, or even to give away varieties that are not on the National List within the Union, although they can be traded outside the EU. New varieties are only listed if they can be shown to be 'distinct, uniform and stable' and their 'value for cultivation and use' is judged to be better than half of the varieties already on the list. Once included, they remain on the list for ten years. They are then dropped, unless the plant-breeder is prepared to pay a fee to renew the registration of the variety. This will only be done if a variety is widely-grown, and therefore profitable to the plant-breeder. Since cereal-farming is a much larger industry than thatching, developing varieties of wheat that have good quality thatching straw does not interest the plant-breeder. It is varieties that suit modern cereal farmers, and are profitable to the breeders that are introduced on to the list and remain on it. Breeding for straw quality would be a case of re-inventing the wheel, anyway, as a return to older varieties and mixtures would be a far more economical route to solving the varietal problem.

It is possible to grow varieties that are not in the National List, but only if a grower collects his or her own seed corn and uses it for replanting. The current legislation is a major technical obstacle not only to expanding the number of varieties of wheat grown that could be beneficial to straw thatching, but even to maintaining existing varieties, suitable for thatching, on the National List. The best prospects for changing this situation lie with a common-sense assumption that the legislation is there to be broken, by effective lobbying by and on behalf of the straw thatching industry and with the hope that future EU legislation designed to protect bio-diversity may pay some attention to the plight of straw thatchers.

John Letts, who approached thatching initially as an archaeo-botanist in the early 1990s but has subsequently become a thatching expert on a number of different fronts, is currently licensed to grow old varieties experimentally at the University of Reading. This research should be a firm foundation on which to carry forward the debate about how to revive and re-introduce varieties and mixtures of varieties that will produce better-quality and longer straw for thatchers.

Growing Methods

Artificial fertilisers were already in use for wheat-growing before World War Two. The use of nitrates rose sharply during the war and increased massively after c.1960. The first item on the agenda of the first-ever national meeting of thatchers in 1949 was 'The effects of artificial manure on the quality of straw', reflecting a real anxiety on the part of thatchers that chemical nitrates, in particular, might damage the quality of straw. Despite a MAFF-funded research at the University of Bath in the late 1970s, prompted partly by a small number of examples of premature decay in thatched roofs in Devon, it has not been possible to establish the precise science of the impact of nitrates on the wheat stem or to prove scientifically that it does affect straw quality. It may be that heavy nitrate use, or large dressings of nitrates at particular stages in the growth of the plant, weakens the straw, and there is some evidence that, by comparison with organically-grown straw, nitrates concentrate in the butt ends of the plant which, in combed straw, are most vulnerable to decay. While the scientific evidence is unclear, most thatchers and growers are convinced that nitrates should be used sparingly when thatching straw is being grown. The experimental work at Bath did establish that thatch should not be too tightly-packed by the thatcher. Ventilation is crucial in allowing thatch to dry out and tightly-packed thatch speeds up the natural rotting process.

© Halsgrove

Harry Dockings with his horse-drawn binder at Southcott Farm, Morchard Bishop in an advertisement for fertiliser between the wars.

The effects of using herbicides and fungicides on wheat have also been debated within the thatching industry. Whether the advantages of these in reducing weeds and protecting the crop from damaging fungal disease are outweighed by possible damage, either to the natural wax that protects the straw from moisture or to the balance of fungi that are present in a thatched roof, is still unknown.

Harvesting

The arrival of the combine harvester severed the connection between mainstream wheat-growing and growing for thatch. The combine, which reaped and threshed in one operation, left only a short stubble in the field. No thatching straw – whether crushed or combed – could be produced when wheat was harvested with a combine. The combine was most efficient on short crops of wheat and worked best when the plants were harvested dead ripe, with little moisture content. The effect of this was to change the 'normal' time of harvest. It is received wisdom that thatching straw is best harvested before the plant has dried out, the moisture remaining in the stem at reaping giving the straw strength.

The combine harvester, this one is used at Clyst William, Plymtree, in the 1980s, reduced the labour and time of harvest dramatically, but created apartheid between the production of grain and the production of thatching straw.

There were 2 500 combines in Britain by 1944 and more than 50 000 by 1960. As with the threshing machine, combines arrived late in Devon relative to the cereal-basket counties of the Midlands and East Anglia. The early combines were large and very expensive, and an investment difficult to justify on the relatively small acreages of wheat in Devon. It was also difficult to get such large objects down Devon's winding, hedge-banked lanes. This meant that the reaper-binder, pulled by tractors rather than teams of horses, continued to be a familiar sight in Devon fields after the war. It also gave the threshing machine a longer life than in other counties and meant that the reed comber attachment could still be used. The development and distribution of smaller combines, however, had its impact on the harvesting machinery of the previous era. New threshing machines were not built much after 1950 and reed combers ceased production in about 1952. After 1952, growers of thatching straw were obliged to keep old machinery in use and could not replace threshing machines and reed combers with new.

One of the economic advantages of the combine was the reduction of labour required at harvest. Growers of thatching straw had to continue to employ, as they still do, levels of manpower at harvest that are rare elsewhere in modern agriculture and which represent a large expense. The minimum number of people needed to man a traditional threshing machine and reed comber is six; more make the operation more efficient. This is a substantial cost for any producer of thatching straw.

The Spread of Combed Straw outside the South West

In the post-war period the Rural Industries Bureau considered the combed straw tradition of the South West to be such a good method of thatching that it was decided to promote it further east as an alternative to crushed straw (long straw) thatch. The thatching officers taught the combed straw method to thatchers outside the South West. With hindsight it is plain that this campaign to shift combed straw to other regions was an insensitive approach to vernacular thatching traditions. It threatened the survival of crushed straw thatch in regions where that method had been commonplace for centuries. It also lost the regional concentration of combed straw, which had previously been exclusive to the South West. The Bureau's priorities were to put thatching on a footing that would provide rural employment and ensure the survival and expansion of the industry. In the 1950s little was understood or valued in any quarter about the regional variations of British thatching and, compared with the last quarter of the 20th century, the state of knowledge about all vernacular building traditions was limited.

The Bureau's attempt to push combed straw further east had unexpected consequences in Devon. As we have seen, the county, along with Somerset, still had the skills and machinery to produce combed straw, although there were finite numbers of reed combers in operation. Devon was not a wealthy county in the 1950s and 1960s and the cost of thatching, although rising, was still cheap relative to the Midlands and especially to those counties where country cottages were being bought up in numbers by commuters. It was possible for Devon growers to get a better price for combed straw by selling it out of the South West, than to local thatchers, at a time when demand had been converted from a regional to a national requirement. Eventually, in 1978, the Bureau's successor organisation, the Council for Small Industries in Rural Areas (COSIRA), tried to deal with the problem by producing drawings from which an all-metal reed comber could be built. In theory, this should have added to the number of machines in existence, expanded the production of combed straw beyond the South West and allowed supply to keep up with demand. In practice, the manufacture of the machine, either as a one-off or in small numbers, proved expensive and was not taken up as extensively as had been hoped. The overall effect of the promotion of combed straw beyond the South West was to leave a shortage at home in Devon and the gap began to be filled by water reed introduced from foreign sources.

One of the Rural Industries Bureau's Thatching Officers teaching thatchers outside the South West how to thatch with combed straw in the 1950s.

The production of combed straw, both for use in Devon and in other counties, continues to be centred on the South West. In 1994 it was estimated by Gordon Glover, an expert on agricultural machinery in the county, that there were about seventeen reed combers still at work in Devon, with a smaller number in use in other counties.[20] Until a new generation of machines is built, this is a limiting factor. Some thatchers are also growers, either on their own land or in partnership with farmers, preserving a direct link with and a measure of quality control over the material they use themselves. They may produce more combed straw that they need, and then also act as agents, selling it on to other thatchers who do not grow their own.

The concentration of the production of combed straw in the South West is partly due to the fact that most of the surviving reed combers are based here. These machines are busy in Devon at harvest. They may be owned by contractors who will come in and harvest the crop for a grower, or individual growers may own their own machinery. Possession of or access to a reed comber alone does not make for an automatically easy harvest. Tradition continues to play its part. The skills needed to keep old belt-driven machinery functioning and to feed the crop into it effectively, are handed down from older to younger men and there is usually an 'old boy' whose experience may be needed, attending in the field. The management of six or more people working in the noise and dust around the machine is also an art in itself. The importance of experience and skill also applies to the techniques of rick-building, in those cases where growers still leave the corn to ripen in ricks. The sight of a South West field in the 21st century, either being harvested, or after harvest, with stooks or ricks invariably means that thatching straw is being produced. It is rare enough to attract the attention of passers-by who remember from childhood that all cornfields once looked like this. It is a scene produced out of hard labour as well as keen judgement. To measure up by eye, for example, the quantity of stooks in a field and then make the base of a rick that will be the right size to contain them all, properly ventilated, is a skilled act of design, without any recourse to measurements or paper. The rick-builder then has to assess accurately, in the middle of all the hurly-burly of bundles of straw pitched up to the men on top, exactly when the shape of the rick needs to be changed to a 'roof' of sufficient pitch to contain all the remaining bundles. It is no wonder that rick-making was once an activity that, like good ploughing, was recognised to require such a combination of skills that there were competitions and prize-winners in the art.

Evidence for Local Technique

Combed Straw
In the 1950s the Devon MTA published a small booklet by R Burnett, a thatcher from Cornwall, *Some Notes on Wheat Reed Thatching*.[21] This is an extremely rare and early example of a publication that includes technical detail of the time: some old, some new. The author was probably the same Burnett described in *The Guardian* 28 April 1965, as living near Truro. He was not from a thatching dynasty. The booklet is undated but on internal evidence is c.1950. It may have been generated by some unflattering remarks on South West thatching made by Norfolk Reed Thatchers of Rickmansworth (established before the war), which led to a flurry of solicitors' letters and a retraction. Whatever the motive for its production, publishing it was a credit to the imagination of the Devon and Cornwall MTA.

Burnett may not have been a native of the West Country, but he clearly observed thatch with care. His publication pointed out the contribution that the production of thatching straw made to the rural economy, underlined the excellent insulation properties of the material and remarked that: 'a well-thatched roof is

a good roof – of good appearance – serviceable – reasonably durable, and with some advantages no other roof covering can offer.'

He emphasised the variety of finished appearance that may come from using one thatcher rather than another:

> *…it does not necessarily mean that one man's work is better than that of the other, although it may indeed be so.*
>
> *Some thatchers give their work a very sharp outline while others prefer the more subdued effect of a blunted edge. Some favour an even plane surface which gives a straight line from ridge to eaves as well as from end to end of the building. Others prefer a curved surface which gives an even plane from the ridge until about three quarters of the distance towards the eaves when it curves more or less sharply downwards. If the curved style is used, the same unvarying curve is maintained throughout, from end to end of the roof. Some craftsmen specialise in fancy ridging, others use a plain ridge or a double ridge or a single-stretcher ridge.*
>
> *All these styles are equally correct and the differences are matters of personal taste rather than craftsmanship. If thatching in a particular style is required it is well to employ a thatcher who habitually uses the shape that is wanted.*[22]

Burnett went on to discuss differences in method. By 1950, it seems he was able to identify at least two different ways, with a variant, of dealing with the eaves of a building which was to have a new coat of wheat reed.

1 The old eaves were cut off flush with the wall, sometimes involving a thin, tight wad of reed fixed laterally along the edge of the thatch to give the kick for the new work, which could be sparred on.

2 The eaves were stripped out completely, in which case the new eaves thatch had to be tied on with tarred twine. In the case of some cob houses, this method 'involves breaking a little off the top of the wall and replacing it with fresh cob into which the new eaves may be sparred'.

Burnett indicates that the latter method:

> *although it requires more work and may therefore be a little more expensive, (it) has the advantage of leaving no old thatch exposed and thus improving the appearance. It is also often more effective in excluding birds, which may break into any old thatch left upon the walls, and later damage the new coat.*

It would seem that as late as 1950 some Devon thatchers were still using cob on the walltops (having removed earlier cob) to get the necessary kick for thatch. This is likely to be an old method and may be one explanation for the 'raise' of cob on the top of stone walling which is sometimes seen on Devon rural houses. This practice was described orally in the 1980s by a thatcher in Barton, Torbay, who had used it in the 1930s. The old cob was knocked off the walltop on to the ground, where it was mixed with unslaked lime and wetted (to begin a slaking process). It was then reinstated with the new eaves thatch sparred into it.[23] Some thatchers working today have also used the method on occasion.[24]

Burnett's publication describes practices in use in the South West with which he was familiar. Its emphasis on regional practice contrasts with the Bureau's book, *The Thatcher's Craft*, first produced in 1960. This useful publication set out to explain the mysteries of the craft to a non-thatching public. Most of the content was a series of photographs showing a thatcher fitting crushed straw, combed straw and water reed to model roofs. The book sought to establish national standards for thatching, and render it an acceptable modern building material and did not cover regional practice in any depth.

The Thatcher's Craft account of combed straw thatching describes the use of lead flashings and aprons, rather than mortar, to make junctions between the thatch and chimneystacks. The use of lead, an expensive material and not produced in the county, is unlikely to have been used on many thatched roofs in Devon before World War One. Similarly, while *The Thatcher's Craft* does show the use of stitching combed straw on to the roof timbers, when thatch is being applied to a stripped or new roof, it is described without much enthusiasm. It describes this technique (known from both documentation and archaeology to be traditional) as 'slower', because it involved an assistant inside the roof, and 'cheaper' than the method of using iron crooks, driven into the rafters to hold the hazel sways. The implication is that the traditional method was old-fashioned, as regards both labour and materials. Some thatchers today use wire instead of hazel sways, completing a gradual transformation from the use of organic to metal fixings.

Wire Netting

The use of wire netting to cover thatch seems to be a post-war introduction in Devon and is only found here and there covering the entire roof, although ridges are often netted to keep the fixings intact for as long as possible. John

Rogers of Modbury describes using wire netting, apparently for the first time, in 1958, on a house in Saltash. Its purpose is principally to prevent bird and rodent damage, although some thatchers consider that it can help to protect gables from wind-damage if a house is very exposed. Some Cornish thatched houses, exposed to Atlantic gales, are known historically to have been given extra protection from old fishing nets, which were tied down to hooks under the verges. Birds sometimes pull straw out from a thatched roof. This is most likely to happen when threshing has left grain amongst the straw. It is a common problem with crushed straw (long straw) roofs where some of the heads as well as the butts of the straw are exposed and these roofs are nearly always netted. Bird attack on combed straw is far less common and is difficult to predict. One roof may be affected while a neighbouring roof is left alone. Netting has its disadvantages. If the netting is tight against the thatch rainwater tends to collect on the wire instead of running off the roof. Netting can also trap leaves which also create damp. Moss growth (which is not necessarily a major problem) can be encouraged by the damp atmosphere created by netting. If there is a thatch fire, netting that is too firmly-fixed can delay fire officers in pulling the thatch off to protect the building and it is very important for it to be fitted so that it can be pulled away very quickly if the need arises.

Water Reed

As we have seen some Devon-grown water reed was in use by the late 19th century, but the source of supply seems to have been limited to Slapton Ley/Dartmouth. In 1959 an individual importer in Newton Abbot imported 100 tons of water reed, landing at Teignmouth, with larger quantities planned for successive years.[25] From the 1960s the use of water reed in Devon increased rapidly until it overtook the combed straw and in 2001 probably 75 per cent or more of thatching in the county is water reed.

A house at Axmouth being thatched with water reed in the 1990s.

© Jo Cox 1990s

Water reed with a block cut ornamental course at the eaves, being put onto a felted roof in Ilfracombe, in 1963.

Loughwood Baptist Chapel at Dalwood in 1998. The water reed was put on in 1969.

Water reed from foreign sources would very probably have arrived in Devon, even without the intervention of the Bureau in the market for combed straw, but perhaps not so soon. In the 1950s water reed was widely regarded, including by the Bureau, as superior to straw for longevity (although more expensive), based on its performance as a single-coat material in the dry climate and steeply-pitched roofs of East Anglia. Without the advantage of the archaeological analysis of thatched roofs, the Bureau also assumed that water reed, as a 'wild' plant, had invariably preceded straw as a thatching material, although it was the perception of its quality, not its antiquity that encouraged its officers to promote its use.[26] From 1965 the Bureau ran courses teaching water reed thatching to trainees at Knuston Hall in Northamptonshire. Courses in thatching with straw were not begun until 1971.

The reason the Bureau promoted combed straw eastwards out of the South West in the 1950s and 1960s, rather than water reed westwards from East Anglia, was that they could not see how native sources of water reed in Norfolk could supply national needs. In the 1950s, it seemed far more practical to try to spread the process of combing straw, which meant applying a particular method of processing to a crop that was grown nationally, than to try to expand the supply of water reed, given that reed beds cannot be moved. Before the British motorway system had been developed, transport costs from Norfolk would, it seemed, have made the price of Norfolk reed prohibitive as a source for the whole of southern England, even if the quantities produced could have been increased. The Bureau did work hard to try to expand the supply of water reed from Norfolk, but there were difficulties at the source, with a shortage of human reed cutters and, for a time, an unexplained reluctance amongst reed bed managers to increase production.

Norfolk was the principal source of British water reed. Some Norfolk water reed was used in Devon after World War Two and is still used from time to time. There were other managed water reed beds nearer at hand in Dorset. At Abbotsbury, north-west of the Chesil Bank in Dorset, 50 acres of commercial reed beds produce a coarse reed known locally as Abbotsbury 'spear'. Its use is recorded in Devon in the early 1960s as well as in John Rogers' biography.[27] Abbotsbury spear was used predominantly on the houses of the Ilsham Estate in Dorset, which owns the reed beds, with any small annual surplus sold off. Abbotsbury spear does not seem to have been used in Devon in the last twenty years, foreign sources being preferred and more plentiful.

The Bureau attempted to develop other coastal reed beds in Dorset, but with limited success. They are also recorded as cutting water reed at Dawlish which they clearly thought had potential for production, but whether Dawlish water reed was ever more than one of their experiments in improving supplies is not clear. Austria, Hungary and Poland were all sources of imported water reed used in Devon in the 1980s and, more recently, Turkish water reed has been extensively used. Water reed from abroad can be purchased directly from agents.

The question of whether the quality of water reed, either coastal or in managed fens, is compromised by nitrate run-off from agriculture into reed beds is unknown. It is one of those things that is 'widely-believed' in thatching, not just in England, but also in the Netherlands, but has not been scientifically proven.

Evidence of Local Technique

Water reed (see colour page 12)
By the time water reed began to be used extensively in Devon, conventional techniques for fitting it had become established in East Anglia. The usual method is to strip the thatch back to the rafters each time the roof is rethatched and to fix on the bundles of water reed with iron crooks, knocked into the rafters. It is now very rare to spar-coat water reed on to water reed in the fashion that combed straw is overcoated. When the water reed coat has been fixed directly to the rafters, and has decayed sufficiently for a rethatch to be required, there simply is not enough material to do this. As a stiff, slippery material, it is difficult to get sufficient grip to add one coat of water reed to another, especially on a steeply-pitched roof where there is a risk that it might slip out of its fixings. There are always exceptions to the rule in thatching and there is some evidence that water reed from Abbotsbury was spar-coated.

The method of stripping all the water reed off when rethatching seems to be an ancient, if not invariable one. What is probably less ancient is the use of metal crooks to fix the bundles of water reed into the rafters. An earlier method was to stitch it onto the rafters. 'Crooking' requires sounder rafters than if the thatch is tied on.

At its most drastic, a change from straw to water reed meant losing all the old layers of straw (including medieval thatch, in some cases) only to discover that roof timbers – adequate for the gentler method of tying thatch on – appeared to be, or were, too feeble to apply the technique of knocking in crooks. The result of this was the unnecessary loss of large quantities of historic carpentry and even whole roofs, especially when the rafters were softwood poles. Fortunately for the survival of historic fabric in the county, most Devon thatchers switching from combed straw to water reed did not follow the practice of their East Anglian colleagues, but treated the material within their own traditional methods of working. To begin with, they did not strip the roofs back to the timbers but chose to spar-coat water reed on to a sound straw base, just as they would apply a new coat of combed straw. There were good practical reasons for this. Completely stripping a straw roof is labour-intensive and costly. Exposing imperfections in roof timbers and then having to make repairs, is expensive and time-consuming.

The switch to water reed for combed straw thatchers was not, technically, very difficult, as there are general similarities in fitting the two materials. Unlike crushed straw (long straw) both combed straw and water reed are dressed into place with a bat-like tool. The Bureau supported Devon thatchers trying out the unfamiliar material by providing on-site training sessions from their thatching officers. Water reed is too stiff to be wrapped over a ridge, so it is accompanied by a straw ridge in Devon (sedge is sometimes used for this purpose in East Anglia). By 1965, a survey for the Bureau showed that, of the 96 thatchers they judged to be working in Devon, all could thatch in combed straw, but 32 could also thatch using what the Bureau called 'Norfolk reed', meaning water reed.

The effect of the method of spar-coating water reed on to straw was one that ensured that the centuries-old tradition of preserving old straw on the roof was continued. It is thanks to this that, in spite of the loss of straw overcoats, early straw continues to survive in the county under many modern water reed overcoats. The loss of straw overcoats has been more controversial. A Devon thatcher, using a fine water reed, thatched 'combed straw' style, can produce a finish that is very difficult to distinguish from a straw roof. Sometimes the only way of spotting the difference is to pull a stem out from the roof and look at it closely.

The colour of water reed is slightly 'greyer' and less rich than combed wheat reed, but the differences are difficult to detect unless they are seen side by side. As a longer, stiffer, and therefore less malleable material than straw, it is not possible to shape water reed in quite the same way as a combed straw roof can be shaped, especially round gables and dormers. This means that water reed can give a much sharper and more angular finish than straw, depending on how the thatcher makes use of it. Like combed straw, water reed is fitted with a kick at the eaves. As a longer material than combed straw, the additional kick it requires is sometimes provided by attaching a board or length of timber to the top of the wall, under the eaves. This can be quite discreet and not readily noticed, but sometimes crudely-finished timber may be used by the thatcher and, if also painted in a contrasting colour to the walls, this can have an intrusive appearance.

What undoubtedly has been lost in the replacement of straw with imported water reed is not only the long Devon tradition of combed straw, but also the old mutuality between Devon farming and Devon thatching, and the vernacular good sense of using a locally-available material on local buildings.

The Vexed Question of the Comparative Durability of Combed Straw and Water Reed

The Bureau believed that, as a general rule to which there would always be exceptions, combed straw lasted longer than crushed straw, and that water reed lasted longest of all. Their publication, *The Thatcher's Craft*, included figures on the durability of the three different methods of thatching. These were hedged round with qualifications, stating that longevity was affected by:

> *…quality of crop and materials, weather conditions, situation with regard to prevailing winds and trees, and of considerable importance, whether or not a skilled thatcher is employed.*

The figures given were: 'Water reed, 50–60 years; Combed wheat reed, 25–40 years; Long straw, 10–20 years'. Produced by the only government organisation with a direct involvement in thatching, the figures for longevity were frequently quoted, without the original qualifications that accompanied them. They played a key role in the national changes of method and materials from the 1960s until c.1990.

Producing reliable figures for the durability of thatch is notoriously difficult and can be very misleading. It is very difficult to compare 'like-with-like' thatched buildings. Each has its own unique combination of factors that affect the life of thatch: pitch of roof (a key factor omitted from the Bureau's qualifications in *The Thatcher's Craft*) skill of thatcher; quality of material; location and aspect of building and proximity to trees or water. If we could compare 'like-with-like' by removing all the variables, a single coat water reed roof in East Anglia will usually last longer than a crushed straw (long straw) roof in the same climate. It was a very large step to assume from this that a spar-coated water reed roof would last longer than a combed straw roof in the very different environment of the South West, but this was done.

By no means all thatchers read *The Thatcher's Craft* and by no means all who did took the figures as gospel, knowing from experience how long the thatching method they used was likely to last in the areas in which they used it. The figures in *The Thatcher's Craft* for the longevity of combed straw, '25–40 years', must have surprised thatchers in Devon who read the book. From 1918 to 1980 figures provided by Devon thatchers, owners and journalists (probably derived from thatchers) quoted in books, articles and diaries, consistently give a range of durability from fifteen to thirty years, most figures given being in the twenty to thirty years bracket. This is somewhat less than the figures for combed wheat reed (combed straw) given in *The Thatcher's Craft*. Most Devon thatchers today would be disappointed and probably rather concerned if a well-thatched combed straw roof, using good quality material and reridged when required, lasted less than fifteen years. Most would consider that, with regular reridging and some patching, twenty to thirty years is still a good rule of thumb, bearing in mind the climatic variations within the county, including dramatic differences in rainfall between, say, the fringes of Dartmoor and East Devon. Of course there will be exceptions, taking into account all the variables that affect the life of thatch, and these exceptions will include combed straw roofs that may last for over forty years.

The figures in *The Thatcher's Craft* exerted a wide influence on newcomer owners and thatchers, as well as Local Planning Authorities, who began to press for the use of water reed, even though, and perhaps because, it was more expensive – and thus seemed 'better' – than combed straw. In recent years doubts have been cast on the assumption that water reed in the South West will last almost twice as long as combed straw. However, it is certainly true that many Devon thatchers

A combed straw roof in Broadhembury in 1959, twenty years after rethatching. It had just been reridged and resheared and was expected to last another ten years.

have lost confidence in the quality and durability of combed straw and prefer to use water reed.

The Thatcher's Craft was produced when long straw was not in official favour with the Bureau, but combed straw was. The figures for durability were produced before there had been any opportunity to see how Norfolk or foreign-sourced water reed performed in the wet climate of the South West. In fact, given that most spar-coated water reed thatch in Devon post-dates 1950, it is not until now – and on to 2010 – that we would be in a position to check whether the Bureau's figures (which certainly referred to single-coat water reed) were right, provided we could identify the roofs in question and compare water reed 'like-for-like'. Such a comparison is impossible because so many different sources of water reed have been used in Devon. Some water reed is fine, some coarse, the conditions in which it is grown are variable and it is unlikely that all will perform in exactly the same way. This is precisely the same problem that made the Broadhembury combed straw experiment fail. Is there any point in having information about the performance of water reed from a particular source, if that source is no longer used?

In recent years it has been suggested that in the wet climate and on the slack-pitched roofs of Devon, there may be little, if any difference in the durability of the two materials because the comparatively woody stems of water reed take longer to dry out than combed straw and this hastens the process of decay.[28] In fact in *Thatch: Thatching in England 1790–1940, English Heritage Research Transactions, Vol 5*, Letts and Moir go so far as to imply that water reed may last less well in the South West than combed straw, describing a ten to twenty year figure for water reed in the South West as 'more appropriate' than the fifty to sixty years quoted in *The Thatcher's Craft*, while describing a figure of about forty years for combed straw in the same region as 'realistic'.[29] This reversal of what was, since the mid 20th century, an assumption on the part of many owners and some thatchers that water reed is the more durable material may be a case of over-correcting the figures in *The Thatcher's Craft*. However, the fact that the jury is still out (and at present lacks the information to make a good judgement) on the comparative durability of combed straw and water reed in Devon cannot be over-emphasised, although strong opinions continue to be voiced on both sides of the argument.

Artificial Thatch

Artificial thatch made a brief appearance in Devon in the 1960s, as surviving advertising material shows. There was still a handful of houses roofed in this fashion in the 1980s and there is at least one thatched this way at the time of writing (2001), in Maidencombe in Torbay. The fibre thatch was attached to a backing, which was then fitted to the roof structure. This version of artificial thatch looks very much what it is, a 'thin' roof on a flexible or flat boarded base with a textured finish. Quite apart from the radical visual difference between it and genuine thatch, it has none of the insulating properties of the genuine article.

Ornament

The previous chapter noted the use of ornamental block-cut ridges used on reconditioned houses between the wars. Burnett's c.1950 description of ornamental ridges employed by some thatchers has been quoted earlier in the chapter. In 1949, the address of the president of the Devonshire Association to its members also referred to the use of ornamental ridges, 'the shaping of an individual coat' used to announce the work of an individual thatcher, as well as an extreme example of using a roof rather like a billboard to advertise the status of its owner. He explained:

> *Each thatcher has his own technique and his one method of ridging, and he loves to apply some simple ornament of his own. It may be cross-strapping or the shaping of an additional coat. Sometimes a really elaborate design is achieved, as on a house at Bishop's Nympton, where the owner's year as Master of a Masonic Lodge was celebrated by suitable ornament in the thatch.*[30]

Artificial thatch, which was used on several Devon buildings in the 1960s/1970s. This version, known as 'Fibrethatch', was glass reinforced roofing panels with a simulated thatch. The literature claimed that tests indicated a life of 100 years.

Block-cut ridges have become more elaborate and far deeper since the 1950s, sometimes asked for by owners who like to put their stamp on the exterior of a building, sometimes insisted on by the thatcher. This fashion is particularly

Above: *A block-cut patterned knuckled ridge at Newport, Barnstaple, c.1949.*

Left: *Using a thatched roof for self-advertisment on a grand scale. The owner of this house in Bishop's Nympton announces that he has been made master of a Masonic Lodge in a unique example of patterned work shown in a photograph of c.1949.*

extreme in East Anglia and can perhaps be traced to a high degree of ornamentation in the 1930s promoted by Farman Brothers, a large water reed firm based in Norfolk. As we have seen, the earliest photographic evidence for ornamental ridges in Devon is in the late 19th century, in contrast with the plain finish to the vast majority of thatched houses. Narrow, ornamental block-cut ridges seem to have become fashionable on renovated houses between the wars, but continue to be very much in the minority in the photographic record. Highly elaborate very deep ridges, patterned with diamonds, the block cut into scallops and V shapes, as well as plainer but very deep block cut ridges, did not arrive in Devon much before the 1980s/1990s. There is no functional advantage in a ridge that is richly patterned.

Straw ornaments, owls, pheasants, rabbits and the like, began to appear in numbers on Devon ridges in the 1980s. No examples have been seen by the authors of this book in 19th century photographs. Their origin is reputed to be the thatched ornaments that were used to decorate ricks. Rick ornaments may be very ancient in origin and part of folk practice at harvest. As noted in the previous chapter, harvest celebrations in Devon, made jolly by large quantities of alcohol (provided as part of wages) celebrated the last sheaf or best ears of corn, accompanied by a chorus or chant. The sheaf was made into an ornament, woven with flowers. Baring-Gould, describing the practice in 1898, says that in living memory then, the ornament was afterwards taken to the granary. He does not give a reason but it may have been for magical 'protection' of the grain store. He does not mention ornaments used for decorating ricks, although this is known from other counties. Baring-Gould writes that, long after the custom had been abandoned, harvest ornaments were given a new and presumably more respectable lease of life, suspended in the church at harvest festival, a church festival which was itself a Victorian invention.

Sid Pearce, thatcher, of Wiltshire with one of his painted pheasant ornaments.

© Jo Cox 1994

Any connection between harvest ornaments and the straw figures that are sometimes added to thatched ridges appears to be tenuous. Their arrival in Devon is more likely to reflect the invention of individual thatchers and the swift transmission of ornamental detail from one part of the country to another after 1945. Mr Sid Pearce, a Wiltshire thatcher, remembers no patterned ridges on houses in Wiltshire (originally a county where crushed straw was used) before World War Two. He had an uncle who thatched in Norfolk and, seeing patterned ridges when visiting, he and his brother decided to try them out in Wiltshire, using card templates to ensure that the pattern was regular. He and his brother also claim to be the first thatchers who used the straw pheasant ornament on a roof, after seeing some real pheasants perching on a house in Woodford in Essex. This has become something of a trademark; Mr Pearce keeping one step ahead of competitors who copied the pheasant, by painting the pheasants he produces.

Thatch on New Houses (see colour page 13)

The revival of Devon thatching since World War Two has not led to many new thatched houses. Devon has been surprisingly slow to add to its historic stock of thatched houses and extend thatching into the modern period. Admirable work in West Dorset District, has ensured that approximately one in six new houses in villages are thatched. Achieving this figure involved close co-operation between Building Control and Fire Officers, which helped to resolve building regulation issues. 'The Dorset Model' is a leaflet explaining how this has been achieved. It ought to be a model for new work in Devon in the 21st century. There has been a revival of interest in Devon cob, including extensions in this material to existing buildings. Cob has been promoted through the Devon Earth Building Association with strong support from research projects at the University of Plymouth. It is disappointing that, to date, this has not developed into more new housing that is roofed with thatch. Both materials have excellent insulating properties and are locally available and renewable, important in an age where energy conservation is a major issue.

There has been a handful of new individual or pairs of thatched houses in the county, most in East Devon, but nothing to compare with Dorset's programme which includes a little hamlet on the outskirts of Abbotsbury where some of the new houses have slate and some thatched roofs. The architectural style of the new thatched buildings in Devon is very diverse. The Dower House at Gittisham, built in 1982, is an early example of a modern thatched house. It is on a particularly sensitive site, adjacent to the parish church and designed to fit into a thatched estate village. Hedgehog Cottage, Talaton, *(see colour page 13, plate 42)* is a 1990s interpretation of an old Devon farmhouse by a Dorset architect and takes many of its elements from the local tradition. Rose Cottage and its neighbour in Upottery, also 1990s, have rounded corners in breeze block, in imitation of the soft outlines of cob. Others have less connection to the plan and character of Devon's traditional buildings but at least their thatched roofs look more comfortable in the local landscape than modern tiled roofs.

The Dower House at Gittisham, a new building of 1982 added to an estate village where most of the roofs are still thatched.

© John R L Thorp 2001

Rediscovering Historic Devon Thatch

A popular interest in the construction and history of traditional regional buildings did not emerge much before before World War Two. There were exceptional authors who had pointed the way before 1945 but the great bulk of work to understand traditional buildings by recording, analysis and documentary research has been undertaken since the mid 1960s. This was not only because many were changing hands and new owners brought a fresh perspective to their new homes, but there was also a broader, historical recognition that these buildings could answer many questions about the history of how ordinary people, who left little in the way of paper documentation behind when they died, lived and worked.

Although the outlines of the development of rural houses in Devon in the 16th century had been established by the work of W G Hoskins, the detailed understanding of how that development had occurred in individual buildings was not clarified until later. As late as the 1960s, when smoke-blackened thatch was noticed, either by owners or thatchers, it was assumed that it was the result of a leaky chimney or unrecorded fire damage in the house. Pioneering work to analyse the development of Devon farmhouses was undertaken from the 1960s, particularly on the specific ways in which open hall houses had been modernised by the introduction of first floors and chimneys. The first recognition, in print, that smoke-blackened thatch had survived from the open hall phase of Devon's old farmhouses was published and illustrated in an article in 1973 in *Medieval Archaeology* by N W Alcock and Michael Laithwaite.

One of a 1990s pair of thatched houses at Colyford.

The 1980s Resurvey of Listed Buildings in Devon

In the 1980s Michael Heseltine, the then Secretary of State for the Department of the Environment, decided that it was time for a resurvey of 'listed' buildings – those buildings with statutory protection – in rural England. Most of rural Devon had previously been surveyed in the 1960s. The inspectors undertaking the work at that time had paid little attention to traditional regional buildings, but had concentrated on country houses and churches. Many important old houses which fulfilled the criteria for listing were missed in the 1960s, both because the interest in traditional buildings was small and specialised in that decade, but also because the age of Devon's farmhouses, in particular, is very difficult to judge from their comparatively plain exteriors.

Thanks to the pioneering work of Alcock and Laithwaite, the fieldworkers who undertook the resurvey in the 1980s and confirmed how many old houses survived in the county, took note of smoke-blackened thatch when they were able to get into attics and identify it. The survival of smoke-blackened thatch was sometimes a contributary factor to a building qualifying for listing, or listing at a high grade. It proved the antiquity of the building, it was recognised as being important fabric and, if it survived, it meant that some, and sometimes all, of the open hall roof structure survived as well.

The 1980s resurvey added large numbers of buildings to the list. Many of these were traditional and many were thatched, or had been thatched in the past. In Cheriton Fitzpaine parish, in Mid Devon, for example, there were six listed buildings prior to the resurvey of 1985. One was the church, only three were thatched houses or cottages. As a result of the resurvey, 40 additional houses, cottages or farm buildings were added to the list. Of the forty additional listings (some including more than one building, e.g. pairs of cottages), 24 were thatched. Six were formerly thatched, their roof coverings having been replaced with other materials.

Today there is a presumption in favour of retaining the thatch on thatched listed buildings. The 4 000 or so thatched listed buildings in Devon should provide assured work for the Devon thatchers maintaining them and secure thatching in Devon for the long-term future. It also means that owners keen to replace corrugated iron or asbestos roofs on their formerly thatched houses are likely to be encouraged to return to thatch, rather than to slate or any other roof covering. However, the statutory protection of listing that was applied to large numbers of thatched buildings in the 1980s, both in Devon and in other counties, opened up a lively national debate on how thatch could best be conserved and showed that the issues could not be adequately tackled solely at the level of statutory control over listed buildings.

Footnotes
[1] Rogers, 1976, 5.
[2] Duncan, 1947, 113.
[3] *Western Morning News*, 27.1.90.
[4] Quoted by Martin Barratt, a loss adjuster, at a conference on fighting thatched fires in 2001.
[5] The authors are grateful to Terry Hughes for information on the regulation of blue slates.
[6] *Western Morning News*, 9.12.46.
[7] Woods, 1949, 205.
[8] RIB minutes 1950-1952, Public RO, MAFF 113/99 XC6552.
[9] Rogers, 1976, 27.
[10] Williams, 1958, 31-32.
[11] Williams, 1958, 33.
[12] Woods, 1949, 205.
[13] Letts in Cox and Letts, 2000, 16-25.
[14] Letts in Cox and Letts, 2000, 18.
[15] Rex Gardner, county organiser of the Devon Rural Industries Committee, *Western Morning News*, 2.12.55.
[16] Letts, Cox and Letts, 2000, 18.
[17] Public RO, MAFF 113/522 Report of the Rural Industries Organiser in Devon 1957.
[18] Letts in Cox and Letts, 2000, 22.
[19] Letts in Cox and Letts, 2000, 16-25.
[20] *Pers. comm.* Mr Glover's knowledge of the history of the reed comber attachment to the threshing machine and its survival was second to none. He reckoned that Murch, one of the three companies who produced the machine, manufactured between 1500 and 2000 in all. His death in 2000 was a serious loss to the history of Devon farming machinery.
[21] He had been a devout Labour Party supporter and stood for Westmorland in 1924 and Lancaster in 1929.

22 Burnett, n.d., c.1950, 12.
23 Larry Keefe, *pers. comm.*
24 Tristan Johnson, *pers. comm.*
25 'Thatch as Thatch Can', *The Field*, 2.6.1960, 1074.
26 *The Thatcher's Craft*, f.p. 1960, 1981 edn., 2.
27 *South Devon Journal*, 31.10. 1962.
28 Moir and Letts, 1999, 95.
29 Moir and Letts, 1999, 98.
30 Oliver, *TDA*, Vol 81, 1949, Plate 16, fig.2.

CONSERVING DEVON'S THATCHING TRADITION

Fears that thatch would be replaced by corrugated iron motivated Mark Kennaway's Devon campaign to promote thatch in the early 20th century. In the same vein, the interventions of the Rural Industries Bureau and its successor organisations from c.1950–1970 were driven by the anxiety that English thatch might disappear, losing useful rural employment. What kind of thatch was preserved was not of prime interest to the Bureau, so long as it performed adequately enough for the demand to hold up in a competitive world. By the late 1980s the fear that English thatch might disappear altogether had receded. Thatch that survived was now safeguarded by the enthusiasm of owners, by the economic value it added to houses, and by the statutory protection given to the majority of thatched buildings listed during the government resurvey of rural buildings *(see colour pages 14 and 15)*. New owners of houses in rural areas were more likely to replace corrugated iron and asbestos with new thatch than the other way round. Confidence in the survival of thatch, as well as the first efforts to apply Listed Building control to thatched buildings, opened up some of the more subtle aspects of how its regional variations and detail might best be conserved.

As we have seen, Devon thatching has contributed far more than practical and appealing roofs to the county's buildings. It also represents a long tradition of craft skills: in thatching, tool-making, machine-building and in farming, passed down by example and practice since before the early 14th century. Combed straw roofs are a distinctive part of the Devon farmed landscape and a powerful link to the absorbing story of the historic economy of the county, its periods of prosperity and comparative poverty. It should be plain that Listed Building control is a limited instrument for tackling all the conservation issues that arise from a good understanding of thatching in Devon. It has the potential to protect the traditional method and appearance of thatched roofs in the county and reduce the risk of losses to archaeology. However, a much broader perspective on Devon thatching is needed if all that is valuable and eloquent about the tradition is to survive.

Conservation of Thatching through Listed Building Control

Devon was not in the forefront of the first efforts by County and District Planning Departments to tackle the conservation of thatch on listed buildings. The fact that overcoated water reed looks very similar to combed straw meant that the change of materials in the county did not usually have a major impact on the appearance of thatched roofs, especially if the finish was plain. The Dartmoor National Park Authority introduced a scheme in the 1980s restricting grant-aid for thatching on listed buildings to combed straw to encourage owners to use the traditional material. The percentage of grant and its size have increased since.[1] Requests for grant-aid for maintaining thatch on listed buildings was one of the considerations that gave thatching a high profile in the 1980s and 1990s. Local Planning Authorities have modest annual budgets for grant-aiding listed build-

Thatch, like cob, is an excellent insulating material. It keeps a house cool in summer and warm in winter. It would have been difficult to resist warming up in the 'Digger's Rest' at Woodbury Salterton in the snow of 1962.

ings and some districts noticed that a high proportion of their limited funds was being spent on thatching. This included thatch that was different in method and detail to what had previously been on the roof. This encouraged conservation officers to undertake research into how? and why? thatch was changing and the rate of change in a selected area. It was the Midlands counties with a crushed straw tradition that took the lead. Conservation officers in Northamptonshire noticed that their regional method of thatching was fast disappearing. It was being replaced, thanks to the success of the Bureau's enthusiasm for combed straw and for water reed, at a pace that, if continued, would result in the complete extinction of crushed straw roofs in the county. The same changes were occurring in other counties, too. The Local Planning Authorities in Northamptonshire decided to control the change by requiring Listed Building Consent for any proposal to replace a crushed straw roof with either water reed or combed straw on a listed building and, as a general rule, refusing consent for the change. Local Planning Authorities in other counties began to follow suit, tailoring policies to the local thatch in their area.

Real problems were encountered in the introduction of thatching policies towards listed buildings. Compared with many other regional building materials, there was a shortage of agreed information on most aspects of thatching. Conservation officers struggled to understand the technicalities of one method of thatching compared with another. Thatchers were the only source of good information and some were understandably reluctant to give away craft secrets, especially to Local Planning Authority officials. In most areas there was little accessible published history or agreement, including amongst thatchers, on which thatching methods and details had been common in the past. Changes since World War Two had obscured the picture of what really was 'traditional' in many places. All the early discussions about the value of maintaining such regional variations that had survived the post 1945 changes were bedevilled by

Symbolic of all the changes to regional thatching traditions since 1950, as well as changes to old buildings, this Bedfordshire house included all three of the principal types of thatch in 1995: crushed straw (long straw) on the house, West Country combed straw on the extension to the right and water reed on the garden room to the front. The visual differences between the types of thatching are dominated by fancy ridges applied to all.

Left and below left: *The Sir John Barleycorn pub in Hampshire in the early 1950s, thatched with crushed straw, Hampshire's traditional straw thatch. Later in the 1950s, it was rethatched in combed straw. This is one of many examples of diluting regional thatching traditions after 1945, helped along by the Rural Industries Bureau.*

the figures for longevity published in *The Thatcher's Craft*. The published figures, even if they had been reliable, did not cover the issue of cost-effectiveness, given that thatching with straw was usually less expensive than using water reed.

In practice, the application of conservation policies and Listed Building Consent to thatching in the 1980s and 1990s reflected different priorities from one Local Planning Authority to another. Stemming the 20th century fashion for deep, patterned ridges was the prime concern in some districts. Conservation officers made the point that the arrival of a patterned ridge on a house was a major change to the proportions, external appearance and therefore to the character of the building. Some Local Planning Authorities therefore required owners to apply for Listed Building Consent when it was proposed to replace the earlier, simpler forms of the flush or narrow block-cut ridges with heavily ornamented ridges.

A deep patterned ridge on a traditional house in Whimple.

Ridges do not last for very long before they need renewing. In some areas they were therefore regarded as a lower priority than ensuring that the previous thatching method on the roof was maintained when a building was rethatched. If houses had been rethatched since 1950 using a method that had previously been unknown in the locality, some Conservation Officers (although not in Devon) tried to persuade the owner to revert to the pre-1950 method of thatching, while others decided that there should be a 'like-for-like' philosophy, and that the previous method of rethatching should be maintained, even if it was a relatively recent change. Both these positions could be justified as good conservation practice, but they were not consistent with each other. The inconsistency was both a puzzle and annoyance to thatchers, some of whom found themselves working in adjacent Local Planning Authorities employing contrasting systems of control.

There were also inconsistencies in the way thatchers reacted to the introduction of Listed Building Consent for proposed changes to thatching. Some were sympathetic, holding strong views on the desirability of maintaining regional thatching materials and methods. A water reed thatcher from Norfolk interviewed by the *Guardian* expressed the sense of possession that some thatchers felt about their local thatching when he complained about water reed from Norfolk being used in the 'straw' counties:

> *They comes and sneaks it away under our noses... By rights they oughter keep to straw, what God made their natural material.* [2]

John Cousins, a Suffolk thatcher, made the same point, this time about the two straw traditions in 1989:

> *I'm damn sure that I don't want to see combed wheat reed in Suffolk and I'm just as sure they don't want to see long straw down in Devon.* [3]

Some thatchers considered that a requirement for a particular method of thatching on the roof of a listed building at least had the advantage of providing a level playing field for pricing up for a job against competition. It cut out the 'sales pitch' in which a thatcher might win a job against competitors on the strength of the argument he or she could make for using one thatching method in favour of another.

Other thatchers were not best pleased to find that there were any restrictions at all on what they might put on the roof, when there had been none before. The fact that thatchers are craftsmen does not automatically mean that they are dedicated to conservation, beyond wishing to see thatch replaced with thatch. Diverse views about the value of conservation were sharpened by existing differences within the thatching industry, particularly concerns about standards and how these related to business practice in an increasingly commercial environment. The economic boom years of the 1980s brought not only new owners of thatched buildings, it also brought newcomer thatchers to what was a moderately profitable occupation. Estimated numbers of thatchers in Devon rose from 45 in 1972 to 78 in 1992. Some had a business background very different from that of old thatching families and pursued work with all the competitive vigour of modern business practice. Like farming, thatching in some quarters became more of a business and less of a way of life. Like farming, there was a huge range of variety in how thatching businesses were run. In the 1980s there was still at least one working thatcher in Devon who did not have a telephone at home, let alone a mobile phone. There were also larger firms, some of whom also grew straw for thatching commercially and imported water reed to supply other thatchers.

Attitudes to Listed Building controls were complicated by commercial and practical considerations. In any region some thatchers specialise in a particular method of thatching. This may be a method traditional to the region, or one that has arrived since 1945. It was inevitable that a thatcher skilled in fitting, say, crushed straw but perhaps unaccustomed to, or even untrained in using water reed, would advise an owner that crushed straw was the right thatching method for the building. Equally, a thatcher who specialised in using water reed and was perhaps also a water reed importer and agent, naturally wanted to see that material used in preference to either of the straws. These were legitimate commercial interests but it was hard to disentangle them from the sincere belief, held by some thatchers, in the superiority of one thatching method over another. It was also quite impossible to disentangle either commercial interests or sincere commitment from 'fact' in the absence of reliable figures for durability or for cost-effectiveness.

Before the vast majority of thatched buildings were given statutory protection by listing, thatchers were the decision-makers about how a building was rethatched and what material was used. Rethatching an old roof occurs when the need arises. It is not usually part of a building project in which anyone other than the thatcher is in charge. The picture was rather different before World War Two, when there were closer links between the owners of thatched houses and thatchers. In straw-thatching regions an owner might well have thatched a rick or farm building himself as well as supplying the material to the thatcher. He was likely to have a much keener appreciation of thatching skills than most owners had in the 1980s and 1990s, and may have discussed the thatcher's work with him from the viewpoint of working knowledge. Non-farming owners of thatched houses found thatching something of a mystery. It was too specialised for an owner to have tried it out themselves, as they might have tried out carpentry or bricklaying. All this contributed to a perception that thatching was an arcane art to non-practitioners of the craft and that only the thatcher, rather than the owner, was placed to take responsibility for the choice of what method of thatching should be employed and the details of finishing the roof. It was difficult for some thatchers to accept that the Local Planning Authority might also have a say in what should go on the roof, but also impossible, given how many thatched buildings had been listed, for them to avoid working on listed buildings.

The application of thatch conservation policies was bound to have teething problems given that they were not always consistent from area to area, and affected an industry that prided itself on independence and had conflicting opinions about the value of those policies. Journalists like stories where there is 'someone to blame'. Thatch stories make good newspaper copy and headlines pleasing to editors: 'the short straw', 'men of straw' and so on. There was a good deal of press attention devoted to local difficulties between thatchers and Local Planning Authorities in the late 1980s and early 1990s. There was also attention directed to disagreements between the two national thatching bodies and between individual thatching firms. At times in the 1990s the mixture of interests seemed explosive and the issues on which everybody agreed (the importance of high standards of craftsmanship and the need to ensure the availability of good quality materials) were set aside. Most of the fireworks went off in the Midlands. Devon, Somerset and Cornwall largely escaped. There was no media attention in counties and districts, Somerset being one, where conservation officers and local thatchers, particularly the MTA, discussed the issues and developed acceptable conservation policies amicably.

As the most fortunate county for the survival of thatch, Devon has also been fortunate, in one sense, in the nature of change after 1960. In contrast to the highly visible changes occurring in the Midlands, the post 1960 change of method in Devon – from combed straw to water reed – can be managed by a skilful thatcher with relatively little impact on the external appearance of a building (*see colour page 12, plates 34 and 35*). Planning committees could see that a fancy ridge – which might be applied for the first time to a house rethatched with either combed straw or water reed – had an impact on the character of a building, but it can be very difficult to distinguish between the texture of a water reed or combed straw overcoat.

The sheer power of the combed straw tradition, as we have seen, meant that Devon thatchers mostly applied water reed, as they had applied combed straw, by overcoating. This meant that the potentially damaging effects of the change – the loss, for example, of smoke-blackened thatch or of old roof timbers – was less prevalent or perhaps less noticed (because of the relatively high level of survival as a starting point) than in other counties.

Nevertheless, losses did occur. Not all Devon thatchers knew that smoke-blackened thatch was likely to be pre-1550, or that it was evidence of the open hall phase of a house. Some smoke-blackened thatch, although we do not know how much, was lost. Roofs are stripped from the outside and the first a thatcher might know of the existence of medieval thatch was the handfuls of blackened material dropped down into the skip. There was no reason why thatchers should know how important historic roof structures are to a good understanding of the development of a building. Roof carpentry – thatching laths, rafters and occasionally entire roofs, including pre-1550 structures – were sometimes replaced by thatchers who did not know their historic value. Thatchers could not be expected automatically to appreciate the rarity of easily-damaged elements of roofs, which they largely saw when working (if they had to strip the thatch back that far) from above and not from inside the attic, where the details can best be appreciated.

The issue of longevity did arise. It was a sensitive one in Devon, in a county that had suffered in the 1970s from 'premature decay' on a handful of both combed straw and, later, water reed roofs. Roofs suffering from premature decay had usually been thatched using materials that gave every appearance of being of good quality. Nevertheless they began to rot in patches, sometimes as soon as eight years, or earlier, after they had been recoated. The problem raised the question of how thatchers can ensure that the material they use is of good quality, and who should be responsible for the cost of rethatching if a roof fails before it should. The problem still occurs, but only very occasionally and is not confined to Devon.

The view that water reed is a more durable material than straw, an inheritance from the Rural Industries Bureau and *The Thatcher's Craft*, persisted. Some Devon thatchers believe it lasts longer than combed straw and owners who also believe this may specifically ask for it to be used in place of combed straw. It cannot be repeated too often that it is far from certain that water reed lasts longer than combed straw in Devon. Very few people familiar with thatch in the county would now claim that overcoated water reed consistently lasts, in the Devon climate, on the shallow-pitched roofs of the county, for the fifty to sixty years quoted, with caveats, in *The Thatcher's Craft*. These figures were provided at a time when there was little water reed used in Devon and were based on the 'strip and single coat' method employed in East Anglia. Whether or not the figures for longevity are actually pretty much the same for water reed and combed straw in Devon, as has been suggested by Moir and Letts, remains to be seen. It would be a long project that could muster statistically-reliable 'general' figures and these could never give a definite figure for an individual building. It would be enormously helpful if thatchers, owners and Local Planning Authorities could co-operate in raising some actual figures for the durability of thatch on individual roofs with information about variety and source as well as the siting of the building.[4]

Some Local Planning Authority documents in Devon gave official status to the assumption that water reed lasted longer than straw in Devon. In the early 1990s a straw grower in South Molton took the North Devon Local Planning Authority to task for producing a leaflet in which it was suggested that water reed was the better of the two materials. He complained in the national press that water reed was changing the appearance of traditional buildings in the county and should be banned. The Director of Planning was unrepentant and responded by saying that:

> given the considerable expense in owning a thatched property and given the fact that it's very difficult to distinguish the types of thatching material visually, it is not thought that there is an overriding case for insisting on the sole use of wheat reed.[5]

There was an attempt in the Dartmoor National Park to confine grant-aid for thatching to combed straw, to encourage its continued use in an area where conservation had an especially high profile. One district decided to introduce

Premature decay. Combed straw in trouble after six years. Premature decay, which was noticed first in Devon but is also known in other counties, affected a small number of combed straw and, later, water reed roofs, particularly in the 1970s and 1980s. The cause or causes are not understood.

a requirement for Listed Building Consent for a change of materials. This was done principally to gain information about the speed of replacement, so that the Local planning Authority could make an informed decision on whether it needed a clear thatching conservation policy, but in practice it has always given consent for a change from combed straw to water reed.

While Devon took a relaxed attitude to the conservation of thatch at the level of building control, the troubles in other counties brought English Heritage, as the lead conservation body in England, into the debate. Research on the archaeo-botany and history of thatch was commissioned. In the late 1990s work by John Letts identified even more smoke-blackened straw thatch in Devon, as well as discovering some, although relatively little, surviving in other counties. This wider view of pre-1550 thatch confirmed just how rare it is, and the unusually high level of survival in Devon. Letts' publication of 1999, *Smoke Blackened Thatch*, analysed the archaeo-botanical interest of the material in detail. The book also brought to light, for the first time, how significant the loss of straw length and the changes in wheat-breeding had been to thatching. Subsequent publications in the English Heritage Research Transactions series on the general history of English thatching provided a background to the importance of thatching and the pattern of change to its traditions. Conferences and seminars aired the issues, both of thatching history and thatch conservation. In November 1999 HRH The Prince of Wales, who has a particular interest in the conservation of historic plants and therefore in the varieties of wheat used in thatch, was one of several speakers at a conference attended by thatchers, growers of thatching straw and conservation officers, with speakers from each group.

Conservation officers, English Heritage inspectors, historians and thatchers at a seminar, including thatching demonstrations, arranged by the National Society of Master Thatchers to discuss research on the history of thatching and conservation issues.

© Jo Cox 1995

In June 2000, English Heritage produced *Thatch and Thatching: a guidance note* outlining their views on 'the question of how far the materials and methods of thatching should be influenced by the concerns of conservation or controlled by the planning process'. This document endeavoured to address all the problems that had arisen during the early efforts to apply Listed Building Consent to thatching as well as the issues of building regulations, fire and safety as they apply to thatched buildings.

The guidance note concluded that, when listed buildings were being re-thatched, Listed Building Consent was required for:

- a proposed removal of material which is clearly of archaelogical or historic importance requires consent. Smoke-blackened material is usually medieval or at the latest seeventeenth century, and always falls into this category, as would be the case with any other material of this age.
- a proposed change of material between water reed and straw, or any other botanically distinct species, requires consent. This includes the covering of one material by another in the technique called 'spar-coating'.
- a proposed change of material between combed wheat reed and long straw, which may be botanically identical but have been differently prepared, requires consent.
- a proposed change of thatching method between the main types as described requires consent.
- a proposed change of external appearance or surface configuration, such as the formation of a different ridge, requires consent.

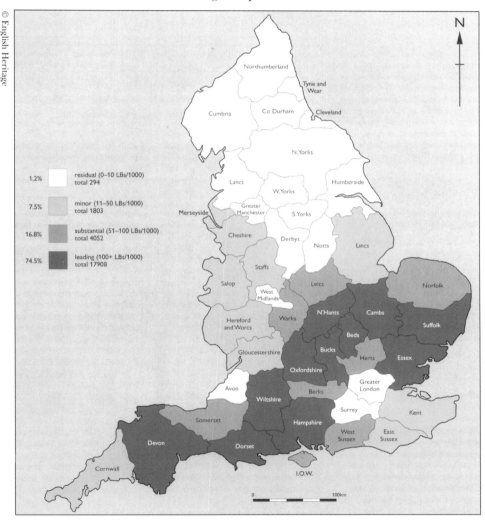

Map showing listed thatched buildings as a proportion of the total listed buildings for each county reproduced from English Heritage's Thatch and Thatching: a guidance note, *2000.*

This, of course, simply represents guidance, and only as it applies to thatching on listed buildings. Each Local Planning Authority in Devon will have to decide whether and how they may wish to apply the guidance, which does not apply to thatched buildings that are not listed. There are also many other changes that an owner might consider making to a listed building that would need Listed Building Consent in addition to the suggested requirements for thatching. Most owners know if their building is listed or not and their thatcher will probably ask them, but if either owner or thatcher is uncertain, they can find out by asking their Local Planning Authority.

Conservation: the wider picture

Extending the Thatching Tradition
As an excellent natural insulating material, all thatch contributes to domestic energy conservation. As a grown material all thatch, in theory, is a renewable resource and therefore truly sustainable. It richly deserves to be used on new houses in the county, following West Dorset's lead. This would help to conserve the tradition by extending it into the future. It would also benefit the appearance of Devon's new housing. Most of this is currently in a national house-builders' style, originally borrowed from the brick and tile vernacular tradition of the South East diluted through generations of suburban houses all over England. It has no roots at all in the county's own building tradition. Encouraging thatch on a percentage of new development in the county would require policies in favour of it in the Local Plans which set out the development control policies of Local Planning Authorities. This would need encouragement from planning and development control officers and the support of local politicians as well as the electorate and house-builders. Designing new houses for thatch requires co-operation between house-builders and thatchers, so that thatchers can explain which forms of roof design are thatchable. Thatchers in Devon are certainly ready to co-operate. If house-builders can manage this with Dorset thatchers there is no reason why it could not be done here. With the county committed to building 75 800 new dwellings within the period 1995–2011, the sooner this happens the better.

Understanding the Performance of Thatch
The performance of thatch – how long it lasts – is a major consideration for owners who pay for it. Performance is affected by a number of factors which will be different for every building. Some have to be lived with, but there are others where the grower, the thatcher and the owner can all contribute in getting the best out of thatch. The location of the building is significant. Water close by or overhanging trees can create persistently damp micro-climates which can speed up decay. Owners should avoid planting trees that overhang thatch and proceed with caution if planning to create large stretches of water close to thatch. On south-facing pitches, thatch can be exposed to extremes of temperature, with a moisture-laden early morning atmosphere succeeded by hot direct sunlight. This can speed up decay and many owners find that the south-facing pitch of their house may need rethatching sooner than the north-facing pitch which is not exposed to the same extreme changes of temperature.

The pitch and design of the roof influence thatch performance. Any proposed changes to the design of a roof, including the insertion of dormers and extensions, should be talked through with a thatcher, as well as the Local Planning Authority if Listed Building Consent is required, to make sure that the design is suitable for thatching. Owners cannot expect to rely on every architect or surveyor to get the design of additions and extensions to the roof right for thatch; not all have the relevant experience. It is cheaper in the long run to pay for the advice of a thatcher from the outset and produce a design that works. The relatively slack pitches of traditional Devon roofs can be exacerbated by methods of rethatching that flatten out the pitch of the thatch. Here the owner needs to rely on the skill and judgment of a good thatcher, taking into consideration the interest of any historic material when stripping off the previous coat. The quality of the thatcher and his technique is critical for a good performance roof.

A good thatcher will adjust technique to get the most out of the materials used on any particular roof. It is worth making every effort to find a good thatcher and waiting for him or her if necessary.

A tree overhanging the right end of this house in Thorverton is responsible for the visible difference in speed of decay of the thatch.

A good thatcher will seek out the best material that can be found, given the constraints of the job but, like the owner, is dependent on a good grower who, in turn, is reliant to some extent on the nature of the season.

Maintenance

Owners can make a major contribution to the conservation of thatch by keeping it well-maintained. Keeping a thatched roof in good condition is crucial to the survival of the house, protecting it from the weather. This must be the first concern of an owner as well as the thatcher. Thatched roofs need regular maintenance to keep them watertight and in good shape. Re-ridging usually needs to be done at intervals of ten to fifteen years, although some may need more frequent attention and six to twelve years may be more appropriate in Devon. Patching can extend the effective working life of a roof. If a roof has been neglected, the thatcher will have to remove more material to find a sound base for fixing the new thatch, and archaeologically interesting old layers of straw may be lost unnecessarily.

Deers Leap and Little Deers Leap in Newton St Cyres, a medieval house divided into two. Patching, like regular reridging, extends the life of thatch.

Good maintenance depends on a good understanding on the part of the owner of the difficulties a thatcher may encounter. It is worth being patient and waiting for a good thatcher, who will be struggling to organise a timetable for work and liable to be affected by bad weather *(see colour page 16)*. If thatchers are pricing up competetively, owners should make sure they are pricing up for the same specification for work. Owners should also discuss with their thatcher the possibility of extra costs that cannot be identified until some stripping has occurred and recognise that, for example, a chimney shaft may be in poor condition and need repair. They should establish whether the thatcher should do this work or arrange for it to be done, or whether the owner might want another contractor to be involved.

Reducing Fire Risk

For the sake, firstly of the people who live in the house and the safety of fire fighters, and then for the preservation of the building and valuables in it, taking sensible precautions to reduce the risk of fire damage is an essential aspect of maintenance for owners. Thatch is much less of a fire risk than was imagined in the 19th century, provided sensible precautions are taken. Nevertheless between 12 and 15 serious thatch fires occur in Devon every year. They are quite different from house fires where thatch is not the roofing material. If they are caught in time, it is the thatch that is usually lost. If the main roof timbers are oak, these sometimes survive. Thatch fires have to be dealt with in a very specialised way by firefighters. Thatch is designed to throw off water, and this means that the most effective approach is to pull off the thatch beyond the fire. Owners and thatchers both have a reponsibility for ensuring that if wire netting is used, it is fixed in such a way that it can be removed easily and quickly by fire fighters. Netting can be a problem if overhead power cabling comes down during a fire and makes the roof 'live'. Although the records of the modern fire brigade show that no lives have been lost in recent years, thatch fires (like any others) potentially put lives at risk and injuries to firefighters dealing with thatch

Lower Southwood, Rockbeare, in 1992, after a thatch fire.

fires are all too common. Quite apart from the potential risk to life, fires where property is damaged and personal possessions are lost are a horrible and traumatic experience. Anyone who has direct experience of a thatch fire knows that it is worth both the owner and thatcher taking trouble to keep risks to a minimum.

Fighting a fire at Buckhurst Cottage, Plymtree in 1997.

All owners and occupiers of thatched houses should be prepared for providing the fire brigade with the information they need, should an emergency arise. This will be the current formally recognised address; a six-figure grid reference and clear instructions for the best way for a large vehicle to get to the building. Firefighters should also be informed of the nearest adequate supplies of water. This information should be in a prominent place, close to the phone for anyone who may be looking after the house. It should also be given to neighbours, along with a key, in case of fire when an owner is away.

Most thatch fires start because of a problem with the chimney or fireplace. Problems include design, condition and use. Sparks from a chimney or any other source landing on the thatch are no longer thought to be a common cause of fire, but the top of the chimney or the chimney pot needs to be sufficiently distant from the thatch to allow free airspace for any burning material from the fire to be blown away. Spark arresters, which were once thought a sensible form of fire protection and were insisted on by some insurance companies, are now generally regarded as more of a hazard than a help. They are difficult to keep well-maintained and without regular maintenance clog up and represent a hazard. The condition of the chimney shaft, especially where it abuts the thatch, is critical and should be kept in good repair. The thatcher is the only person likely to see the 'buried' section of the stack in the thatch and should check the soundness of the construction (which may be masonry, brick, or cob) when rethatching. If the building is listed and either the inspection or remedy (or both) might cause damage to roof timbers, the owner should ask the advice of the conservation officer as well as the local Fire Safety Officer. An owner should ask their thatcher to take full responsibility, if wire netting is being used, for fixing it in a way acceptable to the fire brigade, making sure that it can easily be removed and will cause no delays if there should be a fire and the thatch has to be pulled off the roof.

Most old chimneys in Devon were originally designed when wood was the fuel burned. The fire was likely to be kept in all the year round and at a low temperature for economy's sake and the convenience of cooking. It was also likely to burn in a draughty environment that gave plenty of ventilation. The careful seasoning of firewood in a wood pile and chopping wood into sensible lengths for use were a part of the labour of everyday life. Today, open fires and fires in woodburners are more likely to be lit infrequently, on special occasions, and burnt at a higher temperature using green wood and with less consistent supervision than in a working farmhouse kitchen. The higher temperatures that modern owners expect from fires has meant that Fire Safety Officers now recommend a vertical heat barrier between the chimney shaft and the thatch, within the thatch, to avoid the transmission of heat from the chimney shaft to the thatch, which can become dry, smoulder and eventually burn. These are best fitted when a roof is being rethatched. Flue linings and woodburning stoves, if incorrectly fitted (which they often are), or defective, can cause fire. Chimneys should be regularly swept to clear away combustible soot crust and birds nests. If wood is used it should be seasoned, and logs ready for burning should be stored where they are not at risk from catching fire from a spark. Any proposed change to the way a fireplace is used or the way a room with a fire is ventilated should be thought through in terms of any risks it might bring to the thatch and owners should seek the advice of the Fire Safety Officer. Free advice from this quarter is an under-used service.

Electrical installations in or near thatch are a common cause of fire. Thatch insurance companies have good reasons for insisting on a high standard of safety in electrical installations in thatched houses and most require a smoke alarm under the ridge of the thatch, connected to alarm systems in the rest of the house. If they do not, it is sensible for owners to have one fitted anyway and ensure that it is well-maintained. Modern living in old thatched buildings has often directed a whole range of electrical services into the attic spaces. In principal the use of electrical circuits in or near thatch should be kept to a minimum and, where possible, electrical installations should be designed in conjunction with the advice of Fire Safety Officers. Wiring in or near thatch should be run in trunking or conduits, and lights in roof spaces should be enclosed to protect thatch from heat or electrical faults.

Any contractors, particularly plumbers or painters, who may use equipment or processes that produce heat and are working under or near thatch, should be asked to think of alternative ways of working and produce a written specification to the owner of what they intend to do and a statement of their insurance position. If in doubt, owners can always ask the advice of local Fire Safety Officers or Building Control Officers.

Owners themselves can be responsible for thatch fires. There are numerous horror stories ranging from risky DIY work with heat-producing equipment, to the folly of lighting a barbecue directly under the thatch eaves, bonfires lit near thatch, or even using thatch as a foundation for letting off rockets on November 5th.

There can be conflicts of interest between the needs of fire safety and thatch conservation. Fire resistant board or impermeable membranes introduced under the thatch can reduce ventilation and may reduce the life of thatch, unless carefully designed and kept well back from the underside of the straw or water reed. Soaking thatch with fire retardants before use is known to have been employed in the 1930s, and probably long before. There are modern versions of the system. English Heritage's guidance note states that the balance of evidence 'seems to be against modifying the basic behaviour of the materials, which could adversely affect the roof's performance'.

Some roofspaces are divided up vertically by what can be old and interesting partitions. It makes good sense to have roof hatch access to every compartment of the roof space from the floor below, and big enough for a fire fighter with equipment to get through without a struggle. Good access to all parts of the roof space also allows both thatcher and owner to look at the underside of the roof, check the condition of the thatch and timbers from below and consider the interest of roof timbers and their details. If timbers in a listed building are in poor condition and need repair or replacement the Local Planning Authority should be asked to advise. In listed buildings it is usually less damaging to the historic fabric to make ceiling hatches than trying to cut access through the vertical partitions in the roofspace, but there are exceptions and the advice of the conservation officer should be taken.

Archaeology
On the historical side, from the perspective of archaeology, Devon straw roofs include the physical evidence of crops that may be centuries old. Successive layers are a witness to how cereal crops have changed and what else was growing with them in the fields. Surviving evidence of historic methods of laying and fixing are a record, with unique variations in each roof, of craft practice in the past. Old thatch is part of the historic fabric of a building and can be crucial in explaining its development. As we have seen, the survival of smoke-blackened thatch is proof of the open hall phase of the house and later phases of surviving straw may also be of real interest. A careful balance needs to be struck between the amount of old straw a thatcher needs to strip to get down to a sound base for fixing new thatch and the archaeological interest of what is being stripped. Smoke-blackened thatch should never be stripped off a listed or unlisted building without asking the conservation officer for advice.

Smoke-blackened thatch can only survive on buildings erected before c.1550 and only on houses where the thatched roof has been kept decently maintained ever since. The house must have escaped any single period of serious neglect which required completely stripping the roof. It must have escaped retimbering the roof during periods of change, re-covering the roof in alternative materials, and thatch fire. It is astonishing that we have any left at all and each and every one of the approximately 180 surviving examples in the county deserves to be looked after with the greatest care.

Thatch is literally attached to the carpentry, and may also be fixed to the wall-tops, of the building. Devon's roof carpentry, and the survival of so much early roof carpentry in the county, is as fascinating as its thatch. Before 1700 there are distinctive local styles of roof design developed by local carpenters who converted the resources, supplied by the Devon landscape, into buildings. Oak roof timbers, as has only recently been discovered through tree-ring dating, are a profound connection back to the land management of the past in the pattern and ways of growing and managing oak for building. Like early straw thatch, early oak roof timbers are irreplaceable. In the course of time, as tree-ring dating is more widely applied to softwood, the historic development and pattern of carpentry using pine will also be better understood. It is a rare case where important archaeology, whether straw, old fixings, or carpentry, cannot be kept or carefully repaired, rather than replaced. We have lost quite enough in Devon already. Treating old thatch and old buildings with the respect they and their makers, past and present, deserve is possible, so long as some thought and understanding are applied. This means good communication and good appreciation of the different concerns of owners, thatchers and conservation officers.

The Historic Aesthetics of the Thatched Roof
On traditional Devon buildings, there is no evidence of the use of ornamental ridges before the late 19th century. A real fashion for them does not appear until between World War One and World War Two. Photographs in this book show just how much they can affect the external appearance of a building, espe-

cially one with a simple profile. They have no practical advantage over a plain wrapover or butts up ridge and they are more costly to fit. Whatever Local Planning Authorities decide to do about patterned ridges in the light of the English Heritage guidance note, any owner keen to preserve the traditional character of their building, whether or not it is listed, should ask their thatcher for their flush ridge to be repeated when a house is reridged or should return to one next time the ridge is replaced.

Rethatching can change the shape of a roof. Owners who like the general shape of their roof as it is should discuss this with their thatcher to make sure that they are not disappointed by the results of a rethatch.

The Combed Straw Tradition and Water Reed

Beyond the question of maintaining thatch and guiding change to it in such a way that losses are as small as possible, there is also the wider issue of the contribution combed straw thatch has made, and continues to make, to Devon farming and therefore to the Devon landscape and to the agricultural economy of the county. At the time of writing competition from water reed is brisk and the balance has tilted towards that material since about 1980. The figures for the annual gross aggregate demand for water reed in England in 1989 showed that of the 1 438 500 bunches imported, Devon and Cornwall were estimated to absorb 500 000 bunches, or rather more than one third of the total, as well as more than all the domestic water reed production put together, which was 422 500 bunches.[6]

Although some Devon thatchers continue to use combed straw only, many scarcely ever use the material, the vast bulk of their work being with water reed. The Devon Master Thatchers' Association has already had to consider how existing members might respond to a request for membership from a thatcher whose only experience was water reed, and who was unable to thatch in traditional Devon combed straw. Such a request has not yet been received, but it can only be a matter of time.

Seeking to preserve the tradition of straw roofs in the county is much more than an argument for a traditional local roofing material. The conservation of the combed straw tradition has many layers of importance to the county, some better understood than others. The potential wildlife benefits of the methods of growing thatching straw are unknown but, given the low levels of nitrates generally used and a cautious attitude to herbicides and fungicides, there are undoubtedly some. These are most likely to operate in groups of connected fields on farms where thatching straw has been a speciality for a long period of time. The use of hazel sways and spars for fitting the material helps to sustain the underwood industry and this has benefits to woodland and wildlife.

Thatching straw provides a local market for farmers who produce a crop for which there is a real demand and which can be produced economically on farms that are small by today's standards. It can also be grown in small fields relative to commercial grain crops harvested by combines. There are landscape benefits by virtue of not adding to pressures to enlarge Devon's fields. Combed straw is a crop that provides an option – although not an easy one – for some of Devon's small farms. Growing and producing combed straw is a skilled business and a long way from being a solution to all the problems confronted by small farmers in the county in the 21st century, but it does make a significant contribution to the economy of some small farms.

There are risks attached to growing and producing combed straw. There are good and bad seasons, and these may affect some Devon producers more than others in any one year, depending on localised conditions. A wet spring

followed by a dry summer may mean that the plants have not developed a good enough root system to flourish when there is a shortage of rain. Wind and rain can cause localised or sometimes widespsread 'lodging', when the crop is flattened or buckles in the field. Inclement weather at harvest time can mean that the ideal period of harvest is 'missed'. All these are the age-old problems and risks of farming. They are exacerbated by the unintentionally absurd consequences of the regulations surrounding grain-growing described in Chapter Six.

Devon thatchers who do not grow their own straw generally spend time and energy developing good working relationships with growers to ensure that the material they buy is good quality and that they are prepared in advance for the shortages that accompany a poor season. Water reed is a more conventional commodity. At present, water reed is always available at relatively short notice and can be ordered from an agent at any time of the year. This is convenient for a thatcher pricing up for a house, which he or she may do some months before starting work. Fluctuations in the price of water reed (which also has its good and bad seasons) are generally carried by the seller and prices remain stable for a season. Nevertheless, individual thatchers have preferred sources of supply and some Devon thatchers make occasional or regular visits to Turkey or other sources of the water reed they use, to negotiate terms and note and discuss quality.

Water reed has been used extensively in Devon for 40 years and is undoubtedly an excellent thatching material. Used by a skilful thatcher as an overcoat, it can be made to look very like combed straw. There is no need for additional timbering, to achieve the extra kick at eaves and verges, to be intrusive, as is sometimes the case, so long as the owner and thatcher agree in advance on a discreet design. There is a lot of sense in keeping water reed in the county as an alternative to traditional combed straw, to accommodate seasonal shortages of straw. There is, however, compelling conservation sense in acknowledging that the combed straw tradition is currently at risk in the county and acting to promote its survival and continuation. This would not only maintain a valuable tradition but also avoid a total dependence on an imported material. Combed straw produced in Devon has particularly good green credentials. After half a century of imported water reed, imports of straw into England, including rye straw, is a very recent trend. This is not a sensible answer to the problems of thatching material. It may be as costly in financial terms to produce straw in Devon for use on Devon roofs as to import water reed (or straw) from abroad, but the shorter transport distances involved in using locally-grown straw have obvious benefits to energy conservation, being less polluting than longer travelling distances.

Supplies of water reed sourced from foreign countries cannot be guaranteed always to be as reliable as they are now, nor long-distance transport costs so cheap. The history of switching from one source of supply to another since the 1950s is good evidence that it is difficult to find a source that is consistently reliable for availabilty, quality and price. In the developed world there is a tendency to drain wetlands and put them to more immediately profitable agricultural or even building use. Wetlands in England are far less common than they once were. Norfolk could never supply all the wants of English thatchers. It is significant that much of the water reed used today in thatching comes from countries where it is reasonable to expect intensive development in the near future, Hungary and Poland being two. Quality control over an imported material is complicated. If a consignment of sub-standard water reed arrives the week before it is required for use, it is not easy for the thatcher to return it to the sender. If wetlands are drained and water reed production becomes less common, or international transport costs increase, the price of water reed could rise to uneconomic levels.

There are difficulties with the long-term prospects for combed straw but these problems are relatively well-understood and attempts are already being made to tackle them. Other counties, notably Somerset, which introduced a thatching policy for listed buildings favouring combed straw in the 1980s, regard it as a good quality material and use little water reed. By contrast, many Devon thatchers and owners have lost confidence in combed straw and need to be reassured and confident that good quality material is being grown and is available. The time-lag in producing thatching policies in Devon has meant that demand for straw roofs in this county has fallen to a striking degree in the last twenty years. If it drops too far in Devon, which has so many surviving combed straw roofs, it is difficult to believe that other south-western counties will not also eventually follow suit. Demand below a certain level is also likely to cause the material to rise in price, the impetus to keep machinery going, or to build a new generation of more efficient and safer machines for combing will be lost, and it will be difficult to sustain the experimental work growing old varieties and mixtures to improve quality.

Thatching has not stayed the same in Devon from the open hall period to the present day. Key elements at the heart of the tradition have not changed: the use of combed straw grown locally, the craft principles of fitting it and the method of rethatching by overcoating. There has been a continuous tradition of combed straw but, like most traditions, it has been composed of adaptations and adjustments to changed circumstances. The tradition has been robust enough to withstand numerous obstacles to survival including changes to the design of traditional buildings, variations in status, a period of absurdly high insurance premiums, radical changes in tne varieties of straw available, its production and conversion into combed straw, shortages of thatchers and, recently, sharp competition from water reed. The Devon slate tradition survived, with many adaptations paralleling those of thatch, from at least the 14th century to the late 19th century but finally collapsed in the face of competition from slate, first from Wales and Cornwall, and then from foreign sources. It would be a real loss if Devon combed straw followed the same pattern in the 21st century.

The question of how a better balance can be achieved between water reed and combed straw in Devon cannot be answered solely through the Listed Building Consent system. Adoption of the English Heritage guidelines by Local Planning Authorities would, at least, help to identify the speed of change from straw to water reed and go some way to slow it down. This is only likely to be successful if there is genuinely good communication with local thatchers in implementing the guidance and an acknowledgement that some thatchers will have very real anxieties about returning to combed straw after a long period of using water reed. In practice, adopting the guidelines is very unlikely to put combed wheat back on roofs that have been recoated with water reed in the last fifty or even the last ten years. It can only deal with a limited number of the layers of conservation issues associated with thatching in the county at present. Thatchers, farmers, owners and local politicans must all also be involved in thinking through the implications of what they want to see on Devon's roofs and in the county's fields in future years.

Footnotes

[1] Information from Val Harrison, Conservation Officer.
[2] Cohen, 'Roofs of Reed', undated and unreferenced newspaper cutting in the thatch file in the Suffolk Record Office, Ipswich.
[3] Quoted by Andrew Sim in an article, 'The Changing Face of Thatch' in *Traditional Homes*, May 1989.
[4] The Dartmoor National Park Authority is already undertaking research in this area.
[5] *Western Morning News*, 24.01.91.
[6] Environmental Appraisal Group, School of Environmental Sciences, University of East Anglia, 1991, 62.

GLOSSARY

Barn Comber A machine, either hand operated or sometimes horse- or belt-driven, for combing straw for use in thatching (See also *reed comber*).

Brishing Horse (**Whipping horse**) A device resembling a short curved ladder supported on a frame. Bundles of corn could be threshed by striking them on the 'rungs' of the ladder.

Butt The butt end of a straw is the thick, bottom end of the stem.

Comb (**reed comb**) In thatching a hand tool for combing short straws and rubbish out of a bundle of straw.

Combed Straw (also known as combed wheat, combed wheat reed, wheat reed, Devon reed).
Term used in this book to refer to:
I. A form of thatching straw composed of stems that have been threshed and combed without crushing the stem.
2. The technique of thatching a roof with this material, using the material in bundles, the stems all lying in the same direction. The material is dressed into place and usually secured without external fixings other than at the ridge.

Crook An iron nail with a hooked head used to secure thatch directly to rafters by clasping the *sway* that holds a course of thatch in place. Formerly used only in difficult positions on a roof, hut now used routinely in straw and *water reed* thatching.

Cruck A continuous, curved piece of timber in a building which acts as a combined roof rafter and wall post. In Devon, *jointed crucks* were commonly used in medieval and seventeenth century buildings. These are constructed of separate wall posts and rafters joined together at *eaves* level.

Crushed Straw (**long straw**)
Term used in this book refer to:
1. Straw that has been bruised along its length and towards its lower end by *threshing*.
2. The technique of thatching with this material. The straw is drawn out of a watered heap into *yealms* before being laid on the roof: the straw therefore usually has a proportion of butts pointing up the roof. The roof is crooked into place or is secured to the pre-existing base coat by *spars* and *sways*, rather than dressed into place as in *water reed* or *combed straw* thatching.

Eaves The horizontal edge of the roof, as opposed to the *verges*, the inclined edges.

Eaves Board In thatching, a board or piece of timber attached to the top of a wall to give the thatch a *kick*.

Eaves Hook A tool to trim thatch at the *eaves* and *verges*.

Flail (**hand-flail, drashel**) A device made of two timber sticks, jointed together with leather or wood, and used for *threshing* crops.

Fleeking The practice, and product, of laying a thin coat of *water reed* (or other materials) beneath the lowest layer of the thatch to provide an even surface.

Haulm A term (now obsolete) used for a second cut of straw taken from the field after the upper part of the plant has been harvested.

Kick In thatching, the bend in thatching material at the *eaves* and *verges* which places the underside of the material in tension and the upper side in compression. Crushed straw is laid without a kick.

Lath A thin strip of split or sawn timber used as a groundwork for a roof covering or for plaster.

Leggatt A bat with a short handle and one surface treated to catch the ends of the straw or reed (in *combed straw* or *water reed* thatching), with which the bundles may be beaten up under the *sways* to tighten the coat.

Ligger (rod) A length of roundwood (usually hazel or willow), often split, laid over the upper surface of a thatch to hold **it** in place, with the help of a *spar*, and therefore similar to a *sway* except for its position. Rarely used in modern *water reed* or *combed straw* thatching except on ridges, but used to hold in the eaves and verges of a *crushed straw* roof.

Linhay An open-fronted building, in Devon with a loft, usually used for cattle-keeping.

Lodging The flattening or buckling of crops in the field by the action of wind and rain (or other factors).

Longhouse A house with a *shippon* at one end and domestic accommodation at the other, divided by a passage across the building.

Long Straw see crushed straw

Nitch A bundle of combed wheat reed. Historically 28lbs (12.7 kg), but now sold in bundles half that weight.

Mare In thatching, a type of *reed comb* consisting of a beam supported on a frame with an upright comb in the beam.

Marl Clay mixed with carbonate of lime, useful as a fertilizer.

Marling To fertilize ground with *marl*.

Plug A small handful of new material inserted into a roof in the repair process

Reed Comber Usually used specifically to refer to the mechanical device, invented in the late 19th century, which could be attached to a standard threshing machine for combing straw for thatching (see also *barn comber*) .

Rick A stack of harvested material. Today this is usually corn or hay but in the past there were ricks of other crops as well as wood ricks.

Rick-thatching A method of thatching in which the fixings, either *sways* or, on a *rick*, a straw bond or twine, are not covered by thatch, but left exposed. This is a cheaper and less durable method than when the fixings are covered by the courses of thatch.

Ridge In a roof structure, the horizontal timber at the apex of the roof. In thatching, a ridge is the thatch covering the apex of the roof. There are various types of thatched ridges. A 'wrapover' ridge is formed by wrapping bundles of straw over the apex of the roof. A 'butts-up' ridge uses two bundles of straw which are joined at the ridge. A 'flush' or 'plain' ridge is flush with the plane of the roof. A block-cut ridge projects forward from the plane of the roof. Block-cut ridges can be patterned with scallops and points cut into the straw.

Ridge Roll (dolly) A long roll of tied straw, thatched over to form the *ridge*.

Shingle A wooden tile, historically usually oak, used for roofing.

Shippon A cowhouse.

Smoke Louver A vent in the roof of a room with an open hearth to allow smoke to escape.

Spar (broach) A section of roundwood (usually hazel) split, sharpened. and twisted into a U-shape. Thrust into the thatch, the spar holds one layer to another, usually by holding down a *ligger* or a *sway*.

Spar Coating The fixing of a new layer of thatch on to an existing layer using *spars* and (usually) *sways*.

Stubble The uncrushed residue of the straw left standing in the fields after harvesting, which when tall could be mown and used for thatching. In this form also called *haulm*.

Sway A section of roundwood, formerly of hazel or willow but now often of iron, used horizontally in combination with *spars* or *crooks* to clasp a new course of thatch into position. Each sway is usually concealed in the finished roof by the next course of thatch or by the *ridge*.

Thresh To remove the grain from a ripe plant.

Trimmer An edging timber, often found in association with a void in a system of joists or rafters, e.g. for a stair or for a smoke louver.

Valley The internal angle of two inclined sides of a roof.

Verge The inclined edge of a roof rising along a gable, as opposed to the *eaves*.

Wattling Interwoven pliant branches or twigs.

Water Reed **(Norfolk reed was sometimes used in the past as a generic term for water reed, whatever its place of origin)**

    1. Wetland plant (today *Phragmites australis*) used for thatching.

    2. The technique of thatching with this material, which is carried on to the roof in bundles and secured butts down with *sways* and (today) *crooks*. The reed is driven up under the fixings with a *leggatt to* tighten the roof

Whimble **(wimble, wink)** A device for making straw rope or bond. It is rotated to twist the straw.

Yealm The bundle formed in *crushed straw* thatching from handfuls of straw from the heap of threshed material.

Yealming The practice in *crushed straw* thatching of forming the bundles called *yealms*.

BIBLIOGRAPHY

BOOKS

Baring-Gould, S.	*An Old English Home* (Methuen, 1898)
Beacham, Peter (ed.)	*Devon Building: An introduction to local traditions* (Devon Books, 1990)
Billett, Michael	*Thatching and Thatched Buildings* (Robert Hale, 1979)
Billett, Michael	*Thatched Buildings of Dorset* (Robert Hale, 1984)
Bray, Mrs	*The Borders of the Tamar and the Tavy* (C W Kent & Co, 1879, new edn, 2 vols)
Brockett, P. and Wright, A	*The Care and Repair of Thatched Roofs.* Technical Pamphlet 10. Society for the Protection of Ancient Buildings and Council for Small Industries in Rural England (May 1986)
Burnett, R.	*Some Notes on Wheat Reed Thatching.* Devon Master Thatchers Association (n.d., c1950)
Carew	*Survey of Cornwall* (1602)
Chapple, William	*A Review of part of Risdon's Survey of Devon; containing the General Description of that county with corrections, annotations, and additions* (Exeter 1785, repr. 1970)
CoSIRA	*The Thatcher's Craft.* Council for Small Industries in Rural Areas (1960)
Cox, J. & Letts, J.	*Thatch: Thatching in England 1940-1994.* English Heritage Research Transactions: Research and Case Studies in Architectural Conservation, 6 (2000)
Crossing, W.	*Crossing's Dartmoor Worker.* First published 1966, ed. Brian Le Messurier; facsimile edn of 1992 intro. by Crispin Gill (Peninsula Press, 1992)
Currie, J. R. & Long, W.H.	*An Agricultural Survey of South Devon, Report No 1.* Seal-Hayne Agricultural College & Dartington Hall (August 1929).
Devon Agricultural Study Group	*Devon Farming: A first study incorporating a review and a cartographic & written analysis of cropping and stocking* (1952)
Duncan, Ronald	*Home-Made Home* (Faber and Faber, 1947)
Egeland, Pamela	*Cob and Thatch* (Devon Books, 1988)
Ellacott, S.E.	*Braunton Farms and Farmers* (Aycliffe Press, 1981)
Fearn, Jacqueline	*Thatch and Thatching.* Shire Album 16 (Shire, 1976)
Finberg, H.P.R. (ed.)	*The Agrarian History of England & Wales, IV 1500-1640*

Fraser, Robert	*General View of the County of Devon* (fp 1794, repr. by Porcupines, Barnstaple, 1970)
Haggard, H. Rider	'Devonshire' in *Rural England,* 1 (1902), 175-217
Hartley, D.	*Made in England* (1939)
Hennell, T.	*Change in the Farm* (CUP, 1934)
Hooker, John	*Synopsis Chorographical of Devonshire* (c1600)
Hoskins, W.G.	*Devon* (Devon Books, 1954)
Innocent, C.F.	Chapter XIII in *The Development of English Building Construction* (f.p.1916, repr. 1971)
Kain, R. and Ravenhill, W.	*Historical Atlas of South-West England* (1999)
Kennaway, L. M.	*To Lovers of English Rural Scenery, Landowners, Stockbreeders, and Others* (n.d., c1914)
Kowaleski, M.	*Local Markets and Regional Trade in Medieval Exeter* (CUP, 1995)
Langland, William	*The Vision of Piers Plowman.* A Complete Edition of the B-Text. (ed.) A.V.C. Schmidt (Dent, 1978)
Letts, John	*Smoke-Blackened Thatch*: A unique source of late medieval plant remains from Southern England (English Heritage & University of Reading, 1999)
Lewis, Robert E.	*Middle English Dictionary* (1984)
Marshall, Henry	*Rural Economy of the West of England* 2 Vols, 1 (1796, repr. 1970)
Marshall, Howard	'The Rake's Progress', in Clough Williams-Ellis, *Britain and the Beast* (1937)
Mingay (ed.)	*The Agrarian History of England & Wales,* 6 (1989)
Moir, J. & Letts, J.	*Thatch: Thatching in England 1790-1940.* English Heritage Research Transactions: Research and Case Studies in Architectural Conservation, 5 (1999)
Neve, Richard	*The City and Country Purchaser and Builder's Dictionary*: A Reprint of the Work subtitled The Compleat Builders Guide, published 1726 (Augustus M. Kelley, New York, 1969)
Pearse Chope, E. (ed.)	Count L. Magalotti's 'The Travels of Cosmo III, Grand Duke of Tuscany, through England in 1669', *Early Tours in Devon and Cornwall* (1918, David and Charles reprint, 1967)
Percival, John	*Wheat in Great Britain* (1948)
Polwhele, Rev. Richard	*The History of Devonshire* 3 vols 1797-1808 (reprinted Dorking 1977)
Pyne, G. and Hoare, G.	*Prior's Barn and Gimson's Coxen* (1978).
Ravenhill Mary R., & Rowe, Margery M.,	*Early Devon Maps: Friends of Devon's Archives Occasional Publications* Number 1 (2000)
Risdon, Tristram	*The Chorographical Description or Survey of the County of Devon* (1811)
Rogers, John	*In the Life of a Country Thatcher* (Modbury Local History Society, 1976)
Salzman, L.F.	Chapter 15 in *Building in England down to 1540* (1942)
Scott Wilson, J.A.	'Tradition and Experiment in the West' in *Rural Britain To-day and To-morrow* (1934)
Shears, R.T.	*The Conservation of Devonshire Cottages* (1968)

Shorter, A.H., Ravenhill, W.L.D. and Gregory, K.J.W.G. East (Thomas Nelson, 1969)

South West England. Regions of the British Isles, (ed.)

Skeat, Rev. Walter W. (ed.)

The Book of Husbandry by Master Fitzherbert, reprinted from the edition of 1534 (1882)

Skinner, J.

West Country Tour being the Diary of a Tour through the Counties of Somerset, Devon & Cornwall in 1797 (1985)

Stanes, Robin

The Old Farm (Devon Books, 1990)

Stamp, L.D. (ed)

The Land of Britain. The Report of the Land Utilisation Survey of Britain, Part 92, Devon (1941)

Stephens, Henry

The Book of the Farm, 2 Vols. (Blackwood & Sons, 3rd edn. 1876)

Tanner, Kathy

Around Kingsbridge in Old Photographs (1988)

Thirsk, Joan (ed.)

The Agrarian History of England & Wales, V, 1640-1750 (CUP, 1984)

Torr, Cecil

Small Talk at Wreyland (fp 1918, 1921 & 1923, combined edition fp 1970, OUP paperback edn 1979)

Tusser, Thomas

A Hundred Good Points of Husbandry; first published 1557 (Hartley edn. 85).

Vancouver, Charles

General View of the Agriculture of the County of Devon; with observations on the means of its improvement. Drawn up for the consideration of The Board of Agriculture, and Internal Improvement (Richard Phillips, London, 1808)

Walker, B., McGregor C. &

Thatch and Thatching Techniques: A Guide to Conserving Stark, G. *Scottish Thatching Traditions.* Commissioned by Historic Scotland (Edinburgh, 1996)

Williams, W.M.

The Country Craftsman: A Study of some Rural Crafts and the Rural Industries Organisation in England. Dartington Hall Studies in Rural Sociology (Routledge & Kegan Paul, 1958)

Woods, S.

Uncle Tom Cobley and All: Widecombe-In-The-Moor (2000)

ARTICLES

Barry, Jonathan

'Towns and Processes of Urbanization in the Early Modern Period', *Historical Atlas of South-West England,* eds. R. Kain, and W. Ravenhill, (1999), 415-16

Beacham, Peter

'Local Building Materials and Methods', *Devon Building: An Introduction to Local Traditions* (ed.) Peter Beacham (1990), 13-31

Chapman, G.M.

'An Eighteenth Century East Devon Farm', *Devon & Cornwall Notes and Queries,* 36, Part II (Spring 1988), 101-103

Cherry, B.

'The Devon Country House in the Late Seventeenth and Early Eighteenth Centuries', *Proceedings of the Devon Archaeological Society,* 46 (1988), 91-135

Child, Peter

'Farm Buildings', *Devon Building: An Introduction to Local Traditions* (ed.) Peter Beacham (1990), 61-94

Collins, E.J.T.

'The Diffusion of the Threshing Machine in Britain, 1790-1880', *Tools & Tillage,* 2, 1972-1975, 16-33

Coombes, I.   'Seventeenth Century Thatching', *Devon and Cornwall Notes & Queries* XXX, Part IV (October 1965), 117-118

Fielden, M.E.   'Old-time survivals in Devon', *Transactions of the Devonshire Association*, 66 (1934), 357-373

Fox, Harold S.A.   'Outfield Cultivation in Devon and Cornwall: A Reinterpretation', *Husbandry and Marketing in the South-West 1500-1800* (ed.) Michael Havinden (1973), 19-38

Fox, Harold S.A.   'Servants, Cottagers & Tied Cottages during the Later Middle Ages: Towards a Regional Dimension', *Rural History*, 6, 2, (1995), 125-154

Harwood Long, W   'Factors affecting some types of farming in Devon and Cornwall', *Journal of the Royal Agricultural Society of England* 94 (1933), 42-61

Havinden, M.A.   'Agricultural History in the South-West' in *The South-West and the Land* (ed.) M. Havinden (University of Exeter, 1969), 7-17

Hayter Hames, G. C.   'Devon', *Journal of the Royal Agricultural Society of England*, 103 (1942), 86-90

Jarrett, George   'Growing Wheat Reed for Thatch', *Country Life* (28 January, 1960), 166-168

Jarrett, George   'Wheat for Reed', *Agriculture*, (May, 1960), 85-87

Joce, T. J.   'Cob Cottages for the Twentieth Century', *Transactions of the Devonshire Association*, 51 (1919), 169-174

Jones, John L.   'Growing for the Thatcher, Devon Reed', *Country Life*, (9 April 1981), 970-971

Laycock, Charles   'The Old Devon Farmhouse, Part 1', *Transactions of the Devonshire Association*, 52 (1920), 158-191

Laycock, Charles   'The Round-House or Machine-House', *Devon and Cornwall Notes and Queries*, 11 (1920-1921), 285-286

Meller, Hugh   'A La Ronde', *Devon Buildings Group Newsletter* 11 (February 1992), 10

Moore, H. Ian &   'Some problem areas in the South-West' in *Journal of the*

Macfarlan, P. J.   *Royal Agricultural Society of England*, 112 (John Murray 1951), 15-19

Oliver, Bruce W.   'Address of the President: The Devonshire Cottage', *Transactions of the Devonshire Association*, 81 (1949), 27-45

Pearse Chope, R   'Some Old farm Implements and Operations', *Transactions of the Devonshire Association*, 50 (1918), 268-292

Punchard, F.   'Farming in Devon and Cornwall', *Journal of the Royal Agricultural Society*, 3rd series, 1, (1890), 511-536

Sellman, R.R.   'Captain Swing in Devon', *Devon & Cornwall Notes and Queries*, 35, Part III (Spring 1983), 15-117

Sheldon, Miss Lilian   'Devon Barns', *Transactions of the Devonshire Association*, 64 (1932), 389-395

Stanes, Robin   'A Georgicall Account of Devonshire and Cornwall...' *Transactions of the Devonshire Association*, 96 (1964), 269-303

Stanes, Robin   'Devon Agriculture in the Mid-Eighteenth Century: the Evidence of the Milles Enquiries' in *The South West & the Land: Papers in Economic History* (eds) Havindon and King (University of Exeter 1969), 43-65

Stanes, Robin
'Landlord and Tenant and Husbandry Covenants in Eighteenth-Century Devon', in *Agricultural Improvement: Medieval and Modern*, 14 (ed.) W. Minchinton. Exeter Papers in Economic History (University of Exeter 1981), 41-64

Thorp, John
'Two Hall Houses from a late Medieval Terrace: 8-12 Fore Street, Silverton', *Proceedings of the Devon Archaeological Society* 40 (1982) 171-180.

'Some Thatched Roofs' *Country Life* (21 October 1939)

'Thatch as Thatch Can', *The Field* (2 June 1960)

REPORTS AND GUIDANCE NOTES
Thatch and thatching: a guidance note. English Heritage (2000)

The Dorset Thatching Report. A Report to all Local Authorities in Dorset submitted by the Dorset Conservation Officers Group (December, 1996)

'The Dorset Model' Thatched Buildings, New Properties and Extensions. Local Authority Building Control, Buildings Regulations 1991. West Dorset District Council (October 1998 WD/2797)

Henry, Alison
Thatch in South Somerset: A Guide to Maintenance and Repair. Conservation and Environment Unit, South Somerset District Council (1996)

WEST COUNTRY STUDIES LIBRARY
NEWSPAPER CUTTINGS FILE
Western Morning News 13.7.23; 5.7.35; 8.3.39; 9.12.46; 2.12.55; 27.1.90; 24.1.91
Express & Echo 4.5.28; 18.8.36; 23.9.91
Devon & Exeter Gazette 29.8.29
Western Times 2.10.36
Western Independent and Daily Gazette December 1937
Woolmers Exeter and *Plymouth Gazette* June 2-9, 1938
South Devon Journal 29.4.59; 31.10.62
Exmouth Journal 14.3.80
The Independent 10.7.90
The Times, 'Thatch Roofs of Devon: Causes of Decline', 29.8.36; Letter by J.G. *Cornish*, 28.9.36; letter by Sir Evelyn Wrench, 28.8.36
Exeter Flying Post 9.5.1816; 30.7.1836; 26.10.1837; 21.10.1863

UNPUBLISHED
Brockett, Peter
Combed Wheat Reed - Its Future (a brief view). Rural Development Commission internal note (May 1990)

Environmental Appraisal Group, School of Environmental Sciences, University of East Anglia. Socio-Economic Impact of Changes in the Quality of Thatching Reed on the Future of the Reed-Growing and Thatching Industries and on the Wider Rural Economy', (1991).

Pullen, J.H.
'Growing Wheat Reed for Thatching'. Unpublished ms 1979, (supplied by author).

Wilmot, Sarah
'Land ownership, farm structure and agrarian change in South West England 1800-1900: regional experience and national ideals' PhD Thesis, University of Exeter, 1988.

WEST DEVON RECORD OFFICE
731/34. Church Wardens accounts

DEVON RECORD OFFICE
2065M L3/2
285M/ E4-5
3425M/ E5
2154M/ L14a-b
314M/ E183. Sandford papers
add M/ E18
EDRO PW1 Colebrooke
2644 M/E6
961 add M/E57 E8
3799 Box 27, Seymour Duke of Somerset

THE GUILDHALL LIBRARY
Sun Insurance Records for 1795

PUBLIC RECORD OFFICE
Calendar of State Papers Domestic 1547-1580 Vol.88 (1856)
Rural Industries Bureau minutes 1950-1952
MAF 113/99 XC6552.
D4/421 Rural Industries Inquiry, 1930/1
MAFF 33/770 6510 Executive Committee Meetings of the Rural Industries Bureau 1941-44
MAFF 33/770 6510 'D Straw Thatchers'
MAFF 33/772 6510 Thatching Instruction, Rural Industries Bureau
MAFF 33/772 6510 Training Arrangements
MAFF 113/522 Rural Industries Bureau Council Minutes and Papers 1957-8
MAFF 113/522 Draft of 1957-8 Rural Industries Bureau Annual Report
MAFF 113/98 XC6552 Minutes of the Thatchers' Conference
MFF 113/523 Analysis of returns received by January 1960, to the Rural Industries Bureau's questionnaire on thatched properties

INDEX

GENERAL INDEX